General
Abner M. Perrin,
C.S.A.

General Abner M. Perrin, C.S.A.

A Biography

RON V. KILLIAN

McFarland & Company, Inc., Publishers
Jefferson, North Carolina, and London

LIBRARY OF CONGRESS CATALOGUING-IN-PUBLICATION DATA

Killian, Ron V.
　　General Abner M. Perrin, C.S.A. : a biography / Ron V. Killian.
　　　　p.　　cm.
　　Includes bibliographical references and index.

　　ISBN 978-0-7864-6980-2
　　softcover : acid free paper ∞

　　1. Perrin, Abner M., 1827–1864.　2. Generals — Confederate States of America — Biography.　3. Confederate States of America. Army — Officers — Biography.　4. United States — History — Civil War, 1861–1865 — Biography.　5. United States — History — Civil War, 1861–1865 — Campaigns.　I. Title.
　　E467.1.P46K55　2012
　　355.0092 — dc23
　　[B]　　　　　　　　　　　　　　　　　　　　　　2012002244

BRITISH LIBRARY CATALOGUING DATA ARE AVAILABLE

© 2012 Ron V. Killian. All rights reserved

No part of this book may be reproduced or transmitted in any form or by any means, electronic or mechanical, including photocopying or recording, or by any information storage and retrieval system, without permission in writing from the publisher.

Front cover image: General Abner Monroe Perrin, C.S.A. (1827–1864); cover design by David K. Landis (Shake It Loose Graphics)

Manufactured in the United States of America

McFarland & Company, Inc., Publishers
　Box 611, Jefferson, North Carolina 28640
　　www.mcfarlandpub.com

Acknowledgments

Nonfiction writing requires a lot of assistance, and from many individuals and sources. The people who graciously offered assistance to this writer in the unfolding evolution of this manuscript deserve to be recognized and properly thanked for their help. In this pursuit, the following effort is made.

Spartanburg County Library is a necessary help in all research attempted by this writer. The Interlibrary Loan department under the direction of Betsey Tully always makes a super effort to acquire the materials that make writing easier. Without that help, some sources would be unavailable. In addition, the Kennedy Archives Room offers both direction and additional sources unavailable in libraries located in much larger cities. To these dedicated professionals, this writer owes much.

The Perrin family especially, and in particular Mary Louise Perrin Bailey, offered a great amount of information concerning the Perrins that otherwise would not and could not have been included in this manuscript. In addition, Edward Perrin, a gentleman and scholar, was both helpful and encouraging in many aspects of this manuscript. To them, this writer is thankful, and is in their debt.

To all of the offices, individuals, and various departments and universities in the states of Mississippi, Alabama, and Virginia, and especially the University of South Carolina, a thanks is also given. Special recognition must be given to the Edgefield County Archives Department and the South Carolina Department of Archives and History for information that is likely not available elsewhere.

A succession of small victories over major problems has made the writing of this manuscript less difficult, thanks to many individuals mentioned here.

Table of Contents

Acknowledgments v
Preface 1
Introduction 3

1. A Future Soldier and His Life Between Two Wars 5
2. A Captain in the 14th South Carolina Infantry 16
3. The Maryland Campaign 38
4. The Road to Fredericksburg 58
5. Chancellorsville 75
6. Gettysburg: More Than a Battle 91
7. From the Mine Run Campaign to the Wilderness 125
8. Perrin's Brigade 143
9. The Final Battle 152
10. Bereft of Life and Recognition 170

Epilogue 183
Appendices
    1. Perrin's Remains Located on the Spotsylvania Battlefield ... 185
    2. Letter of Capt. S.J. Quinn of the 14th Mississippi
        Regarding Perrin Family 186
    3. Perrin Obituary, May 25, 1864, *Edgefield Advertiser* 189
    4. Col. Abner M. Perrin Endorsed by McGowan's Brigade 189

Table of Contents

5. Important Dates in Perrin's Life 191
6. Perrin Letter to Governor Bonham, July 29, 1863 191

Chapter Notes 195
Bibliography 211
Index 221

Preface

The American Civil War is unquestionably one of the most momentous and never-to-be-forgotten events in the history of this nation. Mythical heroes were born who were acclaimed to be greater than life itself and who set up "stations of light for men to see in the dark places where reality never shines." To some who took part in this war, the war itself became life and they lost contact with reality for a time.

General Robert E. Lee realized the horror of war and warned against men becoming too fond of it. Isaac Goldberg called war "a disaster to the soldier and a spectacle to the generals." Yet a well-known participant, Gen. Nathan B. Forrest, summed it up with: "War means fightin' and fightin' and means killin'." This may be the most meaningful thing we can conclude about a four-year conflict that brought about 600,000 casualties. Fewer than one hundred brigadier generals lost their lives in this conflict, and Abner Perrin was one of the unfortunate one hundred. Who rounded out the remaining 599,900? How many scientists, poets, historians, physicians, and on and on were lost, how many fathers never came home, how many sons?

The Union was preserved, if one can call the postwar years of political conflict and ill will between the northern and southern United States preservation. Only in the past thirty or so years has the South overcome the catastrophic effects of this conflict, yet it is by no means over.

The Southern states lost more than the war. Leaders such as Abner Perrin gave their lives for this deadly cause, and Abner Perrin, like many other Southerners of his day, viewed the war as an invasion of their homes and their lives. And as well, many people in the north felt they were putting down a rebellion and bringing freedom to people who were in slavery. One can but wonder where and how reason, compromise, and goodwill had fled the scene by 1860.

Preface

Abner Perrin's entire immediate family vanished through death and other, less conspicuous causes related to the war. General Perrin was a creditable soldier and leader and remained so through it all; a man with a somewhat dark personality, but responsible, determined, and always faithful to the values he held. Abner Perrin's problems were not unique, as many other men suffered the same sense of loss and despair, both Confederate and Union soldiers.

The lives of all of these soldiers deserve to be viewed and discussed in word and print so that the part they played in the history of this nation will not be forgotten. For this reason the life of General Perrin is recalled in this manuscript.

Introduction

Abner Perrin and every man who held the rank of brigadier general in the Civil War have one notable and conspicuous as well as fortuitous event in common — their service in America's most defining military conflict. The events of their lives and military service have, for the most part, much like those of Abner Perrin, gone unacknowledged.

More than a thousand men held the rank of brigadier during the war. At best, about 30 percent have received any *substantial* print. This most likely is unintentional, since the Civil War is America's most investigated conflict. The nominal reader is simply unaware of the vast majority of brigadiers and will overlook a book if the name of the general is unknown to him. The result is that a possible 30 percent of the Civil War generals are the subject of 90 percent of the Civil War biographies. Yet, there is little more that can be written about the great heroes that will be read without some sense of redundancy. Perhaps the 70 percent yet to be discussed in print will ultimately surface and their importance acknowledged.

Abner Perrin, much like every Civil War brigadier, has a story to be written and read by the American people. There is no doubt that aspects of these lives will touch the very heart of American culture.

No matter which side of the war one feels drawn toward, the time spent in researching and reading about the war in general, the brigadiers in particular, their lives and service during the war, and the men under their command, will be worth the effort. The sesquicentennial of the Civil War has arrived, and it is the hope of all Civil War historians, enthusiasts, and writers that this will spark renewed interest in learning about the many lesser-known brigadiers who played well more than a casual role in this momentous conflict.

Gen. Abner Perrin is such a man.

CHAPTER 1

A Future Soldier and His Life Between Two Wars

Abner Monroe Perrin III was born on February 2, 1827, and even that important and relevant aspect of his life is in dispute. Some sources list his date of birth as February 2, 1830, which might seem unlikely for reasons that will become apparent. Such was the beginning of an important life that has yet to be given the attention it deserves, the life of Gen. Abner Perrin, CSA.[1]

Abner III hailed from a distinguished and noble family. His ancester was usually addressed as Capt. Abner Perrin to honor his service in the Revolutionary War, and as far as it is possible to ascertain, this branch of the Perrin family originated in Virginia. The Perrin family in South Carolina descended from Joseph Perrin, who lived in Charlotte County, Virginia, as early as 1748. Joseph Perrin and his wife Rebecca had at least eight children, possibly more. Three Perrin brothers married three Clopton sisters, whose ancestors lived in New Kent County, Virginia, as early as the late 1600s. William Perrin was one of the three brothers and Mary Clopton was one of the three sisters mentioned above who relocated to a section of present-day Greenwood County, South Carolina, after receiving a land grant of 315 acres along Hard Labor Creek in southwestern Greenwood County, and established their life there together.

A second of the three Perrin brothers who married Clopton sisters also relocated to Greenwood County. Abner Perrin, the oldest son of William and Mary Perrin, was born in 1763. His father William received a land grant in 1773 of 1,000 acres and received a second grant in 1796. Abner married Sarah Foster, and Abner Jr., their third child, was born on September 23, 1798, in the Edgefield District of South Carolina. A few years after his first birthday, Abner Jr.'s father died, and in 1802 his mother married Robert Perrin, the first cousin of her deceased husband.[2]

Robert was an established merchant living in the area that would ultimately come to be known as Winterseat. It is somewhat difficult to explain exactly what Winterseat was and how it influenced the area around Edgefield. In point of fact, Winterseat was a working plantation, or a very large farm, and in the strict sense of the word, it was not a town, but was the name given to a homesite that was likely built by William Perrin. It is located in present-day Greenwood County, South Carolina, near the community of Troy, which today has about 125 citizens. Winterseat comprised at least 1,500 acres of land. Its earliest date of known existence as a distinct entity is 1831, when the property, or at least some of the property on Long Cane Road, was purchased by Wade S. Cothran, who established a residence on the property and called it Winterseat. It is impossible to determine if William Perrin's home and Wade S. Cothran's residence is the same house, although this is probably the case. It is only possible to note that William Perrin, in the 1770s, was on the property later called Winterseat by Wade S. Cothran, and the property was west of the Abbeville-Charleston road. The Perrins lived in the area around Winterseat and Troy until after 1850.[3] The marriage of Sarah Perrin to Robert Perrin set into motion the progression of the life that Abner Jr. and Abner III would partake of and enjoy from that point onward. This was to be an important family to South Carolina, as well as to the life and culture of this nation.

Abner Jr. married Mary Patterson in 1820, one month before his twenty-second birthday. The union between Abner

Photograph of Abner M. Perrin (Library of Congress Number B812-2982).

1. A Future Soldier and His Life Between Two Wars

Jr. and Mary produced nine children, eight sons and one daughter.[4] Abner Monroe III was the fourth child, born around 1827. There is disagreement as to the year of Abner III's birth; Bailey cites his birth as February 2, 1829, and Watson gives February 2, 1827, and some sources place the year of his birth as 1830. As Abner III's life unfolds in this account, perhaps a determination of the correct year of his birth can be ascertained based upon events which occurred in his life during critical years.[5]

As stated, Abner III had seven brothers and one sister. The siblings of Abner III ultimately were scattered over much of the southern United States in the decade before the Civil War. His oldest brother Josiah died in 1850, in Alabama; the second son was Robert, a physician; Margaret, the only daughter, was born in 1827; William was the fifth child, born in 1831; Telemachus, the sixth sibling, was born in 1832; Napoleon, the seventh child, was born in 1837. Frequently called "Polie," he served with J.E.B. Stuart during the Civil War as an enlisted soldier. James was the eighth child, born in 1840; he also served in the Civil War and was killed in the retreat from Gettysburg. Arthur was the ninth sibling and also served in the war, but survived it and died at some point after 1880. After the war Telemachus moved to New Orleans and Napoleon moved to Arkansas.[6]

Information on Abner Perrin during the years before the Mexican War is very limited, including where and to what extent he was educated. Two sources suggest that he received a private education, and he was probably not tutored, or at least not exclusively so. Abner Jr. joined the Bethany Baptist Church on August 31, 1831; the church had a private school, and it has been suggested that Abner III may have attended that school. More likely he attended the Liberty Hill Academy, a first-rate boys' prep school under the leadership of Headmaster George Galphin. This school was located in present-day McCormick County, about seven miles from the city of McCormick on U.S. Highway 378; it was near the Longmire Store and Post Office that was established in 1809, and was in existence until after 1890. The Longmire Post Office was the postal address used by Abner III until his death in 1864. This school also had some very important graduates: Gen. Matthew C. Butler, CSA, famous cavalry officer of the Civil War, Governor John Sheppard, United States Senator "Pitchfork" Ben Tillman, plus some other important figures of the antebellum period.[7] The historian Francis B. Simkins has suggested that Bethany School and Liberty Hill Academy are different names for the same school at different times, since both schools were under the leadership of the same headmaster, George Galphin, and located in the same confined area in relation to Longmire Store. A member of the extended Perrin family, John Chiles, served as one of the first ordained deacons of the Bethany Church, and this could have been a determining factor in the Perrin family's selection for young Abner's education. A female academy was built to complement the Liberty Academy for males in the 1850s. Both schools existed until the late 1880s.[8]

While there are no records of exactly when and or where Abner III attended school, the facts that he was an attorney and had excellent writing skills speak to the conclusion that he was well educated. He did not attend the South Carolina College (later the University of South Carolina), as no records exist that attest to his attendance. He likely studied law and worked with an attorney to gain the required knowledge to receive a license to practice law, which was commonplace in that period of history.[9] Abner III had a relative in Abbeville, Col. T.C. Perrin, who was a prominent lawyer, and in all likelihood he read law and observed the workings of Col. Perrin's law practice. Abbeville is located very near Edgefield in the western section of South Carolina. Both towns have a long and prestigious history in South Carolina, having supplied many legislators, governors, military figures, and other major contributors to the state's history. Gen. Samuel McGowan, later to be the commander of McGowan's Brigade, of which Abner Perrin would be a part, practiced law with Colonel Perrin. A bond between Abner Perrin and McGowan was formed even before this association when both men served in the Mexican War.[10] Unfortunately, the exact date Perrin's bar admission is questionable, as is the case in some other aspects of his life. The United States Census of 1850 lists the occupation of Abner Perrin III as a lawyer, but records in South Carolina state he was not admitted to the bar to practice law until 1854. If Perrin was born in 1830, he would have been only twenty years of age in 1850 and already a lawyer as well as an officer in the Mexican War of 1846–1848. This all seems rather incredible for one so young, even in 1850, while age twenty-seven (if his date of birth is in fact 1827) makes his admission to the bar in 1854 more believable.[11]

Abner Perrin's service in the Mexican War is yet another puzzle in the life of a man who had an exhaustive list of perplexing riddles concerning the events of his life. One must consider the reason or reasons why a young man of eighteen or nineteen years would forsake a life of ease, comfort, and wealth to volunteer to serve in a war which posed no real threat to the nation, and that offered him no foreseeable personal gain. The fact

1. A Future Soldier and His Life Between Two Wars

that he had no military training makes the issue even more difficult to comprehend. To explain this move in Perrin's life, two things come to mind. First, his grandfather and namesake Captain Abner Perrin was a soldier in the American Revolution, and no doubt this might have spurred Abner III to emulate his grandfather. In addition, his future father-in-law was the colonel of the famous Palmetto Regiment. Abner, though not a member of the regiment, must have been inspired to take part in the conflict with Mexico. Granted, Abner Perrin was a patriotic man, which was evident in his behavior during his entire life.

In any case, Perrin became a member of the 12th U.S. Infantry and was a member of Company A. He was promoted to 1st lieutenant on December 31, 1847. Future South Carolina Governor Luke M. Bonham was a colonel in the 12th Infantry, and Gen. Franklin Pierce, later to become president of the United States, was the brigade commander. Captain Winfield S. Hancock, future major general in the Union Army, served as Bonham's adjutant. Abner rose in rank to become a Captain in the 12th, and Bonham would be a major influence in Perrin's life from this point onward. After three requests, the National Archives could not locate any records of service for Abner Perrin in the Mexican War of 1846–1848, but did offer a reference to his unit and rank. Young Perrin sailed from Charleston to Veracruz on October 19, 1847, to begin his service in the Mexican War.[12]

Several letters written by Perrin to his family concerning his service in the Mexican War survive. In a letter of October 24, 1847, Perrin wrote to his father that he was "making way to Mexico City." His letter is typical of all young men in war writing home to family and friends over the ages. The letter says little but is upbeat and pleasant to quell family fears concerning his safety. He signs the letter, "I am your affectionate son, Abner Perrin." This might seem somewhat stiff and stuffy to modern readers, but in Perrin's era this was a show of respect for his father and his family.[13] In another letter written on July 16, 1848, Perrin writes to his father stating that he is in New Orleans after a pleasant trip across the Gulf of Mexico. He assures his family he is well and will be home soon. He relates that an individual known to his family was killed in combat, but all others are "with me and are well." This is, again, the typical letter of the ages written by a man in the military as he makes his way back home.[14]

On August 6, 1847, Perrin had received a letter from Gen. Maxcy Gregg, the future brigade commander of the famous "Light Division" of

Gen. A.P. Hill, Army of Northern Virginia, in which Perrin would serve some fifteen years hence. Gregg urgently requested that Perrin quickly raise a company of men to take part in the Mexican War. He praised Perrin for his past efforts and states, "There is no need of adding any exhortation to you." This letter exhibits the leadership ability of Abner Perrin and gives insight as to what he would accomplish as a brigadier in General Hill's III Corps sixteen years later.[15] Perrin's service in the Mexican War, while its details are not individually available from the National Archives, were in the campaigns of the U.S. 12th Infantry, commanded by Col. Luke M. Bonham. Colonel Bonham was born in 1813 at Red Bank, Edgefield District, in present day Saluda County, South Carolina. Colonel Bonham seemed to have had a great interest in the military, so much so that President James Polk appointed Bonham to serve as a lieutenant colonel in the 12th Infantry.[16] Bonham was praised for his gallantry by Gen. Franklin Pierce and served as a governor of one of the Mexican provinces for a time after the war.

Doubtless the most important battle in which the 12th Infantry played a role was the Battle of Contreras. Before the actual battle, Colonel Bonham and the 12th Infantry advanced to within 200 yards of the Mexican position. An account of this battle states:

> The Palmetto Regiment arrived at San Geronimo on the evening of the 19th well after dark and bivouacked at Ansaldo.... Only 331 Palmettos were fit for duty, and their commander (Col. Pierce M. Butler) got up from his sick bed to participate in the action....
> The battle was a short affair ... the fire from Colonel Trueman B. Ransom's Ninth Infantry on their front, the impact of Brigadier Gen. Persifor F. Smith's attack on their rear, and the sight of Santa Anna's men retiring from San Angel was too much to bear. [The 12th Infantry of General Bonham and Capt. Abner Perrin was a part of General Smith's command.][17]

Later Colonel Bonham was wounded at the Battle of Churubusco, but soon recovered.[18] Bonham returned home after the war and held a number of positions, including the unexpired term of his cousin Preston S. Brooks as a States' Rights Democrat, where he remained until South Carolina seceded from the Union in 1860.

It bears repeating that Perrin was not a member of the Palmetto Regiment, but was in close contact with the regiment throughout the Mexican War. The experience of being a part of this conflict and the contacts made while serving in the 12th Infantry alongside the Palmetto Regiment would

1. A Future Soldier and His Life Between Two Wars

play a major role in his life and greatly influence the decisions he would later make.

The Mexican War officially ended in February of 1848. By the end of the Mexican War Perrin had risen to the rank of captain, and signed himself as such in two separate letters written to his family in late 1847. Perrin ended his service in the Mexican War on July 25, 1848, when his regiment was mustered out at Carrollton, Louisiana, and he began to make his way toward Edgefield. It is assumable that by this time he had decided to prepare himself for a career as a lawyer, and as was mentioned previously, he listed his occupation as a lawyer in the 1850 U.S. Census.[19]

Abner Perrin's life was about to undergo some major changes. Overall, the 1850s would be a period of blissfulness and contentment with only a few exceptions. It is impossible to know exactly when and how it occurred, but Abner Perrin met a young lady and began a courtship, which led to his marriage. Again, it is impossible to conclude absolutely, but Perrin's Mexican War associations probably had some influence on his marriage. Perrin's father-in-law was the late Colonel Pierce Mason Butler, commander of the famed Palmetto Regiment during the Mexican War. Pierce Mason Butler was born at Mt. Willing in the Edgefield District in 1798. He served in the United States Army for a number of years; he was a trustee of the South Carolina College in 1833, and served as governor of South Carolina from 1836 to 1838. In 1836, President Martin Van Buren appointed Butler to serve as an agent for the Cherokee Indians. Butler organized and led the Palmetto Regiment that served in the Mexican War, resulting in his death at the Battle of Churubusco on August 20, 1847.[20] Governor Butler was a man who received profuse respect and admiration from all the men who served with him, so much so that the thought of behaving in such a way as to disappoint Colonel Butler was more disturbing to his men than any military discipline which might come from that behavior. Historians have reported that Colonel Butler was somewhat of a political opportunist, never missing an opportunity to enhance his image to those in power. Butler and John C. Calhoun shared a close friendship that may have accounted for his appointment as a Cherokee agent. Young Perrin must have idolized such a man, especially when the two men were in close association during the heat of battle.[21]

Doubtless, the association of Abner Perrin and Col. Pierce Butler, both from the Edgefield District of South Carolina, was a factor in Abner's courtship of Colonel Butler's daughter Emmaline Elizabeth, usually addressed as Emily. It can only be surmised that the courtship of Abner and Emily began after the Mexican War, since Abner was away from home and involved in his education, the war, and other such matters, leaving little time for a serious romance. It could be said of Abner and Emily, "She loved me for the dangers I had passed, and I loved her that she did pity them."[22] On November 25, 1851, the Rev. Graham wed Abner M. Perrin and Emmaline Elizabeth Butler at the Edgefield Court House. This was no small unnoticed occasion, as evidenced by the coverage it received. An example is an announcement of the wedding in the *Spartan*, a newspaper that operated over 100 miles from Edgefield. The notice appeared within two weeks of the date of the wedding, a rapid pace in the 1850s.[23]

The next six years were plausibly the best years in the adult life of Abner Perrin. Abner Perrin, Sr., moved his family to Sumter County, Alabama, at some point after 1850, since the family is still listed on the Edgefield County U.S. Census for that year. Abner Sr. was fifty-two and had six children ages eight to twenty-one, and by 1852 the family was settled in Alabama. Abner Monroe did not make the move to Alabama for a number of reasons, presumably the two most important being his education to obtain admission to the South Carolina bar and his ongoing courtship with Emily Butler, soon to be his wife.[24]

In 1853, Abner and Emily Perrin were blessed with the birth of their first child, Pierce Butler Perrin. Pierce appears on the 1860 U.S. Census for South Carolina's Walterboro County as age seven years. From early 1854 until 1860, Abner Perrin was "on a roll," so to speak. He was admitted to South Carolina bar, as mentioned earlier, and his life was moving in a very positive direction. Abner began to buy and sell large amounts of property. Abner Monroe purchased an indenture by way of John Hill's giving Abner rights to a tract of land from the estate of Hugh Quarles for the sum of $300. [25] Abner sold a parcel of land to John Colgan for $900 and the sale was recorded on July 2, 1855.[26] In 1854, Abner purchased another piece of property, one acre, on the edge of the town of Edgefield from Avory Bland for $78.[27] Abner also purchased a second tract of land, which lay between Edgefield and the Cheatham Plank Road, from the same Avory Bland in 1854 for $800.[28]

In 1857, a tragedy of major proportions befell Abner and Emily. Julia Duval Perrin, born on April 16, 1856, died July 29, 1857. This is the most unrelenting pain any parents at any time are forced to suffer. The child

1. A Future Soldier and His Life Between Two Wars

was a namesake of Emily's mother, which of a certainty magnified the pain even more.[29]

In 1858, Abner resumed his land sales and acquisitions. On May 5, 1859, Abner and Emily sold Emily's share of her father's estate, which was one-seventh of the estate in Edgefield County, to Emily's mother, Miranda Julia Butler. Miranda Butler lived in Louisiana at the time. This was a large and valuable tract of land, for which Miranda Butler paid $7,000. It is difficult to determine the precise reason for this land sale; Miranda Butler might have purchased the land as a "helping gesture" to her daughter and son-in-law or for other undisclosed reasons.[30] On the same day Abner and Emily also signed a deed of release of slaves to Miranda Butler *et al*. This may or may not have been a condition of the land sale of Emily's share of the estate of her father, or it could have been a simple example of family goodwill.[31]

The final recorded land transaction of the 1850s is unusual and presents yet another puzzle, one of many in Abner Perrin's life. On September 30, 1859, Abner and Emily sold a tract of land to Emily's brother William, who lived in the Edgefield District, for $333. The sale is not unusual, but other aspects of the sale are, because at some point, Abner and Emily had moved to Notuba County, Mississippi, and claimed residence in that county, which is the area of Philadelphia, Mississippi. The County of Notuba reports that floods destroyed all county records some decades ago and there appear to be no extant records of Abner and Emily living in Mississippi. Perrin had no land or other property to speak of in that area, and one year later, he and Emily would be back in South Carolina, but in a totally different area of the state.[32]

Abner Monroe and Emily Perrin were blessed with a second son, Robert W. Perrin, born in 1859, in the Edgefield District. The U.S. Census of South Carolina, Colleton County, the St. Bartholemew District for 1860, lists Abner, Emily, Pierce, and Robert as residents of Colleton County (Walterboro, South Carolina). Abner's occupation is listed as "planter" or plantation owner; the value of his real estate is placed at $15,000 and his net worth at $51,000, which was a sizable sum of money in 1860. Colleton County reports that all records were lost during the Civil War due to General Sherman's "March to the Sea" in 1865 and the ravaging of floodwaters, and therefore no actual records are available. No response came forth from the St. Bartholemew Genealogy Society, which the Colleton County officials state may have some of the remaining records.[33]

Life for Abner and his family was good: he had a profession, land, money, respect, and a wonderful immediate and extended family, but he was soon to be faced with the most catastrophic event to occur in United States since the American Revolution. His family would be caught up in this whirlwind of events over which he would have no control.

Events determining the political direction in the South, and in South Carolina particularly, were rapidly deteriorating and escalating into a spirit of conflict, and no compromise seemed to be on the horizon. The Southern states felt that slavery was essential to their economic survival, and that they were not receiving fair taxation and tariff rates by the government in Washington. This, plus a host of other complaints, real and imagined, blocked any hopes of a resolution to this constitutional and economic impasse. After Lincoln's election in 1860, South Carolina called a convention to discuss possible secession from the Union. On December 20, 1860, an Ordinance of Secession was passed with no dissent. Within six weeks Mississippi, Florida, Alabama, Louisiana, Georgia, and Texas followed South Carolina's lead. After the fall of Fort Sumter in April of 1861, Virginia, North Carolina, Arkansas, and Tennessee seceded. In Abbeville, South Carolina, Abner Monroe's uncle, Thomas Chiles Perrin, maintained his law practice with Abner's Mexican War comrade, and later brigade commander, Samuel McGowan. Colonel T.C. Perrin, in addition, was the president of the Greenville and Columbia Railroad, a state senator and a representative from Abbeville. His plantation, "Cotton Level," was located on Hard Labor Creek near Abbeville, a town that was heavily involved with the secession movement. On at least one occasion, 2,500 people gathered at Magazine Hill (later called Secession Hill) to hear speakers discuss the issue of secession. Chesterfield was another city in South Carolina where feelings ran very high on this issue. Thomas Chiles was a member of the Secession Committee and voted to leave the Union. While in all probability Abner supported secession, he was bound by blood and family to follow the lead of his fellow South Carolinians.[34]

It was the thinking of many people in the North that the Southern states, and South Carolina in particular, constituted an oligarchy. John W. De Forest exemplifies this thinking in his writings. De Forest was a northerner who visited Charleston in 1860 and concluded that since all military officers, state legislators, and other persons in control generally had similar facial expressions, it stood to reason that no lower class individuals (he used the word plebeians) were allowed in "high places." De Forest concluded that such persons were "leaders of men." When and if war emerged in the nation, this attitude would also be the rule in the Confederate Army. He concluded the common soldiers would, for this reason, have little difficulty in a military structured life since it was exactly what they normally experienced in civilian life.[35] This thinking did, in a sense, prevail in the antebellum South, and, in all likelihood, Abner Perrin was a product of this philosophy. This viewpoint could help explain why he served at such a young age in the Mexican War and immediately felt compelled to offer his services to the Confederate government. Nonetheless, Abner Perrin was, in fact, a leader, and clear evidence of this fact would emerge in the next several years of his life.

CHAPTER 2

A Captain in the 14th South Carolina Infantry

Abner Monroe Perrin joined the Confederate Army on August 10, 1861, and listed his age as 31. Again this brings up the issue of the actual date of his birth. If this record is accurate, then Abner's date of birth is February 2, 1830, rather than 1827, and he would have been 31 years, six months, and eight days old on August 10, 1861. This record is in compliance with the U.S. Census record of 1850 for Edgefield County in South Carolina. It would also mean that Abner M. Perrin was a captain in the 12th United States Infantry at age eighteen during his service in the Mexican War — an incredible accomplishment for one with no military training or experience. Abner's military experience in the Mexican War and the associations he established with leading officers from South Carolina in that war, such as Milledge L. Bonham and Maxcy Gregg, influenced the direction his service in the Confederate Army would take. Abner was an indomitable personality and he tended to be drawn to others who also had doughty and resolute personalities.[1]

The 14th South Carolina, Company D, for which Abner became captain, came to be known as the "Edgefield Rifles." The company would later become a part of the 14th South Carolina Infantry regiment, and was led by Lt. Col. Samuel McGowan. Abner came into contact with McGowan before the war began. McGowan was an associate of Thomas C. Perrin, Abner's uncle, in their law practice in Abbeville. At the beginning of the Civil War, ten volunteer regiments of infantry were raised for state defense in South Carolina and divided into four brigades. Governor Francis Pickens of South Carolina appointed McGowan commander of one of the brigades. The McGowan brigade assisted General Beauregard in the cap-

2. A Captain in the 14th South Carolina Infantry

ture of Fort Sumter. This brigade was transferred to the Confederate Army, where McGowan became an *aide de camp* to Gen. Luke Bonham. Shortly after the battle of First Bull Run (Manassas), McGowan returned to South Carolina and became the colonel of the 14th South Carolina after the resignation of Col. James Jones, the former commander.[2]

The 14th was organized in July of 1861 at Lightwoodknot Springs, near Columbia, South Carolina. The regiment was made up of men from the counties of Edgefield, Darlington, Laurens, Greenville, Spartanburg, and Kershaw. The 12th and 13th SC Infantry regiments were from the same general area and underwent their "basic training" at Lightwoodknot Springs along with the 14th. The 13th was more populated by men from Spartanburg and Greenville, and some from Chester County. By October the regiment had been moved to Pocotaligo, and by early 1862, it was facing attacks from Union gunboats. On April 14, 1862, the regiment was assigned to and became a part of Gregg's Brigade, and its first real battle experience occurred in the Seven Days' Battles. The final regiment added to the makeup of Gregg's Brigade was known as the First Regiment Rifles. The 1st South Carolina Infantry regiment completed its training in Richmond and was originally part of the six-month state volunteer commands. When the men in that command were mustered out, the unit was assigned to Gregg's Brigade. The majority of these men came from Abbeville, Pickens, Anderson, and Marion counties in South Carolina. The unit was usually known as Orr's Rifles and was first stationed at Sullivan's Island (in the Charleston area). Because of the less demanding duty given to the Rifles, it garnered the sobriquet "Pound Cake Regiment."[3]

It would be worthwhile to note some of the officers in the brigade who played a major role in the accomplishments of the famous Gregg's Brigade. The commander of the 1st South Carolina regiment was Col. D.H. Hamilton. The 1st South Carolina was a reorganization of the original six months' regiment led by General Gregg in 1861. Colonel Hamilton would later resign his commission after the Battle of Gettysburg as a result of a command dispute that involved General Perrin. The 1st South Carolina had several interesting aspects, and one in particular. Company E of this regiment was made up of men who had served with General Gregg in the original six months' regiment and had later enlisted for the "duration of the war." Capt. James M. Gadberry of Union, South Carolina, led Company E, which labeled itself the "Minute Men." The company comprised about 125 soldiers, primarily from Union. Captain Gadberry and General

Gregg were close associates before the war and both took a keen interest in politics, particularly the issue of secession.[4]

Colonel Oliver E. Edwards was a lawyer from Spartanburg County who ultimately led the 13th South Carolina regiment. He was originally part of the 5th South Carolina Volunteer regiment, and returned home after the regiment mustered out at the end of their six-month tour. He raised five companies from Spartanburg County that ultimately became part of the 13th South Carolina Infantry. Edwards led the regiment until his death at the Battle of Chancellorsville in 1863. There was notable sentiment for Edwards to be promoted to brigadier and commander of the brigade when Gregg was killed at Fredericksburg. Colonel James M. Perrin, a lt. colonel in Orr's Rifles and a relation of Abner, wrote on January 21, 1863, "I recommend him most cheerfully for promotion and am satisfied he will fill any position awarded to him with credit to himself and service to the Confederacy."[5] Colonel Benjamin T. Brockman took command of the 13th on the death of Colonel Edwards. Colonel Brockman was severely wounded at Spotsylvania on May 12, 1864; he lost his left arm and died one month later. Colonel Isaac Hunt became the commander of the 13th after the death of Colonel Brockman. Colonel Hunt led the regiment until its surrender at Appomattox Court House, after which he returned home, was married, and resumed his life in Greenville, South Carolina.[6]

James L. Orr was the founder and organizer of Orr's Rifles, and hailed from the Anderson District of South Carolina. Governor Francis Pickens granted Orr permission to raise a regiment to fight for the Confederacy, and he was commissioned as a colonel in the Confederate Army. Orr resigned his commission in early 1862 to become a member of the Confederate Congress, where he remained until the end of the war. Orr had served in the United States Congress as Speaker of the House, and after the war served as governor of South Carolina. Colonel John Marshall became the commander of Orr's Rifles after James Orr's departure to the Confederate Congress. Marshall was killed in the Battle of Second Bull Run/Manassas in August of 1862. Colonel Francis Harrison assumed command of the Rifles after Colonel Marshall's death. Harrison's first wife died in 1857 and he later married Mary Perrin, the daughter of Thomas Chiles Perrin. Mary was Abner's cousin, and oddly, upon Mary Perrin's death, Colonel Harrison married a third wife, Lizzie Perrin. Later in the war, Gen. Abner Monroe Perrin said of his cousin by marriage, Colonel Harrison, "I regard him as one of the most efficient officers in the service. He

2. A Captain in the 14th South Carolina Infantry

is prompt, vigilant, energetic, and gallant.... Moreover, I found him to be a high toned patriotic gentleman and he is well fitted in points of ability, education, and experience for any position."[7]

The 12th South Carolina Infantry was a composite of men from the counties of Oconee, York, Lancaster, Kershaw, and Fairfield. As was the case with the 14th South Carolina, it served on the coast near Pocotaligo, and later, in April 1862, moved to Virginia. The 12th served prisoner and ordnance train guard duty during the Chancellorsville Campaign. It rejoined the brigade after Chancellorsville and remained an integral part of the fighting force until the end of the war.[8] The 12th had a number of able colonels, but perhaps the most renowned was Col. Dixon Barnes. Colonel Barnes was from the Kershaw District and a graduate of the South Carolina College. A lawyer and wealthy planter, he is remembered as a "quiet gentleman with a long white beard."[9]

For the first two years of the war, Gen. Maxcy Gregg was the commander of the brigade to which the 14th South Carolina belonged. General Gregg was born in Columbia, South Carolina, in 1814 from a family of northern-based ancestry; in fact, his grandfather was a past president of Brown University in Rhode Island. Gregg was a brilliant student, and a noted expert in the field of astronomy, but unfortunately he had a streak of vanity to accompany his intellect. When he graduated from South Carolina College his scholastic record was tied with another student's as "leading scholar of the class of 1836"; not wanting to share first place, Gregg refused the honor as well as his diploma. Gregg was admitted to the bar in 1839, practicing law in the Columbia area for two decades. General Gregg was first associated with Abner Monroe during the Mexican War. Gregg was given a major's commission in the 12th United States Infantry, where Abner Monroe served as a lieutenant and later captain.[10] On March 24, 1847, Gregg was sent to Mexico but arrived too late to take part in any real battles. Maxcy Gregg was decidedly an advocate for Southern nationalism, and in 1860, he was a member of the Secession Committee. When secession was declared in December of 1860, he was immediately given a colonel's commission in the South Carolina volunteer service. He raised a regiment and was stationed at Morris Island during the bombardment of Ft. Sumter. Later he was transferred to Virginia, becoming part of Gen. Milledge Luke Bonham's brigade, where he took part in the Battle of First Bull Run/Manassas. Four months later, Gregg returned to South Carolina, was promoted to brigadier general and given a regiment, the 1st South

Carolina Infantry. Maxcy Gregg did not look at all like the typical Civil War general. He was short, slightly overweight, and nearly deaf. General Gregg conveyed an aura of calm, a thoughtful elegance, a "straight-arrow will, and absolute honesty." Gregg's 1st South Carolina Infantry, along with the 12th, 13th, and 14th South Carolina Infantry regiments, and the 1st Rifles, or Orr's Rifles, later formed Gregg's Brigade.[11]

An alternate view about Maxcy Gregg exists and will bolster a more balanced view of the personality of the stately general. Gregg was forty-seven years old when he came to Virginia to take part in the Seven Days' Battles. He held passionate convictions about Southern separatism *before* his role in the war, whereas others, such as A.P. Hill, came to that view only after the conflict began. His brigade was made up of equally "fervid and privileged" South Carolinians, as evidenced by the fact that Gregg's original regiment contained twenty-seven doctors and thirty lawyers. Gregg displayed an "aura of gallantry" which set him apart from other civilian generals. He appeared much like a "chevalier of ancient legend" when at the head of his brigade. All of these characteristics gave him a special place in the panoramic long view of Gen. A.P. Hill about the war and the noble cause of which they were a part.[12]

The following list contains the battles in which the 14th South Carolina, as a part of the Gregg's and/or McGowan's or Perrin's Brigade, took part:

Battle	**Date**
Port Royal Ferry	January 1, 1862
Seven Days' Battles	June 25–July1, 1862
Second Bull Run/Manassas	August 28–30, 1862
Chantilly	September 1, 1862
Antietam	September 17, 1862
Shepherdstown Ford	September 20, 1862
Fredericksburg	December 13, 1862
Chancellorsville	May 1–4, 1863
Gettysburg	July 1–3, 1863 (Colonel Perrin led the brigade)
Falling Waters	July 14, 1863
Bristoe Campaign	October 9–22, 1863
Mine Run Campaign	November–December 1863
The Wilderness	May 5–6, 1864

2. A Captain in the 14th South Carolina Infantry

Battle
Spotsylvania Courthouse
North Anna–Appomattox
Court House[13]

Date
May 8–21, 1864

Gen. Maxcy Gregg died of a mortal wound after the Battle of Fredericksburg and General McGowan became the brigade commander. The Bristoe Campaign was the final battle in which General Perrin was a part of the 14th South Carolina and McGowan Brigade. North Anna–Appomattox Court House occurred after the death of General Perrin.

By August 21, events were beginning to heat up along the coast of South Carolina, and Governor Pickens began to realize that he was facing a severe shortage of arms from the Confederate government. In a letter to Secretary of War Judah Benjamin he states, "As I anticipated, they [the Union forces] have passed the batteries, and will take Beaufort. My difficulty is in want of arms. I gave out the last to arm the 4,000 recently mustered in.... If I cannot get arms, can you not spare Gregg's regiment from Suffolk, and order it immediately to Pocotaligo, or near there?"[14] On December 23, 1861, General Gregg was ordered to report to Gen. John Pemberton of future Vicksburg fame. Pemberton was serving as commander of the Fourth Military District, which included South Carolina.[15]

In a report of Gen. G.T. Beauregard, Colonel Gregg was ordered to report with his entire regiment to Morris Island on the South Carolina coast to protect the Confederate works already established there. The report, not dated, was probably written in the spring of 1861, or at some point prior to First Bull Run/Manassas in July.[16] Gregg was still a colonel at this point, which excludes Abner Monroe from having a role in this action.

The first engagement in which *Captain* Perrin was involved probably occurred on January 1, 1862. In a report submitted by Col. James Jones, the first commander of the 14th South Carolina Infantry, Captains Perrin, Carter, and Tomkins were ordered forward under the command of Lt. Col. McGowan to assist and support Captain West at Kean's Neck road, where the enemy was advancing. The action was a part of an engagement at Port Royal Ferry on the Coosaw River. The regiment, along with part of the 12th South Carolina Infantry, was forced to withdraw as the Union forces arrived in large numbers with protection of the guns from three nearby steamers.[17]

In the spring of 1862 General Gregg and his regiments were sent to Virginia, and by late May, the brigade was attached to the famous "Light Division" of Gen. A.P. Hill.[18] On May 24, 1862, prior to becoming a part of the "Light Division," the brigade, along with the rest of the division, was commanded by Gen. Joseph R. Anderson. The division was marched to Richmond, where Gen. Joseph E. Johnson was aligning all the Confederate forces to contest Gen. George McClellan's army. The command reached Richmond around May 30, and here the brigade encamped, about seven miles from Richmond. McIntosh's battery, with four field pieces, was added to Gregg's brigade, which was now made up of five regiments, including McIntosh's battery. The brigade, along with five others (Anderson's, Branch's, Field's, Archer's and Pender's) were officially placed under the command of Gen. A.P. Hill. The command exceeded 25,000, probably closer to 30,000. The "new" soldiers were full of "vim and vigor" and ready for battle, which would come on June 26, 1862. On June 25, Gregg's brigade was ordered to march toward Meadow Bridge, paralleling the Chickahominy River. Unfortunately for Abner Monroe, the 14th South Carolina was left on picket duty at the Chickahominy.[19] Gregg's brigade was a few weeks too late to take part in the Battle of Fair Oaks/Seven Pines, which ended in late May 1862. This battle is significant because Gen. Joseph E. Johnson, who commanded Confederate forces in Virginia, was severely wounded in this battle. His injury opened the way for Gen. Robert E. Lee to gain command of what would ultimately be known as the Army of Northern Virginia.

After they arrived near Richmond and camped on the Chickahominy River at the end of May, little did Gregg's brigade realize that they were about to take part in one of the major battles of the Civil War. The Seven Days' Battles occurred the last week in June in 1862 and would be the last segment of what is generally known as the Peninsula Campaign. Gen. George McClellan, the commander of the Army of the Potomac, formulated the campaign plan after much delay and prodding by the president. Lincoln also offered a plan, which McClellan declined, while seemingly refusing to produce a plan of his own. Finally, in a letter dated February 3, 1862, McClellan sent Lincoln and Secretary of War Edwin Stanton his plan to capture Richmond. In his letter, he reviewed the military situation in general, and in particular discussed two possible plans to advance the Army of the Potomac. McClellan believed that the best plan was to descend down the Potomac, enter the Rappahannock River, land at Urbana for a

2. A Captain in the 14th South Carolina Infantry

base, quickly take the town of West Point at the head of the York River, and thus threaten Richmond before Gen. Joseph E. Johnston's army at Centreville could react and attempt to stop his advance. McClellan hoped to outflank the Confederates far on the left, and shift the major theatre of the war to Richmond. McClellan felt that this plan gave his army the shortest land route to Richmond and stated he would need 140,000 troops to accomplish this feat. Lincoln accepted the plan on March 8, 1862.[20]

Gen. A.P. Hill designated General Gregg's brigade as the 2nd Brigade in the "Light Division" that was under his command. At the time the Seven Days' Battles occurred, Gen. Thomas "Stonewall" Jackson was in command of a part of the army that included the "Light Division." The "Light Division" had six brigades, making it a rather large division, and probably the largest in the Army of Northern Virginia. Gregg's brigade and later McGowan's would remain a part of the "Light Division" until the end of the war. After Jackson's death at Chancellorsville, the army would be reorganized into three corps, and General A.P. Hill would become a corps commander.

Ambrose Powell Hill was a West Point Graduate in the class of 1847. He was a rather small man, 5' 9", and weighing only 145 lbs. He was often called "Little Powell," usually wore a bright red shirt when in battle since he paid little attention to uniform and dress, and always had his pistol, sword, field glasses, and a pipe, which he smoked regularly. Hill was a rather impetuous commander, and was thought of as an aggressive soldier. Hill married the sister of the famous Confederate general John Hunt Morgan, killed in Tennessee by Gen. George Stoneman's Cavalry.[21] An interesting twist of fate is that A.P. Hill was engaged to marry Ellen Marcy, who was also courted by George B. McClellan, whom she ultimately married. Miss Marcy's family was vehemently against her marrying Hill for many reasons, but Hill felt that it was because of "a youthful indiscretion" by which he was infected with a venereal disease in 1855. Hill was highly respected by General Lee, who seems to have had a rather forgiving attitude toward Hill's blunders. Such was the commander of the "Light Division," which opposed McClellan during the Seven Days' Battles in June of 1862.[22]

On June 23, 1862, General Lee called for a meeting of the field commanders of the Army of Northern Virginia to inform them of his plans for the upcoming battle. Often referred to as "General Orders 75," the plan was intended to drive McClellan and the Army of the Potomac from

Richmond. The plan had a number of points in its favor, but hinged on a few crucial elements. For example, a segment of Lee's army would descend upon the Federal right flank and block the bridges crossing the Chickahominy River. This would deny McClellan a passage to supply his army of more than 115,000 men from the White House. He then hoped to successfully attack McClellan north of the Chickahominy, forcing him to the east, thus removing the threat of an invasion of Richmond. Branch's brigade would travel to Half Sink, a crossing on the Chickahominy, and wait for Jackson to arrive in Ashland and establish contact with A.P. Hill's "Light Division." Once alerted of Jackson's arrival, Hill would cross the Meadow Bridge, clearing the way for D.H. Hill's division (of interest, Jackson and Daniel Harvey Hill were brothers-in-law) to cross the Chickahominy. Longstreet would then fall behind A.P. Hill's "Light Division," at which point the entire force would then move down the north side of the Chickahominy and unite with Generals Huger and Magruder for an all-out attack on McClellan from numerous directions. For simplification, McClellan and the Army of the Potomac would be driven down the bank of the Chickahominy River, on the northern side of the river, with no bridges to cross, and no escape other than toward the Chesapeake Bay.[23]

On Wednesday, June 25, Gregg's brigade received orders to prepare to advance. After sundown, the brigade left their compound and marched up the Chickahominy toward Meadow Bridge. Unfortunately, Captain Abner Perrin and the 14th South Carolina Infantry remained on picket duty. After many hours, the brigade arrived at the area near Meadow Bridge, but attempted to remain in seclusion from the enemy. The brigade made no additional movement until 3 P.M. on June 26. By this time, General Hill determined that Jackson's delay might jeopardize the entire operation and thus crossed the Meadow Bridge, with General Field's brigade leading, meeting little resistance, and followed by the brigades of Gregg and Pender. After a general pursuit, the Federals moved toward Mechanicsville.[24] The historian Clifford Dowdey had the following comments about Gregg's brigade as they marched toward Mechanicsville: "The last brigade, Maxey [sic] Gregg's followed the road to Mechanicsville in support of Pender. Gregg, a wealthy South Carolina lawyer, planter, and scholar, was the general next closest to Hill personally. The forty-seven-year-old citizen-soldier held the passionate convictions of separatism which came to Powell Hill and the other professional soldiers only after the invasion." Dowdey continues with these remarks about the men in Gregg's division:

2. A Captain in the 14th South Carolina Infantry

"His brigade was formed of equally fervid South Carolinians, mostly of privileged backgrounds.... Gregg and his hot bloods complemented one another." This statement is probably true of the officers in the brigade, but not of the individual soldiers, who were generally quite ordinary farmers and workers.[25]

General Webb of McClellan's staff gives an account of the battle, stating that the brigades of Archer, Field, Gregg and Pender "came into line but met a terrific artillery fire from the Union line." He continues: "General Branch came up, and was put in support of those already engaged. An attempt was made to turn our left lower down the creek, which failed disastrously. Two regiments of Ripley's brigade, with Pender's brigade, endeavored to flank the position at Ellison's Mill, but being exposed to the magnificent Union artillery, were repulsed with heavy loss." From Webb's account, the only saving grace for the Union force at Mechanicsville seems to have been the artillery.[26] Much has been said about Jackson's tardiness and seeming lack of concern about the battle at Mechanicsville. His chief defender is Lt. Col. G.F.R. Henderson. In his defense of Jackson's no-show at Mechanicsville, Henderson states that Jackson was separated by fifteen miles from A.P. Hill and that communication was to be accomplished by General Branch, but the progress of the battle made it impossible because messengers were stopped by the Union troops or forced to make detours. Thus, neither Jackson nor Hill knew the whereabouts of each other. Henderson continues by saying that the headquarters staff made inadequate arrangements in that a large force could not be expected to maintain a rigid arrival time set so far into the future. Finally, bridges had been burned, and Jackson was unfamiliar with the territory, and knowledgeable guides were not available. Henderson concludes: "The responsibility for Hill's defeat cannot be held to rest on Jackson's shoulders."[27]

Gregg's brigade was placed in the advance position on Friday, June 27, in the attempt to dislodge the Union forces from their position on Beaver Dam Creek, at Ellerson's Mills. Captain Perrin and the 14th regiment had yet to be relieved from picket duty and would not make it in time to take part in the ongoing battle until later in the afternoon. After a march of a few miles, the brigade arrived at Gaines' Mill; skirmishers were immediately sent out and were summarily met with enemy fire. The battle on this day acquired the name of Gaines' Mill because Gaines was the most prominent landowner in the area and was vehement in his support of the Southern cause. In addition, Federal troops had been on and in control of his property for over a month and frequently buried their dead on his land. Two regiments of Gregg's brigade, the 1st and the 12th, moved up and drove the Federal forces away. The Federal troops were most likely Porter's rear guard falling back.

This brief encounter seems to have given Gregg a false impression of Porter's retreat, and for this reason the brigade went rapidly after the retreating Federals, down and across the Cold Harbor Road and down the slope. Hidden guns opened up on the brigade and their irregular lines and the speed of the men probably saved them from extensive loss. By 2 P.M. the brigade was at rest for a time, and Longstreet and Jackson arrived about 3:45 P.M.; meanwhile, the Union and Confederate artillery maintained a constant exchange of fire. At about 4 P.M. the order for an advance was given.[28] The Union skirmishers, who continued to withdraw and hesitate, tempting the brigade to continue the assault, duped Gregg. Gregg moved through the Gaines' Mill area, passed Cold Harbor Road, and continued toward Bostwain's Swamp. At this hour (4 P.M.) Gregg's troops, already weary from the heat and long pursuit, came under intense Union artillery fire. The brigade moved into the swamp until they encountered a stand of trees where they attempted to regroup. General Hill, lacking proper reconnaissance, sent the remaining men in his command into a ravine area, very much unsuited for defense.

The 1st and 12th regiments of Gregg's brigade moved forward and immediately encountered extreme artillery and rifle fire from the frontal and right sides. General Gregg gave the command for Orr's Rifles to charge the Massachusetts battery with fixed bayonets. Colonel Marshall pushed forward, moving across an open field, facing fire from both front and flank. The Rifles gave an excellent account with their actions and sent the artillery battery seeking shelter. The Rifles now faced a new threat, a large aggressive force of New York Zouaves. The Zouaves were part of the division of Gen. George Sykes, V Corps of General Porter, and made up the 5th New York Infantry. General Sykes, often referred to as "Tardy George," was a member of the regular army and commanded the only body of regular troops in the Army of the Potomac. To this day, a unit of the U.S. Army still bears the moniker "Sykes's regulars." General Sykes would command the entire V Corps at Gettysburg. The 5th New York regiment was chiefly two-year enlistment troops, noted for and recognized by their uniforms, which featured red baggy pants and a red cap, as opposed to a hat or kepi-type cap.

2. A Captain in the 14th South Carolina Infantry

Thomas P. Southwick was a sergeant in the 5th and gives an account of the battle at Gaines' Mill:

I heard the battery on the left leaving the field and looking in that direction I saw regiment after regiment of Confederate infantry advancing on us from that flank. Our artillery that we were supporting then fell back and I must confess I felt relieved when I heard the colonel command "about face." We retreated slowly in line halting and turning on the top of every hillock long enough to pour another volley on our advancing foes.

Colonel Duryee was concerned for the safety of his men and told [brigade commander Colonel G.] Warren that if his regiment remained where it was much longer he would not have men enough to go on guard. "How many are left?" asked Warren.... "About a hundred and fifty," said Duryee.... "Well," said Warren, "I'll go and see Sykes." We held the valley and the enemy the battlefield.[29]

If this number is accurate, the 5th New York sustained about a 40 percent casualty rate, and a greater percent would soon occur at the Battle of Second Manassas. After that battle in August and September of 1862, the unit remained intact until May of 1863, when the two-year enlistments ended and only four companies signed reenlistment papers.[30]

At about the time of the Rifles' attack on the Federal artillery, the 14th South Carolina Infantry arrived. Still, with assistance from a regular regiment from Sykes's division, the Zouaves were able to halt the Rifles' assault. The 14th had not been relieved from picket duty on schedule, and they were weary from the long march, the heat, and the frustration of two days and three nights of picket duty; nonetheless they charged into the Union forces. The 14th, along with a North Carolina and a Georgia regiment, were ultimately forced to withdraw to the crest of a ridge, which they held for the duration of the fighting on June 27. The historian Stephen Sears states, "Gregg's brigade was fought to exhaustion. It would suffer 815 casualties on June 27, the largest toll in any brigade in Lee's army." The Rifles alone suffered 309 casualties, about 57 percent of their total force.[31] Dr. Spencer Welch, the physician of the 13th South Carolina regiment, describes a macabre landscape of the death and destruction at Gaines' Mill: "I was on the ground yesterday where some of the hardest fighting took place. The dead were lying everywhere and were very thick in some places. One of our regiments had camped in some woods there and the men were lying among the dead Yankees and seemed unconcerned."[32]

Major E.M. Woodward of the 2nd Pennsylvania Volunteers gives a vivid account of the intensity of the Battle of Gaines' Mill:

Steadily the columns of the foe were advancing on our left, their leading lines dressed in our uniforms, showing no flag and treacherously crying out they were our friends, and not to fire upon them. But we were not deceived, and poured into them a left oblique fire with good effect. But onward they pressed until almost upon us, when they poured into us a deafening roar of musketry. above which the artillery fire at times could scarcely be distinguished. Line after line delivered their fire, and falling to the ground gave range to those behind them. It sounded like one long continuous roar, not a susceptible internal being perceived for several minutes. Overpowered, flanked, and with the enemy in our rear, with scattered remnants of other regiments in the excitement of the moment firing into us, we broke and were scattered through the woods, fighting the best we could from behind trees, until finally we were driven headlong out, with our muskets thoroughly heated, and our ammunition almost exhausted.[33]

Gaines' Mill was the largest and most costly of the battles known as the Seven Days and also of the entire Peninsula Campaign. The battle started at noon and continued until 9 P.M. Neither army had ever taken part in such a battle up to that point in the war. Gen. Jacob Cox made an interesting statement, amounting to an indictment concerning General McClellan's role in this battle, and in the war in total: "It is worse than blindness to continue to repeat assumed facts after they have been shown to be essentially incorrect" [paraphrased].[34] This would be McClellan's style until the end of his career. The Army of Northern Virginia and the Army of the Potomac placed 96,000 men on the battlefield and few later battles in the war would exceed this number.[35]

General Gregg's report on the Seven Days' Battles was delivered after his death in December of 1862 and was prepared by A.C. Haskell, Gregg's assistant adjutant-general, from notes found in Gregg's papers. Gregg states that he sent his aide-de-camp, Capt. Harry Hammond, to relieve the 14th regiment from picket duty and to guide the regiment to the battle area. Colonel McGowan had sent Captains Wood and Taggert to attempt to communicate with Gregg and the brigade. Hammond and Captains Wood and Taggert met at the Chickahominy near a bridge, which had been built by Union troops near Dr. Friend's house, and later burned by retreating Union troops. McGowan's regiment repaired the bridge and came forthwith to the battlefield while under constant fire from enemy batteries. Crenshaw's battery, assigned to General Gregg's brigade, had to cease firing to allow the 14th to pass. The 14th aligned to the right of the 13th South Carolina, and in so doing was able to halt the advancing Federals and prevent the establishment of a battery near the open ground at the crest of the hill, which would have been a major obstacle for the brigade. The 14th established its line along a fence up the hill where it remained until the battle's end. With the help of a North Carolina and a Georgia regiment, the 14th charged the battery, but intense fire and a long traverse over open ground forced the cessation of the charge.[36]

On Saturday, June 28, the brigade was at rest and engaged in the burial of their fallen comrades. On Sunday, June 29, due to McClellan's retreat, the unit began a march toward the James River. The Battle of Savage Station occurred on June 29, but Gregg's brigade did not take part in that combat, instead continuing toward Richmond. The brigade traveled down the Charles City Road, turned on Quaker Road and bivouacked some fifteen miles from Richmond. On Monday, June 30, the march continued and reached Frayser's Farm, where the next encounter with the Union troops occurred. Lee intended to place six divisions in the Glendale or Frayser's Farm engagement. The planned attack was to be somewhat complex, with a frontal, flank, and rear attack occurring simultaneously, designed to create confusion for McClellan's army. Hill's division attacked the Federals at Willis Church and, along with Longstreet, routed McCall's division and captured General McCall. General Huger's division was part of the attack, but his advance was halted on the Charles City Road. General T.H. Holmes was also to be a part of the attack and was supposed to turn McClellan's left flank, but he faltered and was pushed back by gunboats on the James River. Overall, the attack was slow to materialize and made only minimal holes in the Union lines. Lee had determined that with this level of troop involvement he could cut McClellan's army in two; Jackson would then confront McClellan's rear guard, which guarded the White Oak Swamp Crossing. Lee hoped to mass enough manpower to deal with whatever might occur; thus every available soldier under his command would be committed.

This battle has not received the attention it deserves by historians. An authority no less than Gen. Edward Porter Alexander, Longstreet's artillery commander, proclaimed that this battle was the *best* of several chances that could have ended the war with the winning of Confederate independence. The eminent historian Stephen Sears has much to say about this battle. He views it as the most puzzling of Civil War battles. It has many names, which is an indication of the confusion surrounding it. The battle, for once, favored Lee in that McClellan's line of retreat was due south over marshy and boggy terrain and there were few roads for him to take. In addition, McClellan was rattled and making mistakes. The mental stress was taking such a toll that McClellan even indicted the president and other elected officials for his situation.[37] On June 30, McClellan left the battle area for the James River and did not designate any commanding officer to serve in his place. Sears states, "The plain truth of the case is that he deserted his army." McClellan boarded the USS *Galena* and steamed up to River Road to investigate a Confederate column with the artillery fire ringing in his ears. He had a fine meal aboard the *Galena* and repeated the process the next day. Lee, with no knowledge of all this, went about his business and divided his forces into four segments under Generals Huger, Jackson, Holmes, and Magruder. They each had assignments, which none of them carried out; plus, Huger and Holmes were unfit for field command due to age and lack of experience, and Magruder was too "feisty" and eccentric.[38] Stonewall Jackson was absolutely "out of the loop," and speculation seems to suggest that he was exhausted from the battle scene of the past week to the point of breakdown. After a reconnoitering trip, Jackson and D.H. Hill (Jackson's brother-in-law) returned, after which Jackson appeared to have lost any interest in what they had learned and how it could be used. In this weeklong battle scene, Jackson was below par, but at Glendale, he failed to use his 25,000 troops in the battle. Instead, he floundered about seemingly concerned about a bridge he felt was essential, yet his men had several fords available that they could have used. Magruder lost his way to his assigned post and arrived after the battle ended. As mentioned previously, Holmes fired on the wrong Union battery, opening up fire from many batteries, and also from the Union gunboats, and was repulsed completely.[39] Longstreet and A.P. Hill were left to contend with the Union forces, minus about 51,000 men misplaced, squandered, and held back by Holmes, Huger, and Magruder — fully half of Lee's army.[40]

As the scene progressed, about three miles into the march Gregg's brigade encountered Longstreet's division in a battle situation. The Union forces were shelling the Confederates in the hope of delaying any interception as they continued their retreat down Quaker Road. In a rather unusual situation to have occurred in a combat zone, President Jefferson Davis had ventured out to *observe* the battle in progress. He came very near to becoming a death statistic by his presence at the battle, a reckless decision which did not help an already bad situation. Longstreet's division encountered a Union infantry force, and the "Light Division" was sent as reinforcement for Longstreet's division. Captain Abner Perrin's 14th regiment was the only part of Gregg's brigade to actually take part in the battle. The 14th attempted to assist and rescue the brigades of Generals Roger Pryor and Winfield Featherston, both hard pressed and at a late hour, since it was near dark as the brigades came into conflict with General Kearny's division. Colonel McGowan and the 14th were the leading regiment on this march. McGowan sent out skirmishers, who soon reported that General Featherston was located in the "undergrowth, wounded, and about to be taken prisoner." Intense fire was exchanged with the Federals. McGowan reported that his troops shot seventy rounds each. Strangely, both McGowan and the Federals came to believe they were engaged in "friendly fire" and thus ceased firing for a time.

Most likely it was during this period of the battle that the capture of General McCall occurred. Gen. A.P. Hill states in his report that Col. Robert Mayo of the 47th Virginia gained possession of a battery and turned the guns on the enemy, which greatly assisted General Gregg and the 14th South Carolina in its role in the battle. Hill also credits the 47th Virginia with McCall's capture. Yet McCall accidentally blundered into the ranks of the 47th Virginia while attempting to determine his division's location to continue their forward movement.[41] General McCall commanded the 3rd Division of the V Corps and was assigned a position on the left of Long Bridge Road to protect the supply trains advancing from White Oak Creek. General Meade's brigade was posted on the right of McCall's position. By 2 P.M. the division was forced to retreat as the battle raged; McCall was ultimately swept from the field, and Meade was carried from the field seriously wounded. McCall described the battle scene as "the most unequalled wild recklessness I have ever seen."[42]

Also during this time of cessation of firing due to a mistaken impression of "friendly fire," a Union officer came to the 14th South Carolina ranks and asked who they were. McGowan repeated the same query to the Union officer, who said he was with the 20th Indiana and was immediately taken prisoner. In addition prisoners were taken from the 12th Pennsylvania, 40th New York, and an additional fifteen prisoners from the 20th Indiana. Colonel W.L. Brown of the 20th Indiana attributed the capture of his men to "vastly superior numbers of the enemy." Kearny's division loss was 1,017 and the combined loss from the brigades of Pryor, Featherston, and Gregg was 882.[43] (In the mid–1980s, Confederate artifacts [bullets, buttons, etc.] were found on the battlefield and were identified as belonging to the 14th South Carolina. Bones of a buried Confederate soldier were exhumed and reinterred in Columbia in 1985.)

General Lee replied to an officer who asked if McClellan might escape, "Yes, he will get away because I cannot have my orders carried out."[44] General Lee was entirely correct when he gave this reply, having lost one of the best opportunities of the war to capture the entire Army of the Potomac. Lt. George W. Booth of the 1st Maryland Infantry also supports this view of the Battle of Glendale. Lieutenant Booth accepts the view that Jackson may have been ill, exhausted, or otherwise disoriented, but goes on to say: "The consequences were ... far reaching. The bloody repulse at Malvern might have been obviated and the federal retreat seriously jeopardized, had fate ordered otherwise. As it was McClellan succeeded in reaching the Malvern position in fair shape, although his losses in the battle were heavy."[45]

Malvern Hill was the last battle of the Peninsula Campaign for McClellan and the Army of the Potomac. On July 1, 1862, Jackson crossed White Swamp and the battlefield of Frayser's Farm and began to track the Union forces down Willis Church Road. Gregg's brigade played a minor role in this battle and the divisions of D.H. Hill, Huger, and Magruder were the major Confederate combatants. The battle hinged on the Confederates' attacking the artillery units and interaction with the infantry support regiments. In this battle, there was another factor which may also be significant, and yet nearly unknown. General Lee expressed to General Longstreet that he was feeling "fatigued and unwell" and that Longstreet should pass command of his division to General Richard Anderson and continue the march with him. It seems evident that Lee was unsure as to his ability to continue in command and wanted Longstreet available as a backup. This may have been a factor in the outcome of this battle.[46] Lee's extreme fatigue was affecting his judgment. General McLaws testified that he attempted to deliver a report to Lee on July 1 and found him asleep under a tree and that President Davis was present to see that he was not disturbed! General Lee seemed to be out of sync with his subordinates at this point.[47]

Malvern Hill is an elevated plateau, spanning about a mile and a half by about three-fourths of a mile in area, and in 1862 was clear of timber, with several roads converging on and crossing over the plateau. The land slopes gradually toward the north and east. In 1862, this sloping continued

2. A Captain in the 14th South Carolina Infantry

to a heavy wooded area, yet giving good range for artillery. On the northwest side, the plateau falls off abruptly to a deep trench-like ravine, which extends to the James River. On this plateau the Union army placed its artillery on a line running toward a point below Haxall's on the James River. The plateau is about a mile north of the James River, and about 125 feet higher than the river. A creek known as Turkey Island Creek had two tributaries, Turkey Run and Western Run, that framed the plateau. The actual size of the plateau was a disadvantage because only a limited force could be placed in this space. Thus, if a counterforce of Confederates stormed the gun emplacements, then all could be lost before help could arrive. Conversely, this location excelled in its advantage for artillery and the panoramic view that would easily allow the enemy to be immediately sighted.[48] In addition, the Federal battle line flanks rested on the James River, which prevented them from being turned.

An important aspect of this battle is the role of the Union gunboats on the James River. As stated earlier, Malvern Hill is but a mile or so from the river, which placed the gunboats within striking range. Thomas P. Southwick of the New York 5th regiment states, "Soon the battalion we had planted on the hill began to blaze away and then the gunboats on the James River opened fire, sending their huge shells screaming and shrieking through the air over our heads, tearing down the forest trees in the distance with a sound like rumbling thunder." Southwick goes on to say, "The gunboats saved the flank and thus saved the army."[49] Southwick here makes reference to the Confederate Army's attempt to flank the artillery, since it would have been suicide to attempt a frontal attack, given the conditions and location of the guns. Another source states that the Confederate Army attempted to flank both sides of the Sedgwick and Richardson gun emplacements at the same time. The attacks were so fierce that General Slocum was ordered up from the reserve units. Infantry action went on for about two and one-half hours, ending at about 6 P.M.[50] Malvern Hill was an intense battle, second only to Gaines' Mill.

The pressing question one is compelled to ask is why General Lee did not send his entire force against McClellan at Malvern Hill. While it is true that Gregg's brigade and the entire "Light Division" had battled furiously at Gaines' Mill and the 14th South Carolina had been engaged with Longstreet's division at the Battle of Frayser's Farm, a defeat at Malvern Hill would have likely destroyed the Army of the Potomac. This is somewhat the same situation that occurred with McClellan at Gaines' Mill. If

General Abner M. Perrin, C.S.A.

Lee attempted to flank both sides of the Union force at Malvern Hill at once, would not a larger force have possibly been successful? McClellan was forced to called up a reserve unit to prevent being overrun, and it stands to reason that McClellan's army was also just as exhausted as the Confederate Army by 6 P.M. on July 1 after a week-long engagement.

The historian Robert E.L. Krick offers some insight into this situation: "It is clear enough that Lee did not wish to attack Malvern Hill directly." Krick goes on to explain that Lee did finally allow an artillery concentration, as suggested by Longstreet. At about 1:30 P.M. Lee vanished until 4 P.M., searching for a weak spot in the Union lines on the army's left flank. From that point, Krick continues, "He issued orders, based on erroneous, misunderstood information, for a general assault up Malvern Hill. Two hours later he was back in the center of the Confederate line, showing General McLaws where to attack and adjusting the route of Magruder's assault. No one recorded his presence after that, either rallying troops or issuing orders." Lee obviously had little impact on the battle scene. Krick concludes, "The Army of Northern Virginia suffered a breakdown that consumed every branch of the service." Yet another reason for the Confederate defeat at Malvern Hill may have been that Lee was not yet in complete control of the army since he had only been in command for a very short time. In fact, Lee's first victory as commander of the Army of Northern Virginia was Gaines' Mill, only a few days earlier.[51] The Confederates prevented McClellan from entering Richmond and forced his retreat, but the price for this action was very high; an educated assessment states that it was close to 15,000 casualties.[52] At Malvern Hill, Lee had driven McClellan to the last available stronghold he might have used, and the alternative was either the river or a trek back to Harrison's Landing, a couple of miles to the east. Lee had the available manpower to even cut off the escape route to Harrison's Landing and simply hold McClellan at Malvern Hill. He chose to attack instead. This was Lee's mistake and he lost control of the battle as a result. At dark, McClellan withdrew his forces to Harrison's Landing and Lee was deprived of a victory that could have been the end of the Army of the Potomac.

Captain Abner Perrin had "seen the elephant," and his involvement in a major battle of the Civil War, one can reasonably assume, no doubt changed his outlook significantly in many aspects. Perrin, as a captain of a company in a regiment, did not write a report of his company or regiment activities during any of the battles of the Seven Days. In all likelihood he

2. A Captain in the 14th South Carolina Infantry

was not requested nor ordered to write a report concerning these battles. At this point in his career he was still learning the skills and demeanor of an officer in the Confederate Army, as well as the art and science of warfare. In the presence of such men as R.E. Lee, Jackson, the Hills, and Longstreet, he astutely determined that he should remain in the background. In addition, the future general was never a showoff and reserved his comments for the appropriate time and circumstances. In addition, Perrin's regiment was retained on picket duty for two days during the Battle of Mechanicsville, and arrived at 6 P.M. for the conclusion of the Battle of Gaines' Mill, although this was an important contribution. There is little or no information available as to what role Captain Perrin played at Gaines' Mill: the most significant primary source on the Gregg/McGowan brigade of

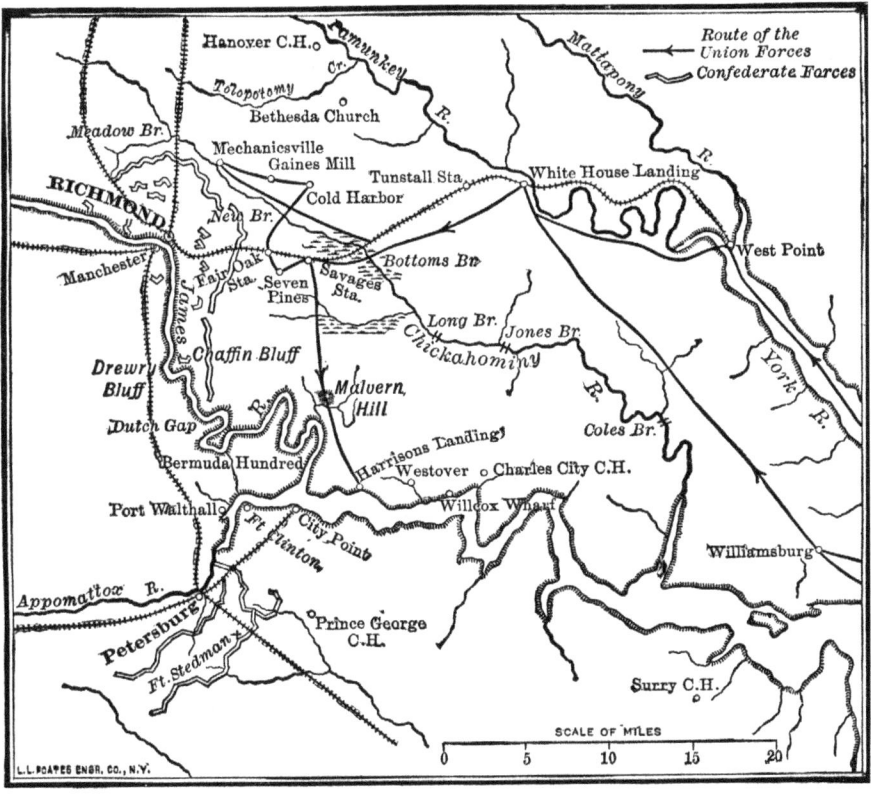

Seven Days' Fighting in Virginia in June of 1862 (Florida Center for Instructional Technology).

which the 14th South Carolina infantry was a part does not mention Perrin, as is the case with all of the other major sources. Without a doubt, Captain Perrin sent letters to his wife and family, but such materials are in private hands, if they exist at all. The 14th regiment was significantly involved with the Battle of Frayser's Farm/Glendale, but Captain Perrin is not mentioned in the reports of Colonel McGowan concerning that battle. It cannot be concluded that Perrin played no role or an insignificant role in the Seven Days' Battles; it is just as likely that his contributions were simply not noted, or occurred behind the scenes. Others may have been credited with his efforts, or reports containing information about Captain Perrin may have been lost, or not included in the *Official Records of the War of the Rebellion* for some reason. Captain Perrin, as will be shown, is an example of the old adage, "Actions speak louder than words." To become a general in the Confederate Army one had to demonstrate leadership and courage in the face of imminent danger and the likelihood of death, and have the trust and respect of the soldiers under his command. For these reasons, Captain Perrin would later become General Perrin.

General Edward Porter Alexander offers a comment about the Peninsula Campaign and Gen. "Stonewall" Jackson's role in the famous campaign that only an actual participant could put forth:

> The Peninsula Campaign and the Seven Days have always been the subject of much controversy, both North and South. The plans of General Lee were bold and excellent, but they fell short of success owing to the faults of his lieutenants, in particular Jackson.
>
> It is difficult to explain the failure of Jackson during the Seven Days. As General Alexander says, "He nowhere, even distantly, approached his record as a soldier won in every other battle, either before or afterward.... Nothing that he had to do was done with the vigor which marked all the rest of his career."[53]

With the presence of individuals who were of such immense importance as General Jackson and General Lee, a captain taking part in his first major battle in the great war between the sections of the United States would likely be overlooked unless he did something of boundless importance. If General Alexander took notice and made a critique of Jackson's *lack* of action in the Seven Days' Battle, it is probable that a captain in a regiment that was part of a brigade and a division under Jackson's command would have been invisible.

Recognition would come later in the life of Captain Perrin and it

2. A Captain in the 14th South Carolina Infantry

would be of grave importance. One can only speculate how Captain Perrin must have felt, the emotions he experienced, the pride that swelled in his thoughts. This was a serious man, a man who took all of his responsibilities as mandates as to how he should live and control his actions and, just as importantly, his reactions. These personality traits would cause him to be misunderstood and in some cases disliked. After all, Abner Perrin was possibly a lieutenant in the United States Army at age eighteen, and this was not a typical occurrence.

CHAPTER 3

The Maryland Campaign

At the close of the battle at Malvern Hill, Gregg's brigade made its way to an area less than ten miles south of Richmond known as Laurel Church, on the River Road. The brigade and much of the Light Division remained in this area until the end of July. Because of poor sanitation, exposure to the elements, and a rather poor and non-nutritive diet, disease became a serious and rampant problem, and in particular typhoid fever and dysentery. The number of men who could not have taken part in a battlefield encounter about equaled those who could. The division was poorly supplied with the basic needs of food, clothing, and shelter. When these conditions are added to the extreme humidity and blazing heat such as are to be found in the coastal Virginia area in July, armies suffer afflictions.

On August 1, the division made an exhausting march to Richmond, boarded railcars on the Central Railroad for the trip to Gordonsville, and remained there until August 6. Another equally dismal and unpleasantly hot trip was then made from Gordonsville to Orange Court House. The troops were then allowed to rest from about midnight until late in the afternoon of August 7.[1]

By this date Jackson had a corps of three divisions: his old division, General Ewell's division, and the Light Division. Gen. John Pope had recently been transferred from the Mississippi area to take charge of a newly created army labeled the Army of Virginia. Pope had experienced some success in the west with a victory at Island 10, and for this reason it was President Lincoln's contention that Pope would be more successful than McClellan in confronting the Confederate Army. "Brash, bombastic John Pope" tempted fate by returning to the old battleground of Manassas. Pope was his own worse enemy: abrasive, conceited, and loudmouthed, he

3. The Maryland Campaign

rubbed people the wrong way. When he returned to Virginia, he managed to alienate his top subordinates almost at once and soon earned the enmity of the common soldiers.[2] Nonetheless, Pope had some reservations about this new command, mainly because he was junior in promotion to a number of the generals that would now be under his command. In a letter published by the *New York Times* July 23, 1862, Pope stressed that he and the other western generals always pursued attack and *not* defense, and that he would seek out the enemy and do it speedily. An interesting description of General Pope is given by George A. Townsend, a war correspondent for the Union army: "In person, he was dark, martial, and handsome—inclined to obesity, richly garbed in civil cloth, possessing a fiery black eye, with luxuriant beard and hair. He smoked incessantly, and talked imprudently ... his vanity was apparent to the most shallow observer ... he inspired distrust by his love of gossip."[3] Pope commanded three corps, which made up the Army of Virginia: the I Corps, commanded by Gen. Franz Sigel; the II Corps, commanded by Gen. Nathaniel Banks; and the III Corps, commanded by Gen. Irvin McDowell. McDowell seems to have been a role model of a sort for Pope and it seemed at first glance that he was dependent upon McDowell's skill and judgment, but that illusion would soon vanish. Pope's army was scattered all over the countryside. The I and II Corps were located at Middletown, and the III Corps was divided, with one division at Manassas and the other at Fredericksburg. Pope immediately ordered the army to assembly at Culpeper Court House, and by July 12, the command occupied the Culpeper Court House area. Jackson's objective in the campaign involving the Battle of Second Manassas was to prevent Pope from connecting with the Army of the Potomac by attacking his three corps before McClellan arrived from the Peninsula.[4]

The first encounter with the Army of Virginia occurred on August 9. Hill's division moved toward Culpeper Court House, crossing the Rapidan River at Barnett's Ford. From that point Gregg's brigade was assigned wagon guard duty, which meant they were to prevent the Federal cavalry from attacking the baggage wagons. Therefore, the brigade did not take part in the battle known as Cedar Mountain on August 9.[5] On August 12, Gregg's brigade continued the march toward Orange Court House, crossed the Rapidan River, and after a rest period resumed the march. At about the halfway point between Gordonsville and Orange Court House, the division halted until morning.

On August 16, the Confederates launched the Maryland Campaign, in which Jackson was to remain to the left of Longstreet's wing and cross the Rapidan River at Somerville Ford. Meanwhile, Stuart went in search of Gen. Fritz Lee, who had strayed too far right toward Fredericksburg and was a day late for the march to Maryland. On this venture Stuart was nearly captured by the Union forces when he made a side excursion to visit a friend. While he was napping in the garden, the Federals approached to within hearing distance, forcing Stuart to flee, leaving his famed plumed hat behind. Stuart's adjutant, Maj. Norman Fitz Hugh, was not so lucky and was captured with a copy of General Lee's marching orders in his possession. This blunder resulted in Lee's having to make a rapid revision in his campaign plan, allowing Pope to escape Culpeper Court House, separating his army from Lee by way of the Rappahannock River. Jackson was now ordered to march toward Stevensburg and Brandy Station, toward the Rappahannock Bridge. Gregg's brigade, along with the Light Division, reached the Somerville Ford on the morning of August 20 and crossed the ford on their way toward Stevensburg.[6]

Beginning on Thursday, August 21, and continuing until Tuesday, August 26, the brigade and the division were on the move, reaching Bristoe Station on the 26th. This location put Jackson behind Pope's army, ending a momentous flanking movement. The march went smoothly, and as was usual, the division as well as the rest of Jackson's forces had no inkling where they were headed. Only one stumbling block stood in the way of a perfect flanking movement, and that was the Thoroughfare Gap in the Bull Run Mountains. Jackson fully expected to encounter Federal troops blocking the way, and sent a cavalry detachment to engage them. He determined that if his movement were detected, even if he subdued the Union troops, word would be sent back to Pope. No Union troops were located, much to Jackson's surprise. In addition, Stuart's cavalry finally arrived, and still no Federal troops had been sighted. Pope's action, or rather inaction, is unexplained. He seems to have made no attempt to determine Jackson's exact location, but persisted in an effort to concentrate his army near the area of Waterloo Bridge, while McDowell was engaged in an artillery duel with Longstreet. Pope continued, or so it seemed, to bank on the assumption that Lee would strike on the Rappahannock at some point.

Mass confusion, faulty information, and a lack of leadership prevailed within the Army of Virginia. Van R. Willard, a soldier in the 3rd Wisconsin Infantry, in the brigade of Gen. Thomas Ruger, Gen. Alphesus Williams's

3. The Maryland Campaign

division, gives a very insightful description of Pope's generalship: "Here the army operations were and still are a mystery to me, and I do not believe that there is a general, not even Pope himself, that can elucidate them. Battles were fought when least expected, portions of the army were separated from the rest, all communications cut off until Pope fled with his army in confusion toward Washington.... Pope was evidently out generaled and most completely bewildered, and finally fled to Alexandria and crept behind the guns of the fortifications."[7] The evidence suggests that General Pope was viewed by the rank-and-file soldiers and subordinate field officers as a fulsome and insipid individual, lacking any real military value.

The three Union corps commanders of the Army of Virginia are also worthy of a descriptive comment. Gen. Franz Sigel had served as a lieutenant in the German army and maintained a saloon in St. Louis. At the beginning of the war, Sigel was given a colonelcy to placate the German-Americans of Missouri. Sigel was a diminutive man, thin and well muscled, somewhat feverish, and sanguine. He made quick decisions, and was more severe than most of the American generals; he preferred to avoid combat if possible, but was ruthless if all else failed. General Banks lived near Boston, was self-educated, and became a legislator, governor, and later a congressman. Banks was a mannerly person, and he possessed considerable ability, "conducting a retreat unequaled in the Civil War." Gen. Irvin McDowell was one of the oldest generals in the Union army. Bull Run had transformed him into a villain who was mistrusted and disliked. Where criticism was concerned, McDowell was stoic, never flinched, and seldom replied to the claims against him. "He was ambitious, but contented himself with subordinate commands. In the mind of many soldiers as well as civilians, he was a traitor, incompetent, and plotted against the nation." As a result of these claims, his role as a general was greatly diminished.[8] The average soldier had contempt for McDowell as well as Pope. In a letter to his family, 2nd Lieutenant Avery Cain, 4th U.S. Infantry stated, "It is said that General Sigel shook his sword in McDowell's face the day of the fight. He was very angry with him — I will resign before I will fight under Gen. McDowell. I do not care to risk my life under such a blockhead as he is."[9]

Captain Abner Perrin, as of August of 1862, had not yet received an opportunity to prove himself to be the competent soldier that he would very soon become. The 14th Regiment had not been involved in some of the action of which the 1st, 12th, and 13th regiments had been a part. This omission was mainly because the regiment spent three nights and two days on picket duty during the battle of the Seven Days, took part in the Battle of Gaines' Mill only in its final hours, and would again be placed on reserve duty during part of the battle of Second Manassas/Bull Run. The frustration level for Perrin because of these standby deployments must have been very high, since he was not one who was content to stand by while others engaged in combat.

On August 27, the division began the march to Manassas Junction, where large Federal stores had been captured. Upon arrival, the men in Gregg's brigade were issued much-needed supplies. Additionally, along the way the brigade had "commissioned" all they desired from a sutler's establishment. After midnight the march to Centreville was begun, once the remaining stores at Manassas Junction were burned. The march continued up the Warrenton Turnpike, crossing Bull Run near Stone Bridge. By sunset, the brigade was mixed with General Ewell on their right, where Gregg's regiments then aligned themselves and remained during the night with their weapons at their sides.

General Lee was extremely fortunate in capturing a copy of Pope's orders, with the troop locations, and more importantly, the location, timing, numbers and other details concerning the reinforcements. Thus, Lee knew that he must bring about the battle before Pope's reinforcements arrived, yet all the while it seems that Pope was totally confused and was busily chasing about looking for Jackson. Early on August 29, Gregg's brigade was posted on a railroad cut, serving as the extreme left of the army, and were aligned in the following order: 13th on the right, then the 1st, then the 12th, and finally the 14th, with Orr's Rifles acting as reserves. The entire brigade was massed only a few feet from the railroad cut, and General Gregg was fifty yards or so behind the regiments. The entire army's position left much to be desired in that the wooded area along the left and center of their line virtually eliminated the use of artillery. This meant fifty guns were silent which could have supported the infantry. In addition, the railroad cut was uneven, too high in spots for the infantrymen to have a proper view, while other areas of the cut were wide-open fields offering no real cover.[10]

Jackson's line was in place when the attack began at about 8 A.M. Schurz's division, on the right of Sigel's Corps, hit Jackson's wing first. This certainly was not the campaign plan that Jackson envisioned, as he had hoped that Longstreet would arrive before the attack began. General Gregg sent the 1st regiment to meet Colonel Krzyzanowski's attack, who

3. The Maryland Campaign

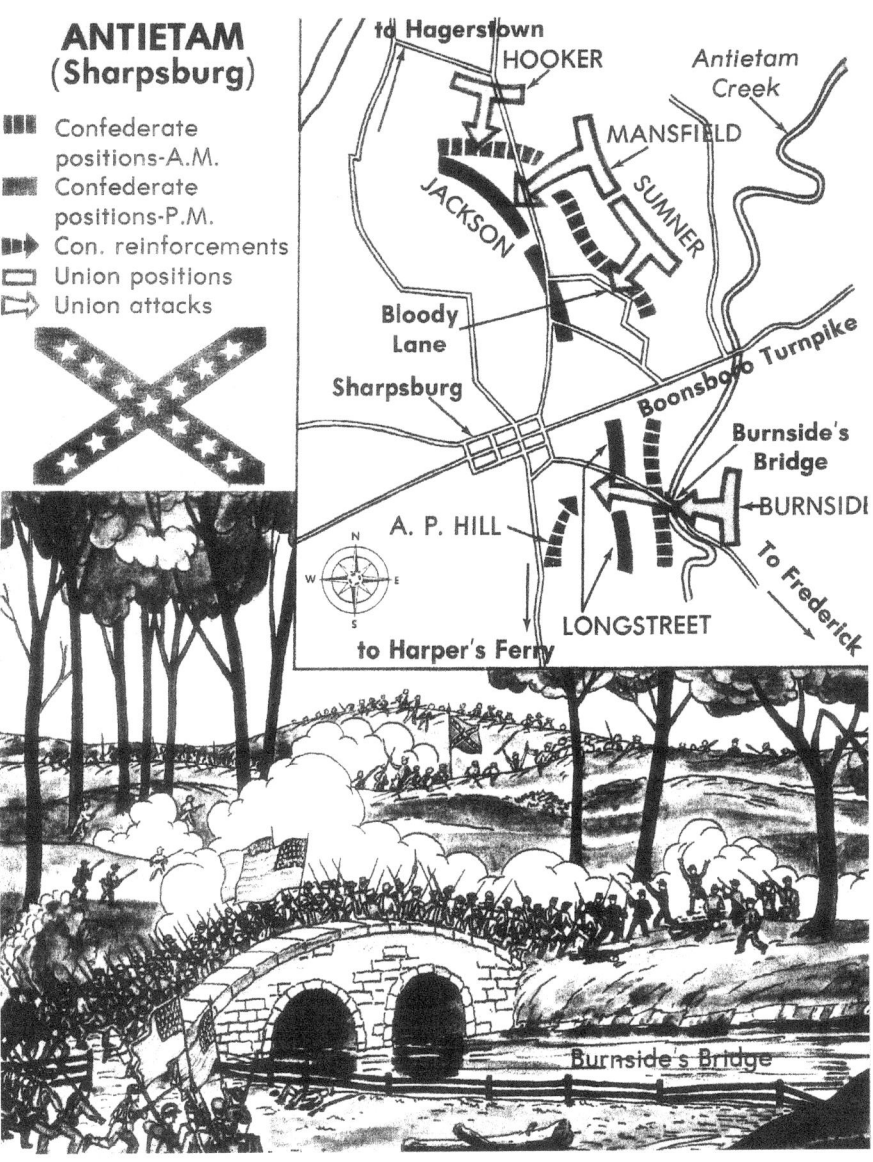

Map showing the Battle of Antietam, September 17, 1862 (© Milliken Publishing Company. All rights reserved).

in turn sent the 54th and 58th New York regiments to attack Gregg's skirmish line. Gregg ordered the 12th South Carolina in, which was then countered by the 75th Pennsylvania. Gregg immediately responded and ordered the 13th South Carolina forward, and the move-countermove contest continued for well over an hour. Gregg's brigade was probably engaged by the full force of the Federal troops by noon based upon Caldwell's account of the battle scene, although it could have been earlier based on other accounts of the battle.

At about 5 P.M. the Union troops engaged their full might and closed in on the Confederates from all directions. As Caldwell stated, "They seemed determined not to abandon the undertaking; we were resolved never to yield."[11] At about 4:30 P.M. Pope decided he should ratchet up the firepower on Hill's line, and he ordered General Hooker to move his division forward. Hooker felt this was a "losing proposition" since he would have no support, and he rapidly contacted Pope and requested that General Phil Kearny also supply troops for this endeavor. Pope consented, and Kearny then ordered Gen. Beverly Robinson's brigade against Gregg's left. Hooker sent Gen. Cuvier Grover to mount his part of the attack at about 5 P.M. Grover's brigade consisted of the 1st, 11th, and 16th Massachusetts regiments, the 2nd New Hampshire, and the 26th Pennsylvania. Kearny and Grover were supposed to attack simultaneously, but for unknown reasons, Kearny's attack was late and aimed farther to the right of the Light Division's line. Grover happened upon a gap in the Confederate line between the brigades of Gregg and Thomas, and the 1st Massachusetts regiment was able to transgress this gap and get behind the 49th Georgia, driving them back to the rear. A second assault was made by Grover, and this time the 49th Georgia, the 14th South Carolina regiment of Gregg's brigade, and men from Gen. Dorsey Pender's brigade trapped the 1st Massachusetts, forcing Grover to end the charge. The attacks were furious, often fought at five to ten paces, with knives, swords, fists, and rocks; General Gregg informed General Hill that he was low on ammunition but "would hold his position with the bayonet." Gen. Gregg made his famous speech to his brigade: "Let us die here today," but fortunately for the Light Division, which was near the breaking point, General Ewell arrived and sent the brigades of Lawton and Early in to assist Hill. The Union troops had battled all day and were weary, much like the Light Division Confederates, and Ewell's two fresh brigades were too much for them to contend with.[12]

3. The Maryland Campaign

Attention was now focused on Gen. Beverly Robinson's brigade from Kearny's division. In his report, Gen. Philip Kearny states: "General Robinson drove forward for several hundred yards, but the center of the main battle being shortly after being driven out of the woods, my detachment, thus exposed, so considerably in front of all others, both flanks in air, was obliged to cease to advance and confine themselves to holding their own." Kearny goes on to say that even bringing up Birney's regiments at about 5 P.M. was not enough. He concludes by stating, "Still our force was too light. The enemy brought up rapidly heavy reserves, so that our farther progress was impeded."[13] The famous sharpshooter Berry Benson offers a brief and concise account of the Battle of Second Manassas/Bull Run: "Fighting almost constantly, our brigade that day [August 29] successfully resisted five charges made by three brigades of Hooker's division, and held the ground all night. But it cost dear. Of 30 men that Co. H carried into action, 18 were killed or wounded. The proportion in Co. L was still greater." Benson served with Jackson's "Foot Calvary" and later in McGowan's Brigade after Jackson death.[14]

Gregg's brigade saw no action on August 30 mainly due to the brigade's weariness after the extreme celerity required on August 29. The action on the 30th involved Longstreet and other brigades of Jackson's wing. Caldwell calls the August 30 battle "one of the greatest battles of the war." The aggregate loss of men in the brigade was 613 killed and wounded, sixty-five of whom were in the 14th (which suffered the fewest casualties).[15] In his report of the Battle of Second Manassas/Bull Run, Gen. A.P. Hill states, "The stubborn tenacity with which Gregg's brigade held its position this day [August 29] is worthy of highest commendation."[16]

On Saturday, August 30, Gregg's brigade did little more than rest and recuperate from the intense battle on the 29th. Thousands of prisoners had to be dealt with, which engaged some of the brigade members, and the dead and dying of the Light Division required attention. Dr. Spencer Welch, a surgeon of the brigade (13th Regiment) gives an account of a soldier, Jake Fellors, who had an arm amputated without chloroform while Welch compressed the artery and Dr. Huot, another brigade surgeon, cut the arm off with the aid of candlelight only! Dr. Welch also gives a rather harsh but bluntly accurate description of the wounded when he said, "...large numbers of wounded [were] lying on the ground as thick as a drove of hogs in a lot." In another account Dr. Welch describes a scene as the brigade moved out: "I passed by where Goggans' body lay. Near him lay the body of Captain Smith of Spartanburg. Both were greatly swollen and had been robbed of their trousers and shoes by our own soldiers, who were ragged and barefooted, and did it from necessity."[17] Dr. Welch also reported that Colonel McGowan was wounded, but not seriously, with a bullet in his thigh.

At the end of the day on August 29, Jackson controlled and occupied about the same territory he had held at the beginning of the day. After two days of fighting, the ranks were thinner and the soldiers were well aware that the sunrise of the next day would cause a resumption of the combat. Even though Gregg's brigade would not be involved in the activity of August 30, the awareness of the possibility of a battle heightened the stress and added discomfort to the life of every member of the brigade.

On September 1, the division moved out toward Fairfax Court House. Again, Captain Perrin had received no opportunity to distinguish himself and he was likely frustrated as a result. On September 5, Perrin was held in Leesburg for an illness, which was not explained as having had a relation to his combat duties. Abner Perrin was not a man to hang back while others were involved in combat that he perceived as his duty to be participating in as well. This is today a recognized source of psychological stress, which can lead to physical illness.

The Army of Virginia made its way toward Centreville and arrived there late in the day on August 30. The army was reinforced with the corps of Sumner and Franklin, about 20,000 fresh troops. Doubtless, Pope and his army had suffered a terrible morale loss, as well as the loss of men and supplies. General Pope summed up the entire debacle with goodly amounts of color and light. In his writings to General Halleck he stated, "The troops are in good heart and marched off the field without the least hurry or confusion. The enemy is badly whipped and we shall do well enough. We have damaged him [the Confederates] heavily, and I think the army entitled to the gratitude of the country."[18]

The weather was horrid the day after the Battle of Second Manassas/Bull Run, and the rain and mud made for impassable roads. The necessity of following up on the victory convinced Lee to push his army to pursue Pope, and thus Jackson led the advance, crossing Bull Run at Sudley Ford toward Little River Turnpike. Jackson left Sudley Ford early on September 1, marching down the turnpike, just pass Ox Hill. The Confederate forces lined themselves facing eastward, with Ox Hill at their back. The Little

3. The Maryland Campaign

River Turnpike and the Warrenton Pike converge at Germantown, which is near Fairfax Court House. With approximately 15,000 troops taking part, this would be the only noteworthy battle of the war fought in Fairfax County, Virginia. The Light Division lined themselves near the Warrenton Pike; Jackson's old division was lined near the Little River Turnpike, with Ewell's division in the center. Gregg's brigade was the left of Hill's line, Field's brigade was in the center, and Branch's brigade held the right end of the line. Thomas and Pender were lined in support of Gregg and Branch, with Archer's brigade held in reserve. After reviewing his line, Hill realized that it was too sparsely spaced, and he immediately pulled Thomas and Pender into the main line, leaving little reserve strength.

Gregg's brigade, in the cornfield, suddenly found themselves under attack from the 50th Pennsylvania and the 26th Massachusetts regiments, and were forced to align themselves under heavy fire. The 13th and 14th regiments were lined in front of Orr's Rifles, with the 13th supporting the Rifles. The 1st regiment was held in reserve. As the battle heated up, the Rifles and the 13th came up into line. The suddenness of the attack stunned Gregg somewhat, and a retreat toward the wood line was ordered. Branch followed, realizing that his brigade would be in the open in the cornfield alone. The two brigades regained their organization and attacked with abandon Col. Bryson Christ's brigade of Stevens's division.[19] Field's brigade was pulled to accommodate a gap in the line, and Pender's brigade came forward to replace Branch, attempting to line as closely as possible with Thomas's Georgians, but the numbers were too small. The 13th and 14th South Carolina regiments were then sent forward to close the gap between Pender and Thomas.

During all of this intense fighting, a torrent of rain was falling and both armies reported being unable to see their opponents, let alone fire at them. The thunder and lightning, along with the wind, muffled the sounds of gunfire, and the rain was so heavy that the cartridges were too wet to fire. Near the cornfield the fighting became completely disordered, hand to hand in a muddy quagmire. All along the line in front of General Stevens's division, the Confederate lines began to break apart. Stevens realized this might be an opportune time to retreat toward the Warrenton Pike and make his way toward the Washington defense area. Suddenly, General Stevens fell dead from a rifle shot fired by a member, most likely, of General Thomas's brigade. The troops of General Stevens's command hovered over their dead commander while under intense Confederate fire.

General Stevens was still holding his division's flag, having just urged his "Highlanders" forward.

Due to the intensity of the battle, a Massachusetts regiment on Stevens's right flank ran headlong into a part of Jackson's command and lost more than 100 men in a few seconds. The remainder of General Stevens's command gave up the wooded position they held and made for the open field, their weapons now failing to fire because of the intense downpour. In addition, General Stevens's son Hazard Stevens was also wounded in the battle, but survived both the battle and the war.

With the death of Gen. Isaac Stevens, the famed division commander, the Federal army lost its cohesion and the various regiments and brigades lost contact with each other, going in different directions, not knowing where or why. It is not difficult to see why the loss of a general of the caliber of Isaac Stevens might cause chaos in the ranks. Stevens was born in Andover, Massachusetts, in 1818 and graduated from West Point in 1839, first in his class. General Stevens was short of stature, only five feet and one inch. After service in the Mexican War, Stevens served for thirteen years in the army before resigning to work for the Northern Pacific Railroad. Rather paradoxically, General Stevens had served as chairman of the 1860 presidential campaign of John C. Breckinridge, later a Confederate general. His request to serve in the Federal Army in 1861 was viewed with some question, but he received a commission, serving in South Carolina. He fought at Second Manassas in the IX Corps under General Reno, and died on September 1, 1862, at Chantilly. He received the rank of major general posthumously, dating from March 12, 1863.[20]

The chaos caused by General Stevens's death indirectly lead to the death of Gen. Philip Kearny. Gen. David Birney alerted General Kearny that a gap existed in the Union line and he immediately began searching to find a way to close the gap. Kearny was noted as a rather headstrong individual; his *aide de camp* Charles Hopkins stated that he attempted to direct General Kearny, but the general set out alone. When Hopkins inquired as to what direction the general took, he realized Kearny was headed toward the Confederate lines. As the scene unfolded, the 49th Georgia had been somewhat spared intense action, as most of the firing had occurred between the Federals and the brigades of Branch and Pender. The 49th expected action soon and finally they heard rumbles. The 21st Massachusetts had been ordered by General Kearny to move forward and attack, but had stopped. Kearny, totally enraged, took command of the

3. The Maryland Campaign

regiment himself, disregarding Colonel Clark, commander of the 21st, who had ordered the regiment's forward movement stopped because he had discovered Confederate troops on his right and front. Kearny was furious at any request to wait for the attack, cursed out all involved, and moved forward. In the rain, mist, and darkness he lost sight of the 21st. He called out to a line of troops that appeared in the distance, asking who they were. The Confederates answered that they were the 49th Georgia regiment. The soldiers of the 49th soon realized that Kearny was a Union officer and ordered him to halt, but he had already turned and was making way toward the cornfield as rapidly as possible. Again he was ordered to halt and dismount, but he ignored the warning and continued. Major Pate of the 49th ordered his men to fire. Kearny was hit by only one lethal ball of about ten or fifteen fired, and he was dead before he fell from his horse.[21] Kearny's body was transported to the Union lines and later buried at Trinity Church in New York City. In 1912 it was exhumed and reinterred in Arlington National Cemetery.

It is worthwhile to investigate and evaluate the opinions of officers and others involved as to the merits and faults of Pope as a general and the methods he employed in his role as commander of the Army of Virginia. The Confederate general E.P. Alexander, Longstreet's artillery commander, felt that Gen. Isaac Stevens, a prominent officer under Pope's command, may have excelled Pope in military skill. It was disclosed later that at the time of his death, he was under consideration for the appointment to the command of the united armies of Pope and McClellan. Alexander also felt Lee made better use of his assets and used Pope's errors to his advantage.[22] Col. G.F.R. Henderson, an English officer and biographer and contemporary of Jackson said of Pope, concluded: "As a tactician, Pope was incapable. As a strategist, he lacked imagination, except for his dispatches. Lee, with his extraordinary insight into character, played on Pope as he had played on McClellan, and his strategy was justified by success."[23] This battle, for all practical purposes, ended Pope's military career. He was sent to the west, to Minnesota, where he remained for the duration of the war.

On September 3, the Light Division resumed marching, passing through Dranesville and Leesburg and on to the Potomac River, crossing at White's Ford on September 5. The army was jubilant after the victories of Second Manassas/Bull Run and Chantilly/Ox Hill. The crossing over the Potomac into Maryland had somewhat of a religious connotation, as if the Potomac were the Jordan River. Jackson's forces had driven the enemy out of Virginia, and now Jackson and his soldiers were crossing into northern territory. As usual, speed was important to Jackson: the army was marching about three miles per hour, eventually stopping at Frederick City and resting until the morning of the 10th. All of the raffish behavior, and the vim and vigor aside, the Confederates were behaving like visiting gentlemen — no destruction of property, harassment of locals, foul language, or any demonstrations of the loss of deportment. Nonetheless, none of the gentlemanly behavior displayed by Jackson's Confederates warmed the thoughts or changed the attitude about the Confederates and their cause to the citizens of Maryland — this would require a war.

On September 10, the army made its way toward Boonsboro. General Lee stressed the importance of good behavior and speed to the army, emphasizing that no help or good will could be expected from this point on in the campaign. On the 11th, the march continued at daylight to Williamsport, at which point the army recrossed the Potomac back into Virginia. From here, the march headed south to Martinsburg, stopping about halfway for the night. On the 12th, Jackson arrived at Martinsburg, Gregg's brigade leading the march, the 1st South Carolina leading the brigade. Martinsburg was a Federal town and problems were expected, though none occurred; in fact the Light Division and the army in total were welcomed, Federal stores were abundant, and locals were generous to a fault. Jackson was mobbed! The ladies cut the buttons from his coat, and even somehow acquired his cap and treated him like a superstar.[24]

September of 1862 included a series of battles as Lee moved into Maryland. Harpers Ferry, Shepherdstown, and many other smaller engagements, leading to the Battle of Antietam present a maze of movements by both armies that is difficult to follow. Readers should be especially attentive to the battles and encounters of Gen. Maxcy Gregg's brigade to make sense of the events that involved Perrin.

On September 13, the corps marched toward Harpers Ferry; early in the day, the Union army tents were seen in the distance on Bolivar Heights. Lee had instructed Jackson to use whatever means he felt necessary and appropriate to take control of the town. Jackson had earlier decided to go to Harpers Ferry via Shepherdstown, but changed his direction when he learned that Gen. Julius White was at Martinsburg, Virginia, with a force of 3,500 troops. General John Wool, at Baltimore, instructed White to seek defense at Harpers Ferry if Jackson approached his position. White soon found that he was unable to retreat northward, since Jackson changed his direction of march from Shepherdstown to Williamsport. This placed Jackson north of White's position, forcing White to retreat to Harpers Ferry. Van Willard of the 3rd Wisconsin Infantry offers an eyewitness description of the town: "It is situated on a point of land just where the lovely, sparkling Shenandoah mingles its waters with those of the grand Potomac. Then there are lofty peaks and craggy bluffs that sentinel the shores, casting their shadows far out upon the stream.... The town is an old one, the buildings are overgrown with moss and look as though they were ready to tumble down. War has done fearful work here."[25]

As the Light Division neared the town, they fired their weapons into the air and made ready to take the town the following day. The Union forces were aligned as follows: 2,000 men on Maryland Heights; 7,000 men on Bolivar Heights, which was near the Shenandoah Valley; and 800 men at Camp Hill. Loudoun Heights, by far the most obvious defense position, was unoccupied. The attack plan was simple: Jackson would move into a position above the town, move back into Virginia, and move down upon the town. McLaws's and Anderson's divisions would continue to move from Frederick City, up the Maryland side of the Potomac, and seize Maryland Heights on the Potomac. Gen. J.G. Walker would travel up the Virginia side of the Potomac. The Light Division was moved towards the Shenandoah on Sunday the 14th. General Pender, with Archer's and Field's brigades, moved to subdue the eminence on the enemy's left side, since no artillery was present there, and Thomas's brigade was held in reserve. Gregg and Branch were to take their brigades, scale the banks of the Shenandoah, and prepare to make a charge. All of the elements of this plan went off like clockwork.[26]

The eminence taken by Pender was used to position the artillery, seven batteries strong. At first light on Monday, the artillery opened fire, as targets had already been selected the night before. Ewell's cannons were added to the artillery force, making an additional ten cannons. Some Federal artillery responded, but Hill placed Pegram's and Crenshaw's batteries at close range to quicken the battle. Within five minutes a white flag was flying on the Federal staff.[27]

Eleven thousand prisoners were taken at Harpers Ferry and Gen. Julius White surrendered. White was arrested, but later exonerated for his decision to surrender Harpers Ferry. Military stores were abundant and greatly needed by Confederate forces. The Light Division held guard duty over the eleven thousand prisoners, who actually poked fun at them because of their shabby dress and "worn and torn" look. As in Martinsburg, the prisoners taken by Jackson asked all sorts of questions about him — his education, his background, and so forth. They even cheered when he came down the road, much like Jackson's troops.[28]

On the 16th, the Light Division marched toward Shepherdstown for a few miles, but later returned and occupied Bolivar Heights. On September 17, the Confederate forces began their trek toward Shepherdstown. A ford across the Potomac River, known as Boteler's Ford, Pack House Ford, Blackford's Ford, and other names, was about a mile downstream from Shepherdstown, Virginia. The ford had been used for time too far back to recall by travelers and native people. After the bridge at Shepherdstown was destroyed early in the war, the ford was a very easy crossing place for people from Confederate Virginia into the border state of Maryland or vice versa.

The Battle of Shepherdstown occurred as the Union troops pursued Lee's army after the Battle of Antietam. Federal cavalry arrived on the Maryland side of the river about dawn and artillery fire began. The Union V Corps arrived and assumed control of the battle, after which the battle intensified. It was a very warm day and the sound of booming cannons was prevalent during the march of the Light Division toward Shepherdstown. By 2 P.M. the army reached Boteler's Ford, where they made a somewhat dangerous and painful crossing, after which they headed toward the battle scene. The Light Division was immediately pushed into action to prevent McClellan from getting between the Confederate Army and the Potomac River. Hill sent his brigades into action in an irregular fashion, based on information he received from Gen. D.R. Jones. As the Light Division came up Sawmill Road from Boteler's Ford, which crossed Harpers Ferry Road, Hill met the brigades at Blackford Farm and attempted to beef up the Confederate right flank. Pender and Brockenbrough were on the extreme right near Antietam Creek; Branch, Gregg, and Archer were on the left, while Thomas was left at Harpers Ferry on post duty. The 14th regiment led Gregg's brigade forward, and was posted behind a low-standing stone fence on the right of the brigade. The 1st, 12th, and 13th regiments went into a nearby cornfield to drive the Federals. There seems to have been some confusion as to direction of the attack: was it to be offensive or defensive? The 12th regiment acted on the belief that the movement was offensive, while the 13th regiment interpreted the command as defensive.

3. The Maryland Campaign

The 1st and 12th regiments pushed on toward the northeast, and suddenly as they came upon the Otto Farm ravine, the 16th Connecticut came into focus at the base of the ravine. This would prove to be very unfortunate for the 16th, which was an inexperienced regiment that had just lost their division commander (Rodman).[29] Their brigade commander, Col. Edward Harland, now in command, gave them explicit orders as to how they should react defensively, and told them they had reinforcements on the way, but to no avail. The 4th Rhode Island was fooled by the Confederates, who used flags taken at Harpers Ferry, into believing they were friendly reinforcements. The situation was still not hopeless until Gregg sent in the 1st South Carolina and Orr's Rifles, a small but experienced and aggressive military unit with only 194 members that blasted the 16th into utter chaos, causing a complete stampede to the rear, with the 4th Rhode Island not far behind. Both regiments sustained very high mortality rates as a result of this exchange; the 16th lost over 150 men killed and wounded. With the appearance of the Light Division, General Porter order the V Corps to return to the Maryland side of the Potomac, since only three federal brigades were on Virginia soil.[30]

The 14th South Carolina while at Sharpsburg was not attacked at their position on the stone wall, and suffered no loss of men or equipment. The 12th South Carolina was not so lucky, suffering the loss of their commanding officer, Col. Dixon Barnes. The night of September 18 was quiet; the brigade remained on the battlefield expecting a Union charge, but none came. As Stephen Sears expounded, "September 18 found Lee holding his lines and defiantly inviting another attack, but McClellan refused the challenge. He [McClellan] was satisfied that his army had survived the battle, and he was unwilling to risk it further by renewing the fighting that day."[31] The *Confederate Veteran* states that Col. Samuel McGowan, commander of the 14th South Carolina, was wounded at Antietam as well as Gen. Maxcy Gregg, although the exact nature of the wound is unclear. In his report, General Hill states that General Gregg was wounded, but no mention is made of General McGowan. In addition, brigade commander Gen. L. O'Brien Branch was killed at Antietam. In the report given by Captain Joseph Brown of the 14th South Carolina, he states that the regiment was placed too far to the right of the brigade to have been actively engaged in the battle. Also, Company E was detached on picket, and was thus half a mile to the right of the regiment until the next morning.[32]

Another telling comment about the Light Division's role in the battle comes from Peter Carmichael: "Wilcox brigade [Federal] moved to attack, he veered far right. This caused a gap in the Union line, causing a loss of continuance on the part of the Union forces. Hill struck when the Federal line was out of balance instead of exploring the gap, however, he smashed Rodman's left flank. The rookie 16th Connecticut received the initial brunt of Hill's attack. A single volley from the flank and rear nearly destroyed the regiment."[33] Col. Joseph B. Curtis of the 4th Rhode Island explains the position of his regiment as the 4th Rhode Island attempted to aid the 16th Connecticut: "I could find no one to whom reply.... He [Colonel Steere of the 4th Rhode Island] then sent to the rear for support. Before they could arrive, the enemy outflanked us with a brigade of infantry [Gregg's brigade], which descended the hill to our left in three lines, one firing over the other and enfilading us."[34]

Shepherdstown was much like the Gettysburg retreat of 1863. Union pursuit resulted in battlefield conflict, and in this case it was a total disaster for the Federal troops. Estimates are that 3,000 men were lost through battlefield fire or drowning, as the Federals were driven toward the river with no options but to jump in and hope for the best. General Hill placed his killed and wounded at 261. Of that total, Captain Perrin and the 14th South Carolina accounted for fifty-five men killed or wounded; the remainder of the brigade suffered eight casualties in the same categories.[35]

The Light Division saved the Army of Northern Virginia from Burnside by being in the right place at the right time. The eminent historian Bruce Catton explained it thusly in article written many years ago:

> Then — at the last minute of the last hour — up came Confederate reinforcements: A.P. Hill's division from Harpers Ferry, exhausted after a seventeen-mile hike in which General Hill personally, with sword in hand, had pricked laggards out from fence corners and out from under shady trees. This Hill was not a cautious man ... with Burnside's blue soldiers preparing to walk in on Sharpsburg and kill the Confederacy forever. A.P. Hill's beat-out soldiers, dust in their mouths and on their clothing, came stomping up the hill from the Potomac and smote Burnside in the flank. It was the push that settled things. The Yankees who were under the gun fell back.[36]

On Friday, September 19, the Light Division made its way toward the Potomac River. Under the command of Capt. J.N. Brown, two companies of the 14th regiment acted as skirmishers and protected the passage of the troops across the river. About 9 A.M. an enemy cavalry unit came on the scene, but were soon routed and dispersed. The brigade crossed Boteler's

3. The Maryland Campaign

Ford, marched four or so miles and bivouacked until the following morning, September 20.

Very early on the 20th, Hill's division was ordered to advance toward the Potomac to halt McClellan's drive into Virginia. The Light Division, about a mile or so from Boteler's Ford, formed two marching lines: Pender, Gregg, and Thomas were placed in a line under Gregg's command; and the brigades of Lane, Archer and Brockenbrough, under Archer's command, made up the second line. Lane was now the commander of Branch's brigade, after Branch's death at Sharpsburg/Antietam. Gen. Thomas now commanded General J.R. Anderson's brigade, and Brockenbrough commanded General Field's brigade since Field had lost a leg at Second Manassas/Bull Run. Colonel Edwards of the 13th South Carolina, senior colonel of the brigade, commanded Gregg's brigade in Gregg's absence due to a wound received during the Antietam/Sharpsburg battle.

The division marched through a cornfield into an open field, at which point the Federal troops opened a blistering rifle fire followed by artillery canisters, causing massive carnage to the seasoned veterans of the Light Division. Orr's Rifles had taken the role of skirmishers and devastated the gunners, forcing many of them into the Potomac River, where they drowned. Nonetheless, the artillery fire continued through most of the day. The 14th regiment suffered fifty-five casualties, nearly seven times more than the rest of the combined regiments.[37]

Federal losses at Shepherdstown are estimated to be about 3,000 from a single brigade, with over 200 prisoners taken.[38] General Porter soon realized that his force at Sherpherdstown was too small to handle the Light Division and ordered an immediate retreat back to Maryland. The retreat began forthwith, but Colonel Charles M. Prevost, the commander of the 118th Pennsylvania, refused to cross the Potomac unless he personally received orders from General Porter. The 118th was a new regiment, known as the "Corn Exchange Regiment," which might explain this decision by Colonel Prevost.

The Light Division smashed into the 118th with vigor. Since this was the first battle for the 118th, they were not yet ready to deal with adversity, especially not when armed with Enfield rifles that would not fire. Captain Francis Donaldson of the 118th explains:

> At this time, something got wrong with the muskets.... I found in many cases, in their haste and confusion they had put the bullet in first, and of course, the gun became useless. One man said that something was the mat-

ter with his musket because he couldn't get the ramrod down. On examination I found he had, in the first instance, put the bullet in first, and the cap exploding, thought he had fired it off, so rammed another and another cartridge until the gun was full.... God! Just think of it!— sending such troops to fight the veterans of A.P. Hill and Stonewall Jackson."[39]

A bayonet charge was attempted, but was a total failure as the regiment crumbled under the pressure of coming into contact with the experienced veterans of the Light Division. Mass confusion resulted as some of the men headed in the wrong direction. When the regiment came into contact with Hill's division in the heat of the exchange, some members of the 118th tumbled into the river. The Confederate troops lined the riverbank and poured fire into the raw troops. The regiment lost 269 men from a total of 700 as they attempted to cross the Potomac. Colonel Prevost was wounded and out of his command for seven months as a result of this battle. McClellan was convinced, as a result of this battle, that Lee was far from defeated and decided to halt any further action pending reinforcements. The Battle of Shepherdstown nonetheless ended Lee's Maryland Campaign, the first northern invasion attempted by the Confederacy.[40]

The reader may perhaps be wondering, where is the future General Abner Perrin? For a number of reasons known only to the general, General Gregg seemed to have relied upon the 12th and 13th regiments more than on the 1st and 14th regiments. In fact, the 14th regiment seems like the "forgotten stepchild" of the brigade. Colonel Barnes was the senior colonel of the brigade, and his death possibly was a factor in determining which troops were used. Colonel Edwards had had a long prewar friendship with General Gregg. Both of these men were highly competent and rendered outstanding service to the Light Division. It seems that Captain Perrin at this point was simply never in a spot where the action was taking place. At Seven Days, the 14th remained on picket duty for three nights and two days, and at Second Manassas/Bull Run the regiment was placed on reserve status. At Antietam the low stone wall position of the 14th was never engaged. Nonetheless, the 14th regiment supplied the next brigade commander. Colonel Perrin would lead the brigade at Chancellorsville for a time, and at Gettysburg, and would later become a brigade commander. One can only wonder what he might have achieved had he been given more leadership and responsibility at an earlier stage of the war.

Captain Brown of the 14th Regiment received several command positions during this battle, yet he was junior in rank to Perrin, who was also

3. The Maryland Campaign

a captain at that point in the war. There is insufficient evidence to determine if any conflict or hostile confrontation ever occurred between the two men over this slight toward Perrin. Colonel Brown's book is cited a number of times in this biography and always is very respectful and complimentary in all aspects concerning General Perrin, yet given Perrin's personality, it is probable that words were exchanged.

CHAPTER 4

The Road to Fredericksburg

In the early morning hours of September 21, the division moved toward Martinsburg, but after a short period, reposed until daylight in the road, later moving to Opequon Creek. At this point, an order was given that all troops must bathe and clean up their clothing and gear. By late afternoon, the brigade had marched to within two miles of Martinsburg, at which point it rested for several days. Promotions and citations were read out for the benefit of all brigade and division members. In general, it was a time for much-needed rest and a few days without pressure, stress and the general hardship which is a natural partner of any combat soldier in any place or time.

After about a week the division moved toward Martinsburg and on toward Winchester. A camp was established at Bunker Hill, ten or so miles from Winchester, and there the division remained until late October. A segment, including Gregg's brigade, was detailed to destroy as much as possible of the Baltimore and Ohio Railroad and was headquartered at Berryville for this duty. The crossties were burned and the rails heated and bent. During this time, and specifically on November 2, a small exchange occurred involving the brigades of Thomas and Gregg with artillery units of McClellan that ultimately also included a segment of the Light Division at Castleman's Ferry. The two brigades were on picket duty to prevent McClellan from crossing at Castleman's Ferry and while no actual crossing was attempted, three members of Gregg's brigade suffered wounds from the artillery exchange. The division remained in the Berryville-Winchester area until November 22, at which point the march to Fredericksburg was begun. From Winchester, they marched through Stevensburg, Strasberg, Woodstock, and on to Mt. Jackson, where the North Fork of the Shenandoah was crossed. From there they turned eastward, later crossing the

4. The Road to Fredericksburg

South Fork of the Shenandoah, going over the Blue Ridge Mountains at Thornton's Gap. From the area of Thornton's Gap, Jackson's Corps traveled to Madison Court House, and then to Orange Court House and finally to Fredericksburg, arriving on December 3. The army covered 175 miles in twelve days, averaging about fifteen miles per day.[1]

This battle would prove to be a major problem in many ways for the Union army, and for reasons not actually considered at that time. Fredericksburg, and the area around the Rappahannock River, is situated on a flood-prone region with high embankments that would tend to act as boundaries to the advancement of troops. The Confederate army used these embankments, flood-prone areas, and the obstacles which they created as impediments toward advancement the Federals wanted to accomplish in their battle plan.

The Federal army had made a number of changes in its command personnel; most notably, McClellan had been replaced by Gen. Ambrose Burnside. The rank and file Union soldier reacted negatively to this change, as Capt. Francis Donaldson of the famous "1st California Regiment" (the 71st Pennsylvania) states: "When the news was first told me, I would not believe it, but when the order was promulgated and the final review ordered, I could no longer contain myself. I entirely lost my self-control, lost my grip, so to speak, and gave way to tears of indignation and words of bitter reproach. Yes! I sat down and cried, and in my distress cared no longer to continue in the service."[2] This was not an isolated occurrence by any means, simply because McClellan, with all of his faults and hesitations, was quite likely the most loved officer in the Army of the Potomac. This attitude of gloom and defeat was picked up by a *New York Times* reporter in a comment made in his report of the upcoming battle: "It was with alarm and pain I found a general want of confidence and gloomy forebodings among some men whose judgement I had learned to trust. The plan of attacking the rebel stronghold directly in front would, it was feared, prove a most hazardous enterprise, and one of which there is no successful example in military history."[3]

Doubtless the reason for McClellan's popularity was, that at least in the mind of the average soldier, McClellan cared for them and looked out for their interests, but what could be said for Gen. Ambrose Burnside? Burnside was born in Indiana in 1824 and was able to obtain a West Point appointment via his father's influence. After graduation in 1847, he was too late to take part in the Mexican War and hence resigned his commission in 1853. Ambrose was an intelligent individual who had a mind for weaponry, to the extent that he invented a breech-loading rifle. The weapon was sound but made no money for him, so he sought another livelihood as a railroad executive with the Illinois Central Railroad from his old friend George B. McClellan. When the war began, Burnside raised a regiment from Rhode Island and made an immediate friendship with President Lincoln. His military record was poor from the start; First Bull Run/Manassas and Antietam/Sharpsburg are examples. Burnside had served as the commander of the IX Corps at Antietam and gave less than a stellar performance. He refused higher command positions on several occasions, realizing his limitations, but finally accepted the command of the Army of the Potomac with reluctance.[4]

One of the first decisions Burnside made as the new commander of the Army of the Potomac was to reduce the number of generals who would report directly to him by a reorganization of the seven existing corps into three so-called grand divisions. Each of the grand division commanders would have direct control over the division he controlled. Each grand division would have two infantry corps, each with three divisions and an artillery force and at least one cavalry brigade. Generals Sumner, Franklin, and Hooker were selected to serve as the lieutenants of the army reporting to Burnside. Franklin and Sumner had had experience at this level during the Antietam campaign, and Hooker had commanded a corps at Antietam, but at a lesser level of responsibility. Burnside, Hooker, and Franklin were West Point graduates, while Sumner had served in the Mexican War and had also served in the army for forty-three years; all things considered, General Sumner was far too old for this position. Franklin graduated from West Point in 1843, had seen action at First Manassas and Antietam, and had served as the VI Corps commander during the Peninsula Campaign after a brigade command at First Manassas. By any measure, Franklin and Sumner were no more than average field officers.[5] In fact, the command structure and internal workings of the Army of the Potomac did need greater precision, but Burnside simply was not the man to make the needed changes. Decision making and the channels to carry out the decisions, with adequate flexibility given to his subordinates to carry out their duties, seems to have been omitted from Burnside's approach.[6] Burnside kept a tight reign on his three subordinate commanders, even though he always seemed to imply this was not his intention.

Burnside made the decision to make a rapid march to Fredericksburg,

4. The Road to Fredericksburg

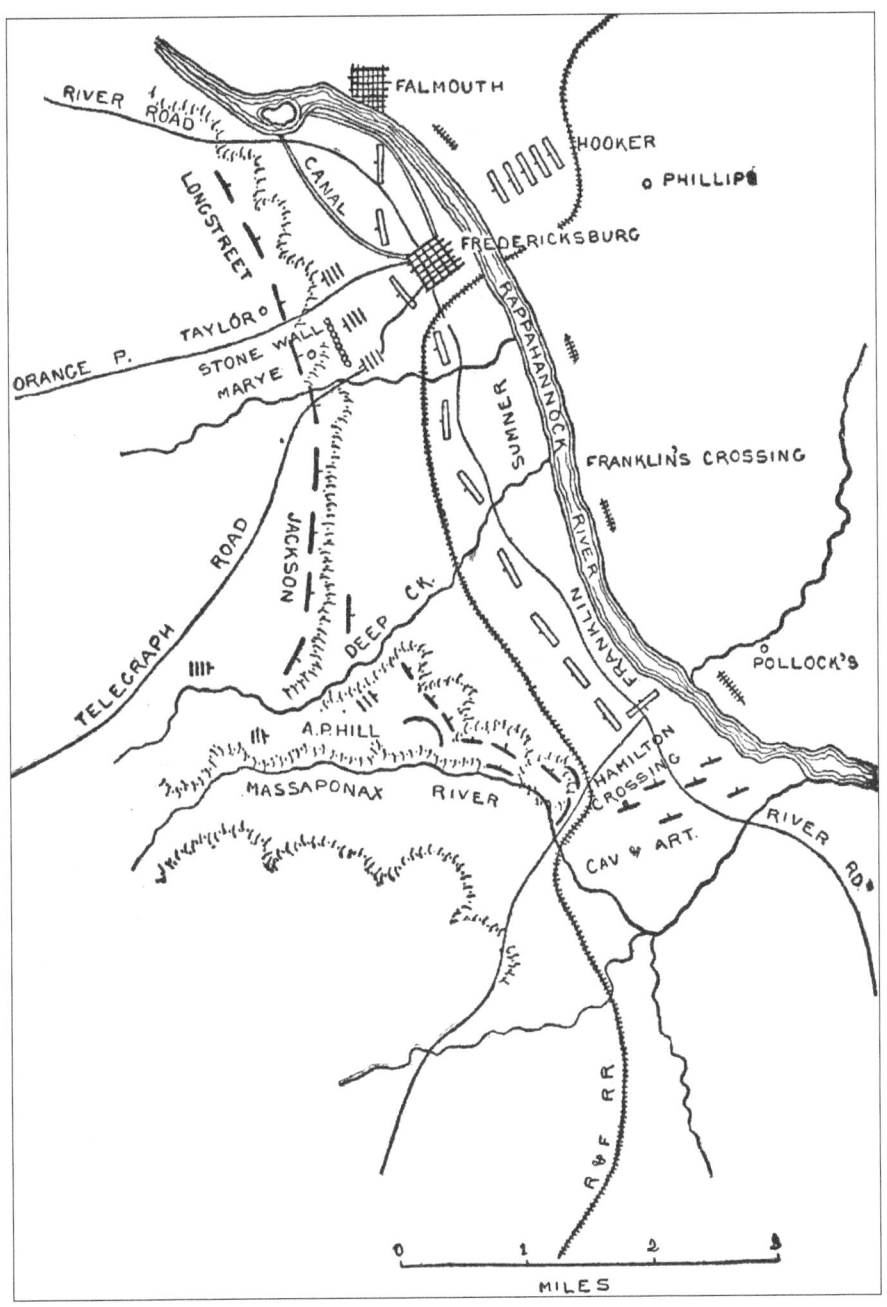

Map of Fredericksburg, December 1862 (Florida Center for Instructional Technology).

then advance along the railroad line to Richmond — all before Lee could locate and intercept him. Burnside's formulated plan was to make an immediate occupation of Fredericksburg, fill his trains with twelve days' provisions, then make a fast movement on Richmond. He began to pour vast numbers of troops into Fredericksburg but made little or no effort to organize any type of creditable attack. Instead, his troops looted and vandalized practically every home and shop in the city. He had ample time to work on an attack plan and ready the situation to his advantage, and he had the manpower and resources to carry out a plan. Unfortunately, his men suffered from his neglect of credible planning. Sumner arrived at Falmouth on November 17; Franklin arrived near Stafford Court House, about ten miles northeast of Fredericksburg, on the 18th; and Hooker moved to Hartwood, about ten miles northwest of Fredericksburg, on November 19. Burnside's plan required pontoons to cross the river, but they did not arrive until November 25, which eliminated any hope of a rapid surprise move toward Richmond. His intent was to cut Lee off from his base of supply. The plan looked favorable at the start, but as often happens, minor mishaps, failures, and poor communications prevented the army from completing the pontoon bridges before Lee was able to move his army on the west side of the river to high ground. This battlefield situation would ultimately play out much like the Battle of Malvern Hill in reverse, demonstrating again that a frontal assault against a combined force of artillery and infantry is a ludicrous military tactic.[7] In his book *Campaigns of the Civil War: The Antietam and Fredericksburg*, Francis Palfrey makes an interesting statement about General Burnside and his actions at Fredericksburg: "It is a familiar military maxim that a general should never do what his adversary wishes him to do. There probably never was an occasion since the first body of troops was arrayed, when a general did more precisely what his adversary wished him to do than Burnside did at Fredericksburg."[8]

On December 3, Gregg's brigade arrived a short distance from Fredericksburg on the Massaponax Hills area. Jackson's corps was sent down river about seven miles to Hamilton Crossing at the base of Prospect Hill. Hamilton Crossing was a small community at the end of the hills which connected Fredericksburg and Marye's Heights. Some of Jackson's troops were as far as twenty miles below Fredericksburg. Jackson's headquarters position was only sixty-five feet above the plain, and this accounts for the layering of his divisions to about a mile deep. In short, his position was

4. The Road to Fredericksburg

less than desirable; in addition, Jackson was opposed to the position of the Fredericksburg location and felt the position could easily be outflanked by crossing the fords above the city. Thus, Jackson wanted the North Anna River position; Lee was in agreement but was forced to acquiesce to Jefferson Davis's concerns. Longstreet arrived on November 19 and was placed at Marye's Heights, a key position on the left of the Confederate line.

Hamilton Crossing and Prospect Hill were the most important locations for the Confederate right in order to assure the protection of the major roads (Mine Road and Military Road) that Lee hoped to use in his defense plan. The Hamilton Crossing landmark was the southern end of a row of hills, about seven miles long, that began on the Rappahannock River. In addition, Hamilton Crossing was necessary for the protection of the Richmond, Fredericksburg, and Potomac Railroad, which ambled and curved toward Fredericksburg as it paralleled the Rappahannock River. On Jackson's right, about a half-mile below Hamilton Crossing, was Massaponax Creek, a dismal, swamplike water flow that was viewed as a tactical asset.

Lee had heard and believed that Federal gunboats were on the Rappahannock, and the situation as he viewed it required Jackson to spread out his line throughout the Hamilton Crossing area and be ready to move on demand. This spread the Second Corps from nine miles south of Hamilton Crossing to the Yerby House, a mile or so southeast of Hamilton Crossing. The Light Division was encamped about two miles south and east of Hamilton Crossing until December 10. The troops of the Light Division seemed to have gained strength and health from the rest, but the weather was very cold and raw, especially to those who were lacking proper clothing and even shoes.

On December 12, General Hill established his line of combat. The right of the line rested on the road leading from Hamilton Crossing, on the railroad to Port Royal Road, and his left was a line about a mile long from the right line running parallel to the river. Fourteen pieces of artillery were placed on the right and two batteries on the left, or eight guns. The front line was made up of two regiments from Brockenbrough's brigade and the brigades of Archer, Lane, and Pender. There was a 600-yard gap between Archer and Lane, and another between Lane and Pender. The second line was on the Military Road, running parallel with the front line, and consisted of two regiments from Brockenbrough's brigade, plus Gregg's brigade, which crossed the interval between Lane and Pender. Hood's division had constructed the Military Road when they occupied that section of the Confederate line. The second line was at the foot of the hills and was concealed from the Federals by a thick forest area. It was felt that the enemy would be unable to penetrate this wooded area due to the low-lying swampy Massaponax Creek.[9] The first line was at the edge of the woods looking out at the open plain, which extended to the river. On the morning of the 13th, the Federals were drawn up into three lines, extending from Hill's right all the way to Fredericksburg, with ten batteries for extra firepower.[10]

General Hill made the same strategic error at Fredericksburg that he had made at Second Manassas: he left too much of a gap in his first line. General Lane was the first brigade commander to call attention to this blank area, but Hill made no effort to correct the situation. General J.E.B. Stuart's attention was also brought to focus on this area by his aide, Major Heros von Brocke, who suggested that the wooded area should be cut to create a barrier, but Stuart felt that artillery could take care of the problem if it arose. General Jackson also noted the gap and even stated that the Union forces would attack that area, yet offered no command that could have corrected the situation.[11]

When the fog lifted on the morning of the 13th, the three lines of Federal troops appeared. The soldiers who would oppose Jackson were under the command of General George Meade, who would later gain fame at Gettysburg. George Meade was born in Spain in 1815 and the family moved to Philadelphia after his father's release from prison, where he had served time as a result of difficulties with the Spanish government. In 1831, Meade entered West Point and graduated in 1835, nineteenth in a class of fifty-six. In 1840, he married Margaret Sargent and later served in the Mexican War with Gen. Zachary Taylor. With the help of Senator David Wilmot in 1861, he was commissioned a brigadier general and reported to General McClellan for duty.[12] Meade later became the 3rd Division commander in the 1st Corps of Gen. John Reynolds. During the Fredericksburg Campaign, Meade served in Gen. William Franklin's Left Grand Division. His troops were Pennsylvania reserves, serving in the brigades of Colonel Magilton, Gen. C.F. Jackson, and Colonel Sinclair, and all were experienced and creditable soldiers. Gen. C.F. Jackson served with McClellan in Virginia at the battles of Mechanicsville, Gaines' Mill, and Glendale, and with Pope at Second Manassas/Bull Run. He would serve at Fredericksburg with General John Reynolds, where he would die on December 13, after a courageous day of battle. Col. A.L. Magilton graduated from West Point in 1846. He commanded the 2nd Brigade, 3rd Division in the Army of the Potomac. Magilton resigned his commission after the Battle of Fredericksburg on December 23, 1862. Col. William Sinclair commanded the 1st Brigade, 3rd Division from November 14 to December 13, 1862. Sinclair graduated from West Point in 1857 and remained in the regular Army until 1899.[13]

The Federals were allowed to move forward and approach the railroad without attack. Meade's division had around 4,000 troops and in order to launch an attack his men had to cross about one-half mile of open ground. From there they had to get over the Richmond, Fredericksburg & Potomac Railroad, and then up the hill and into the woods. When Meade's troops were 800 to 900 yards from the railroad, the Confederate artillery of Colonel Pelham opened a blistering attack, halting the Federals in their tracks for at least thirty minutes. During this half-hour, the Union artillery attempted to silence Pelham's guns. When the Confederate artillery went silent, Meade had his men focus on a triangular patch of woods and then made his charge. When he arrived at the targeted area, much to his surprise it was undefended. He then charged ahead, taking a lot of fire from the brigades of both Archer and Lane. General Reynolds ordered the Federal artillery to fire ahead of Meade, which allowed him to carry the attack into the "impassable gap" directly toward Gregg's brigade. By pure blind luck, Meade had found Jackson's 600 feet of undefended front. Doubleday's division remained more or less untouched and supplied protection from flank attacks for Meade's advance. By 12 P.M. the Pennsylvanians attempted another attack, and again Pelham, along with Colonel Walker, blazed away. Meade's lines were smashed, his skirmishers destroyed, and rapidly he made way toward the Richmond Stage Road while the Union cannons roared against Col. Walker.[14]

It was decided originally by General Reynolds that Meade's division would attempt to gain the crest of the ridge, and then turn toward Jackson's right flank at Hamilton Crossing, the location of much of the Confederate artillery. Gibbon, Meade's backup, would advance to Meade's right, and Doubleday's division would charge straight ahead toward Stuart's cavalry to take the pressure off Meade's advance. The attack had begun about 1 P.M. and had not succeeded. Jackson began to recognize the threat to his corps about 1:30 P.M. and ordered Taliaferro and Early to move their divisions against Meade and Gibbon. The two divisions attacked Meade head-on;

in the interim, Archer and Lane had reestablished their lines, and now Meade was hit on three sides. Meade and Gibbon were essentially unable to attempt another charge and Doubleday's division replaced Meade in the attack plan. By 2:30 P.M. the two armies were exactly back where they were when the attacks had begun.

Demoralization had now infiltrated the Federal army, and support and faith in Burnside had disappeared. Meade stated that he was compelled to fall back to the railroad because after he had held the ground for a long time, no support had arrived. He also stated that the attack was successful for a time, only failing after heavy reinforcements arrived for the Confederate forces. After realizing that no reinforcements were coming to his support and that he was deeply into the Confederate lines with unprotected flanks, he concluded withdrawal was essential. Meade gives "chapter and verse" in the accounting of his killed, wounded, and missing. There were approximately 4,500 (some sources give 3,800) soldiers under his command, among whom 1,770 casualties occurred.[15] General Meade seems to feel that this high casualty rate justified his withdrawal and explained the lack of total success, which might have been attained if other commands had completed their orders.

Gen. John Reynolds, I Corps commander, states that the major cause of the failure to hold the area under Gen. A.P. Hill's command at Hamilton Crossing was "from the dense character of the wood, the connection between his division [Gibbon] and Meade's was broken."[16] Another source seemed to have had a very different concept about the failure of the entire battle, and especially the Marye's Heights area. Color Serg't. H.S. Seage of the 4th Michigan had this to say: "We heard the yell of the Irish Brigade on our right and witnessed that splendid charge.... [W]ith wonderful courage did these brave men charge against that stronghold, until two-thirds of their number strewed the ground. Never in the history of the Army of the Potomac was there such a pitiless, useless, hopeless slaughter. Never did men fight better, or die, alas, more fruitlessly than those thrown against these heights and stone walls.... [N]ight only put and end to the slaughter."[17]

Regardless of Meade's inability to complete the attack, the Pennsylvania reserves were able to drive part of Hill's Light Division back farther into the woods and up the hill. The wooded swampy area that was supposed to be a barrier turned out not to be the case; in fact, the swamp had frozen over, making it not much of an obstacle at all for Meade's troops.

4. The Road to Fredericksburg

In his report General Lee states that the main attack on the right began about 1 P.M. with a serious cannonade followed by the advance of three infantry lines against Hill's front. The firepower of the Confederate batteries checked them for a short while, but they again moved forward until they came into range of the Confederate infantry, after which the contest became hot and bloody.[18] Gregg's brigade was in the second line behind the brigades of Lane and Archer, who were, as stated earlier, 600 or so yards apart, leaving a passageway for Meade to move directly toward Gregg's brigade. Meade's division first attacked Lane's brigade of North Carolinians, who delivered a withering blaze of fire that drove them away to the right. Part of Gen. Ed Thomas's brigade came to Lane's aid to turn the tide, but Meade's troops not involved in this aspect of the strike came toward Gregg's brigade, through the unprotected space between Lane and Archer. General Gregg was aware of the possibility of firing into friendly troops in any woods battle, and therefore ordered his brigade, in the second line, to stack arms and lie down to seek cover from the artillery fire.

During this fire exchange, Archer appealed to Gregg to move up into the space between his brigade and Lane's to aid Lane, whose brigade had become divided due to the Federals' falling back onto Lane's right. Lane also requested assistance from Gregg before Thomas came to his rescue. Gregg was absolutely certain that Meade's troops would not be able to cross the Confederate first line and reach his sector. Caldwell states, "Unfortunately, Gen. Gregg was not aware of the interval between Lane's and Archer's brigades." This seems somewhat spurious in the face of the situation the Confederate army faced on that day. Ellison Capers makes the same statement in his account of South Carolina's role in the war: "Gregg was unaware of the interval between Archer and Lane...."[19] James I. Robertson, in his work on A.P. Hill, states, "Maxey [sic] Gregg knew that his reserve position faced the huge gap in the front line, yet he seems not to have anticipated any involvement in the battle swelling through the woods."[20]

The regiments of Gregg's brigade were aligned from right to left: Orr's Rifles, 1st, 12th, 13th, and 14th. The Pennsylvanians, most probably the 1st and 6th Pennsylvania regiments of Sinclair's brigade, opened fire on Orr's Rifles first, and they scurried for their weapons. General Gregg, who was partially deaf, and was unable to actually see the Federal troops, immediately rode up and ordered the troops to cease firing and restack their arms. By this point, the Union troops were face to face with the

Rifles, who were scrambling for their weapons, and hand-to-hand combat ensued. As it played out, two nearly green regiments did significant damage to an entire brigade of hardened veterans. The Rifles were boxed in, slaughtered, and driven from the scene.

Meade sensed that he had made a breakthrough and that he needed more troops to complete the battle scene. General Gibbon on his right was hopelessly bogged down, so Meade sent an aide to seek help from Gen. David Birney, part of Stoneman's III Corps. Birney refused, saying he only acted on the orders from the corps commander; yet again the request was made and refused. Birney was the only available source to come to Meade's aid since General Franklin had placed the remainder of his troops two miles away near the river to protect the pontoons. If the Confederates obtained control of the pontoons, Franklin would have no escape, since he would be trapped between the river and the Confederate army. Meade was furious and approached Birney himself, explaining he would accept all responsibility for the troop request. Birney complied, but it was too late: Gen. Jubal Early and Gen. William Taliaferro had mounted a counterattack. Meade had broken Hill's line and captured Military Road. It is possible that if Meade had received additional men, the Confederate right would have fallen.

Meanwhile, General Gregg, on horseback and in full brigadier uniform, was the object in each Union soldier's gun sight, and was mortally wounded by a rifle shot to the spine. Berry Benson, a sharpshooter in Gregg's brigade, states that a single Union soldier, who was immediately drilled by all present, killed Gregg.[21] The brigade rallied, and was able survive the attack and launch a defense.[22] The 5th Alabama battalion, the 22nd Virginia battalion, and the 47th Virginia came to aid the brigade in this struggle that finally ended with the retreat of Meade's Pennsylvanians. By 2:30 P.M. both armies were back in their original positions. Meade had lost about 40 percent of his division, and had a near miss when a musket ball passed through his hat.[23]

Four soldiers carried General Gregg from the field on a litter as soon as conditions allowed, and on the way off the battlefield came into contact with the chaplain of the 12th regiment, the Rev. J.M. Anderson. The Rev. Anderson gave the general some whiskey to ease the pain, as the litter made its way toward the Yerby house in the rear of the Confederate lines. The Yerby family received General Gregg with the greatest of kindness and concern. In the course of the next eighteen to twenty-four hours Gen-

4. The Road to Fredericksburg

eral Gregg received a number of visitors. Rev. Anderson visited him and held prayer with him, during which time General Gregg apologized because he was unable to kneel.

Dr. Hunter McGuire, Chief Surgeon of the II Corps, relates a rather unusual request made to him from General Jackson. Jackson requested that McGuire visit Gregg, even though he had just returned from a visit. McGuire agreed, and when he arrived at the Yerby house, Jackson immediately appeared in the hallway. Presumably he followed the doctor very closely and went into Gregg's room with him, and thus the words spoken by the two men will never be known.

Another visitor was Gen. A.P. Hill. In a letter written to Gregg's sisters in Columbia, an unknown caretaker of General Gregg states, "Gen. A.P. Hill, his superior in command spoke to me of him with tears he said he had never seen in his life anything like his perfect calmness and acquiescence in his fate." This writer also commented that Gregg was grateful for the warm touch of a female hand during his last hours. General Gregg died at 5 A.M. on December 15. Before his death, he sent a letter to Governor Pickens of South Carolina expressing hope that the war would end in favor of the Confederacy. This was probably his last official act as a Confederate general.[24] The brigade had a day of rest on December 16, following General Gregg's death on the 15th.

The decision as to who would take command of the brigade now needed to be made. Gen. Wade Hampton was offered the position, but refused it. Colonel Hamilton remained in temporary command of the regiment until January 20, 1863, at which time Col. Samuel McGowan was promoted to brigadier general and assigned command of the brigade. While this was ostensibly the best choice within the brigade at that time, it is remarkable that Colonel Hamilton, second ranking colonel and current commander of the brigade, and Colonel Edwards, the ranking colonel in the brigade, offered no protest to McGowan's appointment.

General McGowan's background was discussed earlier, but a few brief statements are worthwhile at this point. McGowan was born in the Laurens District of South Carolina in 1840. He served in the Mexican War after graduation from South Carolina College (University of South Carolina) in 1841, and was admitted to the bar after working in T.C. Perrin's law office in Abbeville, South Carolina. President Polk appointed McGowan captain on the general quartermaster's staff. In 1860, he was appointed by the governor to command a brigade of volunteers. Later he joined the

Confederate Army and served as aide-de-camp to Gen. M.L. Bonham. Afterwards, he was elected lt. colonel of the 14th South Carolina.

All field officers involved in the Battle of Fredericksburg praised General Gregg for his courage and patriotism to the Confederacy's cause. The *Richmond Examiner* had a very lengthy obituary of General Gregg. The article calls General Gregg the "bravest of the brave who was wounded to death in the glorious victory on the heights of Fredericksburg...." The *Charleston Mercury* expressed similar statements in their obituary: "Simple in habits, pure in his life, his leading characteristics were elevation of sentiment, indomitable courage, strong will, and heartiness of purpose." These are well-deserved comments about the general, and they are essentially accurate. One can but read them with a certain amount of dolefulness in that such statements are seldom made today about fallen military heroes.[25] Gregg was buried in the Elmwood Cemetery in Columbia.

The Battle of Fredericksburg was two distinctly different battles. Hamilton Crossing and Prospect Hill, the area defended by Hill's Light Division, were the scene of massive Confederate casualties: killed, wounded, and captured/missing, according to General Jackson's report, totaled 2,120. This is a little out of proportion with the total Confederate forces that took part in the battle. Longstreet's I Corps had about 1,875 casualties in the same categories. The question remains as to why such a large percentage of troops were lost in only a segment of the battle. Longstreet's Corps was involved with the area of Marye's Heights, which was far more defensible from enemy attack, and thus easier to defend. Jackson's defense line was a mile and a half long, with gaps in the line of over a quarter of a mile, and therefore more difficult to defend. The following statement will lend insight to this question:

> A very general impression prevails, and it is in great measure confirmed by writers on Fredericksburg, that Jackson's lines were strongly fortified. This is not correct: we had no time to construct anything like fortifications.... The next morning the scenes of carnage were heart sickening. To intensify the horrible picture the dead and the wounded were in many instances burned in the sedge-grass, which was set on fire by bursting shells.[26]

This could explain the difficulty Hill faced in placing his brigades, and the difficulty the brigade commanders encountered in carrying out the assignments given to them. There was simply not enough *time* to prepare a defense, nor did the landscape lend itself to a solid defensive stance.

Additionally, Longstreet states, "Towards the latter part of the month,

4. The Road to Fredericksburg

General Jackson was called down and assigned the position on the right near Hamilton Crossing and Massaponax. He objected to the position, preferring the North Anna area, but General Lee had already decided in favor of Fredericksburg."[27] Hood's division had been in the area of Hamilton Crossing long enough to create a service road (Military Road) to bring in artillery. Even though Marye's Heights is most often thought of as the major area of the Battle of Fredericksburg, the real battle was actually fought at Hamilton Crossing and Prospect Hill.

As the sun came up on the morning of December 14, 1862, an unearthly sight must have confronted any individual who viewed the battlefield. The bodies of the Union dead were stripped of their clothing and their bodies frozen into macabre positions. The average Union soldier in the ranks must have pondered how this had all happened. An interesting human-relations event occurred in the early morning hours after the battle. The famous "Iron Brigade" of Doubleday's division was on picket duty on the south end of the battlefield. The brigade established a truce with the Confederate pickets in Jackson's command, which was a common practice. The original "Iron Brigade" regiment was relieved, but failed to inform the incoming regiment of the truce, and the relief regiment immediately fired on the Confederate pickets. After a time, two of the soldiers, one on each side, had had all they could deal with: they threw down their weapons, charged into the open field and slugged it out. Both sides of the dispute had a cheering section, and after a reasonable period, the fight ended in a draw, and a new truce was declared.[28]

It was enough to be defeated in battle, yet to suffer this particular defeat as a result of such blatant incompetence was too much to bear. From the Federal troops' point of view, Burnside had to be replaced. Still, it must have occurred to the private soldiers, as well as to those making command decisions, to wonder whether another attack would or should be launched on December 14.

Gen. Rush Hawkins of Burnside's staff relates how the decision not to make an attack had been reached the night before. General Hawkins states that a number of officers convinced him to go to General Burnside's headquarters and convince him to withdraw. Hawkins states that at 9 P.M. he traveled to the Phillips house to make the case. When he arrived he found Generals Sumner, Hooker, Franklin, and Hardie present, along with Colonel Taylor; he was told that General Burnside had just departed but would return soon. The generals were convinced that an attack was

> **Death of Gen. Maxcy Gregg**
>
> Gen. Maxcy Gregg was mortally wounded at the battle of Fredericksburg on December 13 and died on December 15, 1862. General Gregg is buried in the Elmwood Cemetery in Columbia, South Carolina. A fitting epitaph on Gregg's gravestone reads:
>
> > If I am to die now, I give my life cheerfully
> > for the Independence of South Carolina
>
> General Gregg played a major role in the military career of General Perrin from his enlistment in the Mexican War until Gregg's death at Fredericksburg.

unwise and that General Hawkins should await Burnside's return, which occurred at 1 A.M. General Burnside announced that an attack would take place and gave all of the details of his plan. Afterwards, there was dead silence, after which General Hawkins then made his case against the attack: the troops were too fatigued, too much privation had taken place, and morale was too low after the battle on the 13th. The order to attack was never given after the end of the discussion.[29]

Another issue concerning Fredericksburg is the often-asked question: why did General Lee not mount an attack on December 14? The Federal army was in Fredericksburg, packed tightly, and the Confederate artillerists could easily have shelled them into oblivion. Some historians feel this was not done in respect for the safety of the civilians still in Fredericksburg, while others state it would have damaged the city's homes and businesses to the extreme. Others suggest the ammunition was not available. Regardless of the reason, this opportunity would not arise again for the Army of Northern Virginia.[30]

In the recent past, with new material coming forth on the goals and aspirations of the Confederacy, it is believed by many historians that Gen. R.E. Lee was seeking the supreme battle of annihilation to end the war and achieve Southern independence. Frank A. O'Reilly, a noted authority on the Battle of Fredericksburg as well as the Civil War in general, had this to say about Fredericksburg:

> The Army of Northern Virginia commander had fought a battle not of his choosing on ground not of his liking. He achieved an astounding victory but took little pride from it. Fredericksburg became synonymous with Confederate invincibility, but Lee knew it was devoid of meaningful, long-term

4. The Road to Fredericksburg

results. The Union army had been embarrassed at Fredericksburg — but not destroyed. Lee knew that Southern resources had dwindled by the end of 1862 and shortages of men and munitions would only get worse in the coming year. He had desperately wanted a decisive victory before the impending crisis weakened the Confederacy.[31]

Needless to say, the battle of annihilation was never to come for the Confederacy.

A soldier in the 121St Pennsylvania made an astute observation about the Battle of Fredericksburg, "The dreadful slaughter in front of Marye's Hill at no time approached success, but however brave, the efforts of the troops at that point were from the first utterly hopeless. Meade's were the only troops that broke through the enemy's lines, and saw victory for a short time, perched upon their banners."[32]

Again, one must ponder and question the role of then Capt. Abner Perrin of the 14th South Carolina. Events were occurring in his life within and outside of the war itself. Perrin's wife Emily passed away in late November of 1862. The *Edgefield Advertiser* gives the date as November 26. The *Advertiser* gave a stirring and doleful obituary on the death of Emily Perrin — in fact, a far more extensive obituary than that which Gen. Abner M. Perrin would later receive. At the very least, the death of his wife must have been an extreme burden to bear for General Perrin during war. There is no evidence that Perrin was even able to attend her funeral.

Emily's brother had also died in early 1862 in the defense of Richmond. The weight of evidence places Emily Perrin and her two sons, Pierce and Robert Perrin, in Bossier City, Louisiana, living with her mother Julia Butler and her brothers. Emily had sold her share of her inheritance from her father to her mother, who had resided in Bossier City before the war, since May 1859. There is no evidence that she lived in Edgefield, or in any other town in South Carolina. Her gravesite is undetermined by sources consulted in Edgefield. After the war ended, the son of Abner Monroe and Emily Perrin, Pierce Perrin, was listed as a resident of Bossier Parish, Louisiana, in the 1890 census.

Events of the Battle of Fredericksburg, the death of Gen. Maxcy Gregg, and the promotion of Gen. Samuel McGowan, would rapidly alter Perrin's circumstances in the Confederate Army.[33] The death of General Gregg was probably far more traumatic than the existing information suggests. Perrin and Maxcy Gregg's relationship went back to Perrin's early years, to the late 1840s. General Gregg was a somewhat close associate of

Perrin's during the Mexican War and was instrumental in Perrin's connection with the 14th South Carolina regiment and events in General Perrin's military life prior to 1863. Thus, General Gregg's death was yet another tragedy to bear among many for Abner Perrin in the 1860s.

Abner Perrin's role in the Battle of Fredericksburg was minimal, and for that matter, the 14th South Carolina's role was also greatly subdued. General Gregg's position on the "friendly fire" issue prevented his brigade's participation in the battle and resulted in his death. For this reason, there is little that can be conveyed to enhance understanding about the soldier that Perrin would soon become, but General Gregg's death made a dolorous and rancorous impression on Perrin. This combination of sadness and anger would play a role in the general's life and later would account for some of the impressions he would leave on associates and men under his command.

It has been cited in a number of sources that General Lee experienced a heart attack after the Battle of Fredericksburg and before the onset of Chancellorsville. Lee reported that his army was living on "a pound of flour and four ounces of fat meat per man per day." He stated to the Secretary of War that the army was beginning to experience health problems as a result of this inadequate food supply. General Lee ended his comments to the Secretary of War with, "Old age & sorrow is wearing me away, & constant anxiety & labour, day and night leaves me but little repose." Lee resorted to dispatching Longstreet's corps to Southside, below Richmond, to find forage and actually to feed itself. Things were so desperate that Lee made a trip to Richmond, quite unsuccessfully, to persuade the government to make an effort to locate and supply the army with more and better rations. On March 30, 1863, it is reported that Lee suffered a heart attack, yet it seems to have been more likely an angina attack. It is somewhat of a stretch of the imagination to assume that an individual could experience a heart attack and two months later lead an army into a major battle involving hundreds of thousands of men, and still be standing. The reader must reach his own conclusions concerning this account of General Lee's health on March 30, 1863.[34]

CHAPTER 5

Chancellorsville

From about December 20, 1862, until early April of 1863, very little military activity took place that involved the Army of Northern Virginia in general and the Light Division in particular. Promotions were made and other changes occurred in the command system. General Samuel McGowan was now the commander of the brigade formally commanded by Gen. Maxcy Gregg. Capt. Abner M. Perrin was promoted to command of the 14th South Carolina, and Lt. Col. James Monroe Perrin, Abner Monroe's cousin, was placed in command of Orr's Rifles. Col. Abner Perrin's rise to command came about in rapid leaps. Within a period of six to eight weeks he went from captain to colonel.[1]

The Army of the Potomac had also made a command change that would be of great interest to the Army of Northern Virginia. Gen. Joseph Hooker replaced Gen. Ambrose Burnside as the overall commander of the army. General Hooker was born in Massachusetts in 1814 and graduated from West Point in 1837 in the "dead middle" of his class, which also included Braxton Bragg, Jubal Early, and John Sedgwick. Hooker served in Florida, the Canadian border area, and at West Point. Additionally, General Hooker was in the Mexican War, after which he resigned his commission in 1853. Hooker had several vexatious personality traits. He was boastful, highly critical, tended toward an autocratic style of leadership, and was often inclined to be argumentative with his peers. Conversely, Hooker also had a number of positives to his credit. He reorganized the Army of the Potomac, improved the morale of the troops, and also upgraded the living conditions of the army as a whole during the winter months. Hooker was often accused of excessive drinking in critical periods of his command, although he denied these accusations. Before his appointment by Lincoln to command the army, "Fighting Joe" Hooker commanded the I Corps of the Army of the Potomac.² A close-up personal observation of General Hooker by George Townsend, a writer and news correspondent of the period, reveals some interesting sidelights about the general:

> Joseph Hooker was a New Englander, reputed to be the handsomest man in the army. He fought bravely in the Mexican War, and afterwards retired to San Francisco where he passed a Bohemian existence at the Union Club House. He disliked McClellan, was beloved by his men, and was generally known as "Old Joe." He has been one of the most successful Federal leaders, and seems to hold a charmed life. In all probability, he will become Commander-in-Chief of one of the grand armies.³

On April 29, McGowan's brigade received orders to prepare to march on short notice, but little did the brigade realize just how short the notice would be. The same day the Light Division was ordered to proceed toward Hamilton Crossing on the RF&P Railroad. The Federals had crossed a small force over Deep Run, giving signs that it intended to make an advance and overrun the Confederate positions. McGowan's men soon reached the same area they had occupied during the Fredericksburg campaign and remained there unoccupied for some time; April 30 was also a quiet day. On Friday, May 1, the Light Division moved at daylight upriver toward the Plank Road that ran from Fredericksburg to Orange Court House.

General Hooker was determined to defeat the Army of Northern Virginia and see to it that they paid dearly for the humiliation and disgrace they had put upon the Army of the Potomac in general, and upon Hooker, as he viewed it, in particular. Hooker felt he could devise a plan to bring an end to war in the east, and he set out to accomplish this at Chancellorsville.

How could a simple crossroads, which could hardly be considered even a village, become one of the major battlefields of the Civil War? The Chancellorsville campaign, together with Fredericksburg, was often referred to as the "Dare Mark" Campaign by many Confederate soldiers. Some Civil War enthusiasts may not be familiar with this term. The origin of the term had to do with the "mark" in Virginia beyond which the Union troops were dared to attempt to cross. That mark was the Rappahannock River, which was the "gateway" to Richmond and the parts of Virginia which the Confederates held to be territory not to be given up to the Union no matter the cost in life or pain.

5. Chancellorsville

The Federal Army desired to get its forces below the Rappahannock River and make an advance on Richmond. They had tried and failed at Fredericksburg on two separate occasions, but Hooker determined that he could come up with a plan to achieve this goal. He was well aware that the Rappahannock and Rapidan Rivers came together above the United States Ford, and at the conjunction, the two rivers formed a loop. If the Federal cavalry crossed the upper fords of the Rappahannock, then took a northern loop, and then a southwestern swing, they would cross the railroads north of Richmond, creating havoc for the Army of Northern Virginia. The Federal infantry would then cross the Rappahannock River at Kelley's Ford, and the Rapidan River at Germanna and Ely's Fords, then go down river to Banks' Ford, getting in the rear of Lee's army. Meanwhile a smaller force, the VI Corps and Gibbon's division, would attack Fredericksburg and draw the Confederates away from the main goal of the campaign.

This plan had problems, mainly due to the fact that below the Rapidan River, where it converges with the Rappahannock, there was an area referred to as the Wilderness. Chancellorsville was on the edge of this area, an intensely thick growth of vines, trees, bush and brambles, with few roads and even fewer cleared spaces, making artillery nearly useless in this place. To make the task Herculean, Hooker had to get his army in place before the Confederates were aware of his presence, and Chancellorsville was located about ten miles behind what was General Lee's extreme left lines. Hooker reasoned that he could then exit the Wilderness southwest of Fredericksburg, and move on Richmond.[4]

A very important part of Hooker's plan concerned the role of the cavalry. Gen. George Stoneman, the Army of the Potomac's cavalry commander, was scheduled to make a sweep around the Army of Northern Virginia about two weeks before the infantry moved on Lee's army. The goal of this aspect of the campaign was intended to separate Lee from Richmond and force a rapid withdrawal. Stoneman was to begin his assault with about 10,000 cavalrymen — the entire cavalry of the Army of the Potomac, with the exception of one brigade — on April 13. The weather intervened and rain delayed the assault for several weeks. Hooker gave Stoneman extremely explicit orders; in short, the campaign's success or failure depended upon his action, or lack thereof. On April 28, new orders were issued to Stoneman, whereby he was instructed to cross the Rappahannock River at a point of his determination between Kelly's and

Rappahannock Fords. He was then ordered to send part of his force toward Raccoon Ford and Louisa Court House, and the remaining part of his cavalry was to destroy the Orange and Alexandria, and the Aguia and Richmond Railroads. At some point, his cavalrymen would reunite, hopefully at the Pamunkey River, so as to cut off the enemy's retreat. In his orders of the 12th, he was instructed to take note that the primary objective of his mission was to cut the enemy's connections with Richmond via the Fredericksburg route. This aspect of the orders was strongly reiterated again.[5]

It was an essential part of Hooker's plan that the cavalry operations should begin about two weeks before the infantry marched, and if the cavalry did their part, Lee would be out of provisions. Union intelligence determined that the Confederate cavalry strength was at about 3,000 men and Hooker was satisfied that Stoneman would have little difficulty. Hooker became impatient, and when the rain ceased, he sent all his forces — infantry, cavalry, and artillery — out together.[6]

On May 1, the Light Division was on the march before daybreak, upriver toward the Plank Road that ran from Fredericksburg to Orange Court House. By this time, Hooker had crossed the Rappahannock and was attempting to gain some sort of position on the Confederate left flank. Longstreet's Corps was also on the move, passing the Light Division on the left. Movement continued until dark with no sighting of the Union forces and only artillery action noted in the distance. After the march ended at dusk, skirmishers were sent out, and Union skirmishers quickly engaged them. No major encounter occurred during the night, although Confederate artillery shelled Union wagons attempting to offload supplies.[7]

The brigade commanders of the Light Division were: Gen. Dorsey Pender, Gen. James Lane, Gen. James Archer, Gen. Edward Thomas, Gen. Samuel McGowan, and Gen. Harry Heth, who would soon receive a division command. Each of these men had special abilities and individual limitations. This group of generals would lead the division past the Gettysburg Campaign, and for that reason a short sketch of several of them will be of value at this point.

Gen. James J. Archer was born in Bel Air, Maryland, in 1817. Archer graduated from Princeton in 1835 and studied law at the University of Maryland, after which he opened a law practice in Maryland. Obtaining a captain's commission, Archer took part in the Mexican War, winning a citation of gallantry at Chapultepec. After the war, he left the military and returned to his law practice in Maryland. In 1855, Archer re-enlisted in the army as a captain in the 9th U.S. Infantry. General Archer resigned his commission in 1861 and became a colonel in the 5th Texas, Confederate Army. On June 11, 1862, Archer was promoted to brigadier general and given a brigade command that consisted of the 1st, 7th, and 14th Tennessee, the 19th Georgia, and the 5th Alabama Battalion, as part of A.P. Hill's Light Division. General Archer was captured at Gettysburg and held prisoner for a year at Johnson's Island. He returned to duty briefly, and died in Richmond in October 1864.[8]

Gen. James H. Lane was born in Matthews Court House, Virginia, in 1833. Lane graduated from Virginia Military Institute in 1854, and afterwards graduated from the University of Virginia with a degree in science in 1857. Lane became an assistant professor of mathematics at V.M.I., and later at Florida State Seminary. Ultimately he became a professor at the North Carolina Military Institute in Charlotte, where he taught philosophy and military studies. In 1861, Lane helped to raise and train soldiers for the Confederacy. He was commissioned a major in the 1st North Carolina under Col. D.H. Hill, and took part in the Battle of Big Bethel. Often referred to as the "Little Major" because of his short stature, Lane became a lieutenant colonel when Hill was promoted to brigadier. After the death of Gen. L.O. Branch, Lane was promoted to brigadier and took command of the brigade made up of the 7th, 18th, 28th, 33rd, and 37th North Carolina regiments. After the war, Lane taught at a number of universities, and for the last twenty-six years of his life was a professor of mathematics and engineering at present-day Auburn University. General Lane was a highly respected officer both during and after the war, and as a mark of this high respect, he was a part of the honor guard at the funeral of Jefferson Davis. General Lane died in 1907 at Auburn, Alabama.[9]

Gen. William Dorsey Pender was born in Edgecombe County, North Carolina, in 1834, and after a local education in the county schools and a stint of work at his brother's store in Tarboro, North Carolina, Pender graduated from West Point in 1850. J.E.B. Stuart, O.O. Howard, and Stephen D. Lee were Pender's classmates in the graduating class of 1850. After graduation, General Pender served on the West Coast frontier as a lieutenant and was involved in a number of Indian fights. In 1859, he returned to North Carolina for a time and married Fanny Shepperd, after which the couple returned to California to complete Pender's last two years in the Federal army. In March of 1861, Pender resigned his commission and was elected colonel of the 3rd North Carolina, and later the 6th North Carolina. At the Battle of Seven Pines, Pender made an outstanding maneuver as Jefferson Davis looked on, and was immediately promoted to brigadier by Davis. Pender was a noted disciplinarian who worked diligently to reduce desertions, which made him unpopular with some of the enlisted personnel. He was disliked, and extremely so, by Gen. James Archer, who felt that he, rather than Pender, should have been promoted as the commander of the Light Division after Gen. A.P. Hill was promoted to corps commander. Hill had high regard for Pender and actively sought his promotion to major general. After the death of General Jackson at Chancellorsville, Pender was promoted to commander the Light Division. The Army of Northern Virginia was reorganized and Pender took command of only four of the brigades — those of Archer, McGowan, Thomas, and Lane — of the original Light Division. The remainder went to Gen. Harry Heth, who was promoted and given a division after the restructure of the army. Pender was wounded at Gettysburg with shell fragments to the leg. It appeared not to be life-threatening, but a ruptured artery took his life in late July of 1863.[10]

Gen. Edward L. Thomas was born in Clarke County, Georgia, in 1825. Thomas graduated from Emory College in 1846 and volunteered for service in the Mexican War, serving as a 2nd lieutenant with the Georgia Mounted Volunteers, under the command of Gen. Winfield Scott. After the war Thomas chose to return to Georgia, as opposed to taking a commission in the army. When the Civil War began, General Thomas did not immediately join the Confederate Army, but later was authorized to raise a unit and was appointed the colonel of the 35th Georgia by Jefferson Davis. By mid–1862, the 35th Georgia was in Virginia under the command of Gen. James Pettigrew. The regiment later became part of Gen. Joseph R. Anderson's brigade in the Light Division. After distinguished service by Thomas in the Seven Days' campaign, in which General Anderson was wounded, Thomas took command of the brigade until the war's end. After the realignment of the army into three corps, Thomas's brigade became part of Pender's division. Pender's death at Gettysburg opened the possibility that General Thomas might be the new division commander. Lee declined the promotion, claiming it "might create dissatisfaction among the two brigades of North Carolinians and the brigade of South Carolinians." Many historians view this as unlikely to have occurred, and have dismissed it as the real reason for the rejection of the promotion. For a time during the winter of 1864, Thomas's brigade served with Gen. Jubal Early's command in the Shenandoah Valley, but later returned to Wilcox's division, Gen. Wilcox having replaced Pender as the Light Division commander. General Thomas was one of the most steady, reliable, and dependable brigadiers in the Army of Northern Virginia, yet was never fully credited for his service. After the war, General Thomas returned to Georgia. In 1885, President Cleveland appointed him to a position in the Land Bureau in the Oklahoma Territory, where he died in 1898.[11]

By May 1, Lee and Jackson were both aware that options were few as to how they might deal with Hooker and the sheer number of troops at his command. The high streambeds, the poor roads, the dense Wilderness — all closed many attack and defense doors. The engineering officers of both Lee and Jackson were sent to survey the land and see what, if any, options they deemed available. Major T.M.R. Talcott of Lee's staff and J. Keith Boswell of Jackson's staff returned with the same discouraging conclusion that no attack options toward the Federal center existed. But it was suggested by other scouts that a possible rear attack could take place if troops were sent toward the west, completely across the Federal front, and around the right segment of the Union line. A minister friend of Jackson's, Beverly Tucker Lacy, had a brother who knew the area well: Charles Beverly Wellford, who ran the famous Catherine Furnace (named for the female head of the Wellford clan) and owned a large amount of land in the area. Jackson's mapmaker, Jedediah Hotchkiss, and the brothers Lacy and Wellford, went out and surveyed the land, and Hotchkiss put together a possible route for troop use. It was conceivable to swing around south by west by north in an arc fashion, reaching the Orange Turnpike at Wilderness Tavern about five miles west of Chancellorsville, which would put the Confederates in Hooker's rear. Gens. J.E.B. Stuart and Fritz Lee both concurred with this route, having viewed the land firsthand.

After numerous reports, discussion and questions, Lee reached a decision in the early hours of May 2 to allow Jackson to take well over half of the army on a march south by west by north to attack Hooker's army of 100,000-plus from the rear. Jackson had about 34,000 men (three divisions: Rodes, Colston, and Hill), twenty-seven batteries of artillery (108 guns), and three and a half regiments of cavalry. Lee would be left with 14,000 men and six batteries (24 guns). Gen. Jubal Early had about 12,000 troops in a strong position at Fredericksburg, who could come to Lee's aid if needed. All told, this was an extremely dangerous move: any serious movement against Lee by Hooker would have destroyed the army.[12]

At this point, Hooker had crossed most of his army over the North Fork of the Rappahannock, and over the fords of the Rapidan. Hooker's lines extended from Chancellorsville to the Rapidan, to the flank of Lee's line at Fredericksburg, and they were as close to Richmond as the Confederates were.

Early on the morning of May 2, Jackson began his twelve-mile march around Hooker's forces, and by late afternoon had his 30,000 man army placed behind the unenlightened Hooker. Jackson's force was a ten-mile-long column; Rodes's division was in front, followed by Colston and A.P. Hill. At about 4 P.M. he reached his destination and was about three miles in the rear of Chancellorsville; however, along the route to his location, some problems were encountered. As the army approached Catherine Furnace a sizable force advanced and attempted to capture the army. Jackson had placed the 23rd Georgia in position to guard his flank, and as fate would have it, Lt. Col. J.T. Brown's artillery was passing and placed a battery in position to aid in deterring the attack, along with two companies of the 14th Tennessee of Archer's brigade. The attack was stalled until Jackson's trains had passed, but Federal forces captured most of the 23rd Georgia afterwards. Additional Confederate forces were sent from the commands of Gens. Posey and Ambrose Wright to end the Federal advance. After placing the divisions in right-angle order in relation to the road, Jackson readied the attack and placed Maj. Eugene Blackford in command of the skrimishers to draw out the Union forces. As stated earlier, Lee retained the I Corps divisions of McLaws and Richard Anderson, around 13,000 muskets and twenty-four pieces of artillery, in order to provide a demonstration to convince the Federals that they were confronting Lee's entire army.[13]

At about 6 P.M. the attack was ordered and the Union XI Corps under Gen. O.O. Howard was rolled up like driftwood on the tide. Artillery was captured, and every attempt by Howard to regroup his forces was stalled. A very complex and obsequious individual, Oliver Howard was born in Leeds, Maine, in 1830. An uncle raised him after his father's death in 1839. A reasonably good student, Howard graduated from Bowdoin College in 1850, and from the United States Military Academy in 1854, number four in his class. General Howard lost an arm in the Battle of Fair Oaks, but soon returned to duty. His courage and good political connections led to

5. Chancellorsville

a rapid rise in rank. Due to his Chancellorsville and Gettysburg performances, he was transferred to the western theater of the war, obtaining a corps command under Sherman in the Army of the Tennessee, and ultimately the command of the Army of the Tennessee. After the war, he headed the Freedmen's Bureau, and in 1893, he received the Medal of Honor for his courage at Fair Oaks.[14] General Howard suffered great disgrace for the turn of events at Chancellorsville, as expressed by Sergeant James Peabody: "Howard must needs rush among his own men, swing his revolver and whine, 'I am ruined.' No, the Eleventh Corps did not ruin General Howard; but he ruined the reputation of the Eleventh Corps forever."[15]

In the pursuit of the enemy, the divisions of Rodes and Colston became meshed into a single force. The advance continued past the house of Melzie Chancellor and beyond until dark. Jackson ordered Hill's division forward and as they moved into position, Jackson and his staff were returning from the front when they came into contact with Hill's skirmishers. They were mistaken for enemy soldiers by the 18th North Carolina of Lane's division. The skirmishers opened fire. Capt. J.K. Boswell, chief engineer of Jackson's corps, was killed, along with others, and a number of men were wounded. Jackson received what ultimately would be a mortal wound. Command of Jackson's Corps fell upon General Hill.

Artillery fire was opened on Hill's division, but with the efforts of Col. Francis Mallory of the 55th Virginia (killed in the advance), the attack was repulsed.[16] General Hill was also wounded in the artillery advance and was unable to continue his position of command. Gen. J.E.B. Stuart was summoned to take command of Jackson's Corps and immediately reformed the army's lines. General Rodes refused to take command of the II Corps; thus General Stuart was the logical choice. Jackson expressed to Stuart that he had full confidence in his ability and that Stuart should use his own judgment. Hooker launched counterattacks against Stuart's right, and the right of Hill's Light Division was now under attack from the Union troops who had been driven back toward Chancellorsville to avoid being cut off from the Union command by Jackson's advance. Hooker was successful early, but later withdrew his line, once again giving up a position which could have placed him between Lee's divided army.[17]

On Sunday morning, May 3, from about 2 A.M., the Light Division was under cover until daylight. The enemy had been only marginally engaged up to this point by McGowan's brigade. The first strike of the brigade was near Hazel Grove. The brigade caught one of Gen. Dan Sickles's regiments, the 37th New York (the Irish Rifles) in marching formation, doling the 37th a loss of about 222 men. Maj. William DeLacy of the 37th New York states: "[4 A.M., May 3] Our brigade was moving to the rear, and, as we were about to follow the Seventeenth Maine Regiment, we were ordered to file into line, but before half the regiment was formed the enemy opened a deadly fire on our front and left flank, which caused a little confusion in consequence of the regiment not being formed, which compelled us to fall back." Major DeLacy goes on to say, "The regiment was again rallied and took the same position, and after some hard fighting, fell back to the rear about half a mile."[18]

McGowan would next encounter Gen. Thomas Ruger's brigade of the XII Corps. General Ruger was an extraordinary soldier. Born in New York, he graduated from West Point in 1854, resigning his commission after one year of duty in New Orleans. Ruger lived in Janesville, Wisconsin, and practiced law there from 1856 until he rejoined the army in 1861 as a colonel. Ruger was given a lt. colonel's commission in the 3rd Wisconsin, and took part in most of the early battles of the war. General Ruger became a brigade commander in the XII Corps and later a division commander in the XXIII Corps in 1864. After the war, he was the military commander of the Department of the South until 1878.[19]

Colonel Perrin's 14th South Carolina was aligned on the left of the brigade and immediately on the right of Lane's brigade. Perrin states that at this point confusion reigned due to the thick woods and undergrowth, and also because the plan of advancement had not been communicated to him. Perrin continues in his report of the battle stating that the plan seems to have been to wheel left, making General Lane's brigade the pivot, which he determined after he discovered that the brigade line was not parallel with the Union line of battle. The enemy's line was too close to General Lane's front and receding too far back on his right. In the forward movement, Perrin's regiment was disengaged and separated from Lane's right, with no support on his left. The 14th South Carolina came, somehow, between two lines of Union field works, one of which appeared to be abandoned. Immediately a strong Union attack began on the right of the brigade, and Perrin continued to move his regiment forward until he encountered musketry fire. The entire brigade's forward motion seemed to have stopped, he explains, and the musketry duel continued for at least thirty minutes, after which the 14th moved forward.[20]

Col. Silas Colgrove of the 27th Indiana presents the Battle of Hazel

5. Chancellorsville

Grove in his report as "an out and out slaughter."[21] While there is little doubt that General Ruger's brigade achieved a sound victory (Lane's brigade suffered the highest killed, wounded, and missing totals in either army at 909 men; General Ruger's brigade lost 614 men), Colonel Colgrove seems to have somewhat stylized the situation, especially with the statement, "Regiment after regiment was poured into the battle to break the line." From where did all of these regiments come, as Colonel Colgrove was involved with Lane's brigade for the most part?[22] One is led to believe that the 27th Indiana *alone* was facing a division rather than a brigade. Lt. Col. Francis Price, 7th New Jersey; Capt. George Beardsley, of Ruger's brigade; Col. Louis Francine also of the 7th New Jersey; and Col. Samuel Quincy of the 2nd Massachusetts of Ruger's brigade, all give a much more balanced report. The report of General Ruger's brigade and the regiments from Sickles's III Corps concerning the engagement with the Light Division on the morning of May 3, as given by Colonel Colgrove, seems extra spectacular.[23] Another viewpoint, as given by Colonel Quincy of the 2nd Massachusetts might be somewhat more accurate and creditable: "For two hours our brigade fought like devils ... our last round of ammunition brought down the colors of the 1st South Carolina ... the battle thunder rose and fell & the yellow smoke rose above the trees and floated up in the clear sunshine while we lay by the roadside and made coffee ... once more I have by the grace of God come out safely from about as much hell as a man often experiences in this world."[24]

This duel, in the main, occurred between McGowan *et al.* and the division of Gen. Alpheus Williams's second line. General Williams was a division commander in the XII Corps, of which General Ruger's 3rd brigade was a part, and a very creditable soldier. Born in Connecticut in 1810, Williams graduated from Yale in 1831, afterwards studying law and traveling extensively. Williams established a law practice in Detroit and later married in 1839. Ten years later, his wife died, after the birth of their five children. In 1840, he became a probate judge; he later served in the Mexican War and was mustered out as a lieutenant colonel. In 1861, the president appointed Williams a brigadier, assigned to Banks's command. General Williams held many different command positions, at times even a corps command. He left the army in 1865.[25]

When General Archer realigned at Hazel Grove, McGowan's right was unprotected and was counterattacked by General Ruger, as mentioned earlier. Regiments on Perrin's right continued to experience intense fire, and they began to fall back. Perrin, along with the 13th South Carolina, was ordered to fall back; they did so until they reached the Union's first line of breastworks, or about 300 yards back. Several brigades of Rodes's division advanced toward the Federals, pursuing them toward Chancellorsville. By this time, the McGowan's brigade had become somewhat unraveled. The 13th South Carolina, a part of the 1st South Carolina, a fragment of the Orr's Rifles, and the 14th South Carolina made up the brigade. Perrin states, "For some reason, unknown to me, the First and Rifles had moved to the rear. I was informed by this officer that our troops in front had driven the enemy from some redoubts, and that they were almost without ammunition and that the enemy was about to flank them on our left."[26] Colonel Edwards of the 13th South Carolina was wounded, and Lt. Colonel Brockman took command of the 13th, making Colonel Perrin the ranking officer in the brigade at that time. General McGowan had suffered a severe knee wound and would be unable to command the brigade until after the Battle of Gettysburg, then remaining in command into early 1864.

Perrin moved the brigade forward, attempting to gain cover from a hill in front of the brigade en route to a wooded area, but was directed to continue forward by Gen. J.E.B. Stuart, now in command of the corps. The brigade then attempted to move toward a battery and an area of woods. They were near the wooded area, and were within 250 yards of the battery, when a hail of musketry fire erupted from the left and rear of the brigade. Confusion and disorientation reigned, even though Perrin attempted to calm the men and finally regrouped them, but the battle was now in its final stages. General Trimble's division and General Archer's brigade were moving on the left and right of the woods and Plank Road, and it was evident the battle had been won by the Confederates.[27] Hazel Grove was one of several high points in the landscape of the Chancellorsville battlefield. Once Hazel Grove came under Confederate control, at least thirty guns were placed on this high point, giving the Confederates considerable leverage. The Federals also began to move guns toward Fairview, soon to be the target of massive Confederate artillery fire.

Colonel Hamilton of the 1st South Carolina stated in his report, in an attempt to explain why his regiment moved to the rear breastworks, that the 1st South Carolina and Orr's Rifles were in fact out of ammunition and deemed retreating to the rear breastworks their only option. After the brigade was reunited, Hamilton (now leading the brigade as senior colonel)

5. Chancellorsville

stated that he was ordered by General Pender to move the brigade to a position on the left of the Plank Road.[28] Colonel Edwards of the 13th South Carolina, the senior colonel of the brigade previous to this point, was mortally wounded. As he walked on top of the works, waving his sword to encourage his men, he was shot through the shoulder, and was carried from the field. Col. James M. Perrin, a relative of Col. Abner Perrin, received a mortal body wound, and later died in great pain. The *Charleston Mercury* printed a very praiseworthy obituary for Col. James Perrin, which was well deserved.[29] The brigade suffered a loss of 455 men killed, wounded, and missing. The 14th regiment, at 145, had the most severe losses overall.

Col. David G. McIntosh of the Pee Dee Artillery battalion made a very interesting observation concerning the battle:

> The battle of Chancellorsville was probably the most difficult of all General Lee's battles. At the same time it was his greatest success. At no time if we except the closing chapter of the war, did he have to face such overwhelming odds. After the battle of Fredericksburg he was reluctantly compelled to detach Longstreet and two of his best divisions and send them south of Richmond, beyond his reach.... The situation was full of peril and might well appall the stoutest heart. That General Lee was able to meet it successfully proved him to be a master in the art of war, and made it his greatest triumph.[30]

This is an accurate statement concerning the Battle of Chancellorsville, yet Lee was a general who kept all Union generals guessing as to what his next move might be. If war is a chess game, "Fighting Joe" Hooker was checkmated at Chancellorsville.

Depending on one's viewpoint, the Union army was not defeated at Chancellorsville, but they were "outgeneraled." General Hooker was a competent officer, and perhaps at a later time in his career as the General of the Army of the Potomac, this battle might have ended differently. After the battle "Fighting Joe" made an interesting comment about it: "I felt confident when I reached it [the battlefield] that I had eighty chances in a hundred to win."[31]

Could Hooker have won at Chancellorsville? The eminent historian Stephen Sears feels that it was possible until Hooker was thrown on the front porch of the Chancellors' house on Sunday morning, May 3. Hooker was unconscious for nearly three-quarters of an hour. His doctors felt he would not survive, and others thought he was dead. When he finally regained semiconsciousness and attempted to mount his horse, he fell off and began to vomit. Throughout the day he was in and out of consciousness, vague, sleepy, lacking any decision-making power. These symptoms are the typical signs of concussion. Hooker likely remained in a less than alert condition for a few days, at least. Some felt that General Hooker was "prostrated by too much abstemiousness," which may or may not have been the case. Within two months, he was relieved of command of the Army of the Potomac. One must decide if this had any effect on the outcome of the Battle of Chancellorsville, as the information suggests.[32]

Col. Theodore Dodge of the 119th New York list twelve "failures" of General Hooker at Chancellorsville: (1) failure to move the entire army into open space and seize Banks' Ford; (2) failure to move the cavalry effectively; (3) failure to make a firm push toward Banks' Ford on Friday morning; (4) withdrawing into the Wilderness to fight a defensive battle; (5) failure to cover his right flank after 9:30 A.M. on Saturday; (6) failure in allowing a weak, partial, and an ineffective movement against a foe of Jackson's ability; (7) failure to not attack one of Lee's separate wings Saturday afternoon; (8) failure to hold Hazel Grove; (9) failure to support the struggle at Fairview with one of his unused divisions; (10) failure to support Sedgwick's advance at Salem Church; (11) failure to properly ration his army when communications were open to do so; and (12) failure to keep Sedgwick on the south side of the river to make a new advance.[33] In more general terms, Lee was successful because Hooker made too many mistakes. Hooker did not engage a full one-third of his army, a mistake he had made previous engagements; and in addition, poor coordination, inadequate intelligence, bad decisions, and slow reaction to "things that didn't work" were also factors in his defeat.

There are some factors concerning this battle from the Confederate position, which might have made a significant difference in the outcome of the battle. The death of General Jackson doubtless had an effect on the outlook and morale of the army and how the battle was conducted. Jackson wanted a battle of annihilation and he seemed to have felt it was possible. Arguably, that may not have been the case, given all the constraints the Confederate army faced in this battle, the greatest being the relative size of the two armies. A second constraint, which would have altered the difference in the size of the armies, is the fact that Longstreet's Corps was not present to take part in the battle. Had this part of the army been available to General Lee, a more formable attack could have been launched

5. Chancellorsville

from whatever might have been the most advantageous position. Unfortunately the age-old proverb is correct: hindsight is 20/20. But we'll never know for sure.

Col. Abner Monroe Perrin of the 14th South Carolina began his rise to leadership in the battle of Chancellorsville. For the first time, Colonel Perrin was able to submit a report to be included in the official records of the war. Far more importantly, Perrin's leadership was recognized by the high command of the army during the short period that he actually commanded the brigade due to the wounding of Colonel Edwards and General McGowan. This leadership role would shortly result in an extensive and protracted conflict with another colonel in McGowan's brigade. General McGowan would be unable to take command again until after the Mine Run Campaign. With the death of Colonel Edwards of the 13th regiment, Perrin was now the second-ranking colonel in the brigade. Colonel Daniel Hamilton of the 1st regiment was the ranking colonel and asserted his seniority before the Battle of Chancellorsville ended. Colonel Hamilton was unavailable for a time after the wounded McGowan and Edwards left the field, but assumed command on his return. The struggle between the two men, more intense on the part of Hamilton, would not end until the Battle of Gettysburg, at which time Hamilton would be transferred to the coastal defense force of South Carolina, and resign his commission shortly thereafter.

General Jackson died on May 10, and it was halcyon and somehow proper that General Jackson "passed over the shore" that day, which was Sunday. Jackson had always stated that he wanted his final day on earth to be on a Sunday, and he got his wish. In his final hours, he spoke in semiconsciousness to General Hill, saying, "Order A.P. Hill to prepare for action! Pass the infantry to the front immediately!"[34] Although General Hill had, by default, become the commanding general of Jackson's corps, it was not yet official. In fact, there were six candidates: A.P. Hill, Richard Ewell, D.H. Hill, Richard H. Anderson, Lafayette McLaws, and John B. Hood. Hill received the acclamation from General Lee, who said: "[Hill] is the best soldier of his grade with me."[35]

In addition, a new division was to be created and attached to the III Corps. General Hill strongly suggested that General Heth be placed in command of that division, and also that Gen. Dorsey Pender be given command of the Light Division. Lee concurred with both requests and the promotions were made. Heth's division included his old brigade,

Archer's brigade, Johnson Pettigrew's North Carolina brigade, and Joseph Davis's Mississippi brigade. Pender's division was made up of his old brigade, now commanded by Alfred M. Scales, and the brigades of McGowan, Thomas, and Lane. Anderson's division, made up of the brigades of Mahone, Perry, Posey, Wilcox and Wright, comprised the III Corps of Lt. Gen. A.P. Hill. The corps was over 20,000 soldiers.[36]

Col. G.N. Saussy gave an interesting observation about General Lee, printed in the English magazine *The Strand*:

> His presence was a signal for one of these unaccountable outbursts of enthusiasm which none can appreciate who have not witnessed them. The fierce soldiers, their faces blackened with the smoke of battle, the wounded crawling with feeble limbs from the fury of the devouring flames, all seemed possessed with a common impulse. One long unbroken cheer, in which the feeble cry of those who lay helpless on the earth blended with the strong voices of those who still fought, rose high above the roar of battle and hailed the presence of the victorious chief.... I thought it must have been from such [a] scene that men in ancient days ascended to the dignity of the gods.

This seems a fitting statement concerning Lee's victory at Chancellorsville. Such awe and admiration probably was worth more than an additional infantry corps.[37]

CHAPTER 6

Gettysburg: More Than a Battle

Unknown Soldiers
Stranger! Tell the people of Spoon River two things:
First that we lie here, obeying their words;
And next had we known what was back of these words
We should not be lying here![1]

On the last day of the Battle of Chancellorsville, McGowan's brigade remained in battle formation the greater part of the afternoon and night. Everything that could ignite seemed to have done so, probably from the exploding ammunition. The blaze approached a furious level, burning breastworks, trees, both dead and alive, undergrowth, and most indecently, the bodies of the wounded and dead from the momentous battle of the last few days. The scene was absolutely ghastly: heads blown off, bodies crushed, limbs mangled, and an odor straight from hell itself. The brigade remained in this situation until May 6, and by that time, Hooker had recrossed the Rappahannock and was in the position he held before the Battle of Chancellorsville, Stafford Heights.

By May 7, the division had made its way to Moss Neck on the Rappahannock. This was the location of the division prior to the Chancellorsville battle and they expected some semblance of order when they arrived. Much to their sorrow, however, the place was in shambles: all of their belongings had been packed up, moved or destroyed, tents were burned, and private baggage was simply left to the elements. While this was an extreme frustration, the spring weather made up for the disappointment to a degree. After a short break to recover from battle, military regime was resumed with drills, guard duty, picket duty, and other camp activities that produced much displeasure and complaint.

General Abner M. Perrin, C.S.A.

General Lee in mid-May reviewed the Light Division for the last time before the brigades were reassigned to various commands. Gens. Ewell and Hill were promoted to lieutenant general, and Heth and Pender to major general. The Army of Northern Virginia now consisted of three corps: Longstreet, I Corps, with Hood's, McLaws's, and Pickett's divisions; Ewell, II Corps, with Early's, Rodes's, and Trimble's divisions; and Hill, III Corps, with Anderson's, Heth's, and Pender's divisions. The idea of military medals was also discussed and the decision was made, at that time, to reject idea.[2]

About June 6, the division, along with the army as a whole, was ordered to prepare to move from Moss Neck and begin a march. This was a crucial point in the career of Col. Abner M. Perrin. Col. David Hamilton, the senior colonel of the brigade, had been ill for some time and had left the camp, turning over the command of the brigade to Colonel Perrin. As stated earlier, General McGowan had been seriously wounded at Chancellorsville and would not resume command of the brigade until early in 1864. Lt. Col. J.N. Brown was placed in command of the 14th regiment.

The division marched onward until it reached Hamilton Crossing, near Fredericksburg. Federal troops had attacked and later captured a Florida regiment on picket duty at nearby Deep Run. The division also encountered resistance that resulted in setting up defenses and preparing for an attack. A Federal assault was made, but was repelled by Scales's brigade (Scales was now in command of Pender's old brigade) and driven back to the Rappahannock. Since the Federals controlled the road toward Fredericksburg and erected a large barricade to halt passage, the Light Division also placed an equally large barricade. A standoff resulted for a time, and even though both armies had pickets in place, no combat resulted from the standoff. This situation continued until the middle of June, when it was discovered that General Hooker had chosen to abandon his positions on the both sides of the Rappahannock as well as Stafford Hills and had moved up river.[3]

On June 15, the army moved up the river, followed the plank road between Fredericksburg and Orange Court House, passed over the Chancellorsville battlefield, and moving due west, crossed the Rapidan at Ely's Ford. On Tuesday the 16th the march continued to Stevensburg, where the army stopped and bivouacked for the night. On the 17th a long march was completed in which the army was a few miles beyond Culpeper Court House, about twenty miles from their starting point at Stevensburg. This

6. Gettysburg: More Than a Battle

was exceptional speed in light of the intense heat and the fact that each man was carrying more baggage than usual. The movement continued on Thursday the 18th after a pleasant rain on Wednesday night that reduced the dust and allayed the heat somewhat, ending at Gaines' Cross Roads. The rain returned in force, unfortunately, and the army was reduced to halting on a bare hillside until morning. By Friday night, the army had reached Chester Gap in the Blue Ridge and was still dealing with the intense rain.[4] The III Corps on June 20 marched to Front Royal, on June 21 stopped at White Post for the night, then passed through Berryville, reaching Smithfield on Tuesday, June 23. On Wednesday, June 24, the corps passed near Shepherdstown, reaching the Potomac on Thursday, June 25. By nightfall of the 25th, Hill's corps was a few miles from Hagerstown, Maryland, and on the night of the 26th, near Leitersville, reaching Funkstown, Pennsylvania, on the 27th. The corps remained in Funkstown until June 30 and then began the march to Cashtown.[5]

This was the second campaign into the enemy's territory, and the

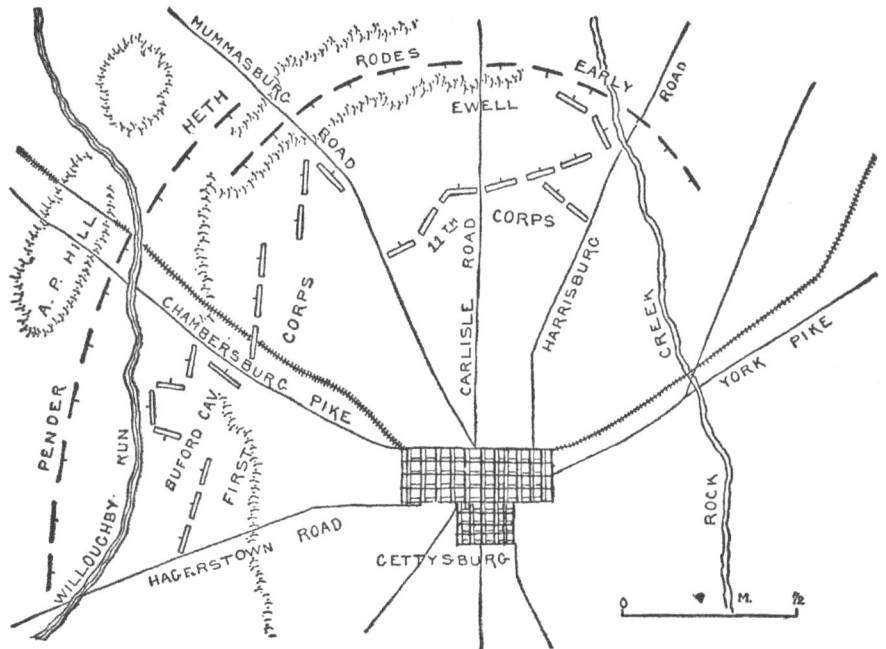

Map showing the essential battle area around Gettysburg in July 1863 (Florida Center for Instructional Technology).

results of the Battle of Antietam were not a very satisfying memory to the men of the Army of Northern Virginia. Was there anything different in the psychological attitude and outlook of the Confederate soldiers concerning this campaign? Dr. Spencer G. Welch, a surgeon of the 13th South Carolina, had this to say about the army's disposition: "I have never seen our army so healthy and in such a gay spirit. How can they be whipped? Troops have so much better health on the march.... Last year when invading Maryland we were almost starved, and of course anyone would be disheartened."[6] Another account of this changed attitude is offered by the famed historian of Hill's III Corps, William Hassler: "The conquerors presented a marked contrast to their haggard appearance the previous fall.... Nowhere was the change more evident than in Powell Hill. Instead of walking grimly at the rear of his division while under arrest, he now rode proudly at the head of his corps where he frequently enjoyed the company of the commanding General."[7]

If better health, pride in the cause, and a rebounded spirit exhibited by the commanding officer were among the plus factors, then what were the constraints faced by the army as it went into Pennsylvania? Much has been said about this area of the campaign, and Joseph T. Glatthaar gives one of the most enlightening accounts of these factors. Glatthaar identifies plundering as a serious problem among Confederate soldiers in this campaign. This would have been a problem with any army that had faced such deprivation as that which the Confederates had endured for most of the war. Ewell's troops were breaking into stores and committing all sorts of problems for the locals. "Plundering dulled the edge of the Confederate soldier, discipline slipped and the army lost its focus." The supply of essentials as well as luxuries was too great a temptation for men who had been without them for so long. Concentration slipped when it should have strengthened; "officers give in to the wishes and desires of the men." These problems would carry on into the battle as well. The march to Pennsylvania took a huge amount of energy that must have had adverse effects on the troops. The heat, relaxed discipline, and loss of focus may well have tipped the battle in favor of the Union army. Glatthaar sums up his points of presentation: "Throughout the campaign, the distractions of invasion — amid a hostile populace and novel surroundings, living off the countryside and plundering Yankee households — may have stripped the Confederate troops of their fighting edge. The distractions and festivities of the raid eroded their discipline and focus."[8]

6. Gettysburg: More Than a Battle

On Wednesday, July 1, soon after sunrise, Pender's division was given a loud and urgent reveille; preparations were made and the march toward Gettysburg was begun. Rain was falling and the day would be hot and humid, much like a day in South Carolina in July when rain falls. McGowan's Brigade was under the command of Col. Abner M. Perrin of the 14th South Carolina, and Lt. Col. J.N. Brown commanded the 14th South Carolina in Colonel Perrin's absence. Somewhere around 10 A.M. the command halted for a short break, after which the march then resumed for a few miles. Then a right turn was made and the division formed a line of battle facing toward Gettysburg. The brigade formation was Lane on the right, Perrin next, then Scales, and finally Thomas was on the left. Perrin's brigade's order was 13th on the right, next the 14th, then the 12th, and the 1st was on the left. The Rifles remained at the previous night's campsite. The brigade numbered about 2,000 strong, but without the Rifles, about 1,500. Rifle and cannon fire continued as it had from the beginning of the march, likely coming from General Heth's division and the dismounted cavalry of General Buford's Federal troops. On June 29, the Federal cavalry commander, Gen. Alfred Pleasonton, ordered the 1st Division of the Army of the Potomac to send any two of its brigades toward Emmitsburg, Maryland. From Emmitsburg the brigades were to proceed on to Gettysburg, Pennsylvania, and attempt to locate the Army of Northern Virginia and determine what they were attempting to accomplish and any additional information they could ascertain.

After even a casual perusal of a map of the state of Pennsylvania as it existed in 1860, Gettysburg immediately can be seen as a "hub" city, with major roads passing through the town in all four directions and toward other major cities within the state and elsewhere. The fact that Gettysburg was the site of what is perhaps the major battle of the American Civil War was no accident. Still, the events that launched the battle and the timing of those events were likely not under the control of either army to the extent they would have preferred.

Gen. John Buford was placed in command of the two brigades of his choice to locate and monitor the Army of Northern Virginia as they attempted to launch a campaign into Pennsylvania. Buford was born in Woodford County, Kentucky, in 1826. His half-brother was Union Gen. Napoleon Buford, and his cousin was Confederate Gen. Abraham Buford. The Buford family moved to Rock Island, Illinois, in the 1840s. Buford obtained an appointment to West Point. After graduation he served in the west, and in 1861, he became a captain in the 2nd Cavalry. In 1862, he became a brigadier in the Army of Virginia, serving with Gen. John Pope. Buford was in the Battles of Second Manassas (where he was badly wounded), Antietam, and Fredericksburg, as well as Chancellorsville. As is evidenced by his background, General Buford was an extremely capable general and the result of his efforts enabled him to become a division commander in the Army of the Potomac.[9]

Buford selected the two brigades with his most reliable commanders to accompany him to Emmitsburg and on to Gettysburg. General Thomas C. Devin was commander of the 2nd Brigade of the 1st Cavalry Division and one of Buford's most steadfast and reliable officers. No less an officer than Gen. Ulysses Grant stated that Devin was "the best cavalry officer in the Union army." Devin was born in New York City in 1822; by profession he was a printer, and he worked at that profession until the outbreak of the Civil War, at which time he entered the army as a colonel in November of 1861 in the New York 6th Cavalry. General Devin took part in most of the Army of the Potomac's major battles and served with General Sickles for a time. At the time of the Battle of Gettysburg, Devin was still a colonel; he was promoted to brigadier in August of 1864 and played a major role at the Battle of Five Forks. He remained in the army until 1877.[10]

Colonel William Gamble was, like Colonel Devin, a trusted and reliable brigade commander in General Buford's command. Gamble was born in Ireland in 1818; after completing his education he became a civil engineer in Northern Ireland, later emigrating to the United States in 1838. About 1840, Gamble enlisted in the army and ultimately became the sergeant major of the 1st Cavalry, before his tour of duty ended in 1843. After his military service Gamble worked in Chicago as an engineer until the outbreak of the Civil War, when he received a commission as a lieutenant colonel of the 8th Illinois Cavalry in 1862. Colonel Gamble was severely wounded at Malvern Hill, but returned to his command during the Fredericksburg Campaign. As events unfolded, Colonel Gamble would command the regiment that fired the opening rounds of the Battle of Gettysburg.[11]

On June 29, Devin and Gamble crossed into Pennsylvania by late afternoon and bivouacked at Fountaindale. Before dawn, General Buford arrived, and the march continued to Fairfield. Contact was made about daylight with two regiments of General Harry Heth's division of the III Corps. Buford determined that he must not allow his command to be delayed in reaching Gettysburg. He dismounted one of Colonel Devin's

6. Gettysburg: More Than a Battle

cavalry regiments in an attempt to allow the command to countermarch into Maryland (Emmitsburg). Buford apprised General Reynolds of the situation, since Reynold's I Corps was also en route to Gettysburg. Gamble and Devin made their way to Gettysburg and arrived there by about 11:30 A.M.[12]

The first serious exchange of fire on July 1 occurred on the Chambersburg Pike at about 7:30 A.M. between the skirmishers of Heth's division and Gamble's pickets. In his account of the exchange, General Heth asserts that he ordered General Pettigrew to "take his brigade to Gettysburg, search the town for army supplies (especially shoes) and return the same day." Heth notes that Pettigrew had encountered a large force of cavalry near the town, with infantry support, and, as commanded, had returned to Cashtown. General Hill was informed of the situation upon his arrival in Cashtown on June 30. On July 1, Heth's division and Pegram's artillery battalion departed Cashtown at 5:00 A.M. By the time the division reached the summit of the second ridge of hills west of Gettysburg, Heth states that he realized that Federal cavalry, artillery, and infantry were around and in Gettysburg. Heth was unaware of the size and seriousness of the situation as he pushed toward Gettysburg and assumed he was dealing with Home Guard troops. In his own words, Gen. Harry Heth said, "I was ignorant what force was at or near Gettysburg, and supposed it consisted of cavalry, most probably supported by a brigade or two of infantry."[13] Since General Stuart and his cavalry were not on the scene, the Army of Northern Virginia lacked any significant intelligence about the Union troops, such as their numbers or whereabouts.

In a message to Stuart on June 23, Lee advised Stuart to post two brigades to monitor Hooker if he remained inactive, to judge if he (Stuart) felt he could pass around the Federal army without hindrance, and to detect the right of Ewell's Corps and collect information. Finally Stuart was advised "to be watchful and circumspect in all of his movements."[14] It appears he was not. Major General Sir Frederick Maurice, in his 1914 work, *Robert E. Lee: The Soldier*, observed: "But it was dangerous to give so vague and general direction to a commander of Stuart's well known enterprise and penchant for sweeping raids...." Maurice continues, "It apparently did not occur to Lee that Hooker's army might move promptly, get between his infantry columns and his cavalry, and make it impossible for Stuart to rejoin him in time to be of service. This is what actually happened."[15]

General Abner M. Perrin, C.S.A.

Consequently, by 8:00 A.M., Gamble and Devin were in position on the top of McPherson Ridge, about a quarter of a mile west of Seminary Ridge. Skirmishers of both armies clashed as Gamble and Devin's troops moved toward Herr's Ridge, about a half mile west of McPherson Ridge, and Heth's division moved toward McPherson Ridge. It was nearing 9:00 A.M. before Heth's division was able to move the scrappy Union forces back toward McPherson's Ridge and securely hold Herr's Ridge.[16] In this exchange, General Archer and about sixty men of his brigade, of Heth's division, were captured by the Federal troops. The historian Warren H. Hassler accounts in his excellent work on the first day's battle at Gettysburg:

> The fate of the first day of battle at Gettysburg seemed to hinge upon which side could obtain reinforcements first. Heth was aware that the powerful elements of Ewell's Second Corps were expected to arrive shortly from the North and northwest, which would place them on the right flank or right rear of the Federal Forces on McPherson Ridge then contending with Heth.... Doubleday realized the vast forces converging against him, and looked anxiously for the arrival on the field from the south of the remainder of his First Corps, as well as for the expected appearance of Howard's Eleventh Corps from the same direction.... At about 11:15 A.M. the remaining divisions of Doubleday's corps arrived on the field.[17]

Buford was aware of the movements of the Confederate army to a large degree, far more so than the Confederate army's knowledge of the Union army's movements. On June 30, at 10:40 P.M., General Buford sent the following to General Pleasonton:

> I have the honor to state the following facts: A.P. Hill's Corps, composed of Anderson, Heth, and Pender, is massed back of Cashtown, 9 miles from this place. His pickets, composed of infantry and artillery, are in sight of mine.... Rumor says that Ewell is coming over the mountains from Carlisle. One of his escorts was captured to-day near Hiedlersberg. He says Rodes, commanding a division of Ewell's has already crossed the mountains from Carlisle....[18]

General Maurice offered the opinion that if Stuart had been in position at Gettysburg on June 30, Gettysburg would have either fallen to Hill's III Corps, with a major defeat for the Army of the Potomac, or the battle would have occurred at South Mountain, and Meade would have been forced to attack Lee in order to save Washington and Baltimore.[19]

In another message sent to Pleasanton, Buford states, "The enemy's

6. Gettysburg: More Than a Battle

force [A.P. Hill's] are advancing on me at this point, and driving my pickets and skirmishers very rapidly.... I am positive that the whole of A.P. Hill's force is advancing." This was sent on July 1, at 10:10 A.M. At 3:20 P.M. on July 1, Buford sent another message to Pleasanton stating, "I am satisfied that Longstreet and Hill have made a junction. A tremendous battle has been raging since 9:30 A.M., with varying success.... General Reynolds was killed this morning. In my opinion, there seems to be no directing person."[20] General Heth states that the first volley fired by Pegram's artillery killed General Reynolds. This is in contrast to many accounts that state General Reynolds's death came from a sharpshooter's musket. The time of Reynolds's death may have influenced the progress of the battle.[21] If Pegram's artillery was the cause of Reynolds's death, then he was likely killed much earlier in the day than if his death was due to a sharpshooter's bullet.

Gen. John Reynolds was an extraordinary soldier and was both loved and admired by those under his command, and genuinely respected by most officers in the Confederate army. General Reynolds was born in Lancaster, Pennsylvania, less than sixty miles from Gettysburg. He graduated from West Point in 1841, and served in the Mexican War, and later was an instructor at West Point. In 1860, Reynolds was named commandant of cadets at the Academy. At the outbreak of the war, he was given a brigadier of volunteers commission and commanded a brigade in McCall's division of the V Corps. The Confederates, during the Peninsula Campaign, captured Reynolds for a short while, but he was exchanged at the end of the campaign. He served in most of the significant battles of the war, and in November of 1862, he was promoted to major general. Reynolds was disgruntled with Hooker's leadership at Chancellorsville, after which Reynolds was offered the command of the Army of the Potomac. He refused the position unless Lincoln agreed to remove himself from the military aspects of the army's responsibilities. Reynolds commanded three army corps at Gettysburg and was killed in action while attempting to reinforce General Buford's position on July 1, 1863.[22] General Reynolds is credited with immediately ascertaining the value of Cemetery Hill. Some accounts say that actually the credit for the importance of Cemetery Hill should go to General Buford, as he may well have observed this area from his position on Seminary Ridge and informed General Reynolds of its potential.[23]

As a result of the death of General Reynolds, command changes immediately took place in the Army of the Potomac I Corps. General

Doubleday became the commander of the I Corps and General Thomas Rowley replaced Doubleday as commander of the 3rd Division. Col. Chapman Biddle was now in command of the 1st Brigade of the 3rd Division, replacing General Rowley. Before his death, General Reynolds had requested the XI Corps to make its way to Gettysburg. Upon the arrival of the XI Corps, and the death of General Reynolds, Gen. O.O. Howard, XI Corps commander, was now in command of the Union forces at Gettysburg, as he outranked General Doubleday.

As the battle began to take shape, the Federal line was in the form of a crescent, with the apex on the Chambersburg Pike, and it extended from Hagerstown Road on the left to Rock Creek, north of Gettysburg, and a few hundred yards beyond the point where the Harrisburg Road crosses the stream. Von Gilsa's brigade of Barlow's division was on the extreme right, and to his left was Wadsworth's 1st division, with Rowley's 3rd division beyond Wadsworth.[24]

General James Wadsworth, whose command (among others) opposed Colonel Perrin at Gettysburg, was born in Geneseo, New York, in 1807. Wadsworth attended Harvard for two years, later studied law and was admitted to the bar in 1833. He later inherited an estate of 15,000 acres of very valuable farmland, and thus lived comfortably. A Democrat in his young years, Wadsworth later became part of the antislavery movement and was a presidential elector in the 1860 election, which probably influenced his determination to join the army and assist in the fight to reunite the Union. He received a major general's commission in the New York State Militia, which was later withdrawn. At the outbreak of the war, and at his own expense, Wadsworth sent two shiploads of supplies to Annapolis, where he attended personally to their delivery. Later serving as a major on General McDowell's staff, Wadsworth received a brigadier's commission from President Lincoln in late 1861, after which General McClellan assigned him to a brigade command of New York troops. In December of 1862, Wadsworth was given command of the 1st Division of the I Corps. General Wadsworth took part in most of the major battles of the war, and was most distinguished at Gettysburg. After the combining of the I & V Corps in 1864, Wadsworth was assigned the command of the 4th Division, V Corps. On the second day, May 6, of the Battle of the Wilderness in 1864, Wadsworth received a mortal head wound. General James Wadsworth was an exceptional person, in private as well as military life.[25]

As the Light Division moved toward Gettysburg, a line of battle was

6. Gettysburg: More Than a Battle

formed with Lane's brigade on the right, McGowan's brigade in the center and Scales's brigade on the left. Thomas's brigade had been pulled to act as a coordinating unit between the corps as they came together for the battle. Colonel Perrin, in his account, says: "We remained in this position until about 3 o'clock [line of battle three miles from Gettysburg with the brigades of Lane and Scales] and were again ordered forward, and again advanced about a half mile when we came close to General Heth's division pressing the enemy within a short distance in front of us."[26] Perrin gave the orders at about 4:00 P.M. to the officers and staff, and then to men in the ranks, that the troops were to move forward without firing, and that they should not stop for any reason, stay close in, be aggressive and press the enemy and attempt to extract them from their position. In addition, they were to pass Heth's division if it was halted, or otherwise assist Heth's division if possible. Sergeant B.F. Brown of the 1st South Carolina relates that Colonel Perrin said, "Men, the order is to advance; you will go to the crest of the hill. If Heth does not need you, lie down and protect yourself as well as you can; if he needs you, go to his assistance at once. Do not fire your guns; give them the bayonet; if they run, see if they can outrun the bullet."[27] Artillery fire became more intense, as did the small arms fire. This situation prevailed for several hours as the brigade came closer to the actual battle area. Soldiers, both retreating and wounded, gave various accounts of the battle scene ahead.

By 4:00 P.M. the situation began to change. The Union troops had retreated or fallen back to a line of loosely constructed earthworks (logs, rails, and earth) on the rise in front of the seminary, located about a mile or so from the town of Gettysburg. This line of earthworks continued with a loose connection to a stone fence about one to two hundred yards south of the Lutheran Seminary to a brick structure (Harman's house), then running along the crest of Seminary Ridge. On the turnpike, near the Seminary, Union artillery was located on the left of the division. This situation put General Scales in great peril, with the artillery on his front, and also the earthworks with Union troops, who were still able to deliver small arms fire. McGowan's brigade (Perrin) faced the same earthworks, while Lane's brigade faced dismounted cavalry behind the stone fence, armed with repeating rifles. The terrain in the area was sloping down slightly, then leveling off, and finally a gradual hillside led to the crest of the ridge. This deployment put McGowan's brigade at great risk, in that if either of the brigades fell by the wayside during the attack, the

General Abner M. Perrin, C.S.A.

brigade in the center, McGowan's, would be facing fire from several directions.[28]

As the advance order was given, again it was stressed to press forward and close in on the enemy. As the division moved forward, the brigade passed General Pettigrew's brigade, who had fought a gallant struggle, but had been forced to withdraw and were seeking a short break to regroup before resuming the battle. At this point, Colonel Perrin used a ravine, probably the indentation sloping down to Willoughby Run, to shelter his men from the enemy's artillery as he reformed his line and again reiterated the no-firing command. The command moved forward, attempting to remain aligned with General Scales's command. When the brigade began the uphill movement, from the left of the road came a hailstorm of lead from the Federal batteries and the Union rifles; yet the Confederates continued the charge, driving the Federals in their front. The forward movement continued, and when the brigade reached a point about two hundred yards or so near a grove of trees near the seminary (likely McPherson's Ridge), the most destructive rifle fire yet experienced by the brigade erupted, disorienting the 14th South Carolina. Some of this fire came from the famous Iron Brigade, doubtless the finest fighting force in the Army of the Potomac. The brigade was made up of regiments from Wisconsin, Michigan and Indiana, and was the only completely Midwestern unit in the Army of the Potomac. The brigade was part of Gen. James Wadsworth's 1st Division, which was part of the I Corps.

The commander of the Iron Brigade was Gen. Solomon Meredith. General Meredith was born in Guilford County, North Carolina, in 1810 to a conservative Quaker family. Meredith was a giant of a man, six feet, seven inches tall. When the family moved to Indiana when Meredith was nineteen, he walked from the North Carolina coast to Indiana. After arriving in Indiana, Solomon worked and paid his own way. He earned enough for an education and became the sheriff of Wayne County, Indiana, at age twenty-four. He later served in the Indiana legislature, and eventually served as a U.S. Marshal. At the outbreak of the war, Governor Oliver Morton appointed Meredith as a colonel of the 19th Indiana, and in 1862 Colonel Meredith was promoted to brigadier. "Long Sol," as he was called, was not popular with his first command, the colonelcy of the 19th Indiana, and some said "he had absolutely no military sense whatever." Severely wounded at Gettysburg, Meredith was out of service until November of 1863. In 1864, he was assigned a command in Cairo, Illinois, and later

6. Gettysburg: More Than a Battle

moved to Kentucky, where he ended his Civil War career. General Meredith lost two sons in the war. He died in 1875.[29]

The Iron Brigade was in support of Col. Chapman Biddle's 1st Brigade of the 3rd Division. The brigade was made up of the famous Ulster Guard (20th New York State Militia), the 121st, 142nd, and 151st (Teacher's Regiment) Pennsylvania regiments. Biddle's brigade had been in hot conflict with General Pettigrew's brigade of Heth's Division of the III Corps for some time. Biddle was finally outflanked and forced to withdraw toward the seminary. When Colonel Perrin and the brigades of Lane and Scales moved forward, Biddle's brigade gave way. Perrin was about to completely cut off their retreat, but their retreat was orderly, although with deliberate haste toward Cemetery Hill in the direction of the stone wall over looking Taneytown Road.

Questions have arisen and much has been said about the commander of the 3rd Division of the I Corps, Gen. Thomas Rowley, and whether or not his actions and inactions influenced the performance of Colonel Biddle's brigade at the Battle of Gettysburg. It seems Colonel Biddle was given orders, which seemed aimless as to their direction and purpose, after which Gen. Rowley issued additional seemingly bizarre orders the entire day of July 1. Col. Rufus Dawes of the 6th Wisconsin took note of Rowley's behavior, and contacted the 1st Division Provost Marshal; Lt. Clayton Rogers proceeded to arrest Gen. Rowley, who later was given a court-martial in April of 1864. Charged with drunkenness, conduct unbecoming an officer, and disobeying a direct order, he was convicted of all charges. A number of other officers concurred with Colonel Dawes, including Gen. Lysander Cutler. Secretary of War Edwin Stanton felt the evidence was inconclusive and refused to cashier Rowley. Instead, Rowley was transferred to the Department of the Monongahela, from which he resigned in December of 1864.[30] Regardless of Rowley's orders and their effect, Perrin and the 26th North Carolina regiment were on both sides of the Union brigade of Colonel Biddle. The 142nd Pennsylvania was nearly captured, as well as the artillery battalion of Captain Cooper.[31]

Rufus Harling of company K of the 14th South Carolina describes the intense fire on the brigade by Biddle and the Iron Brigade: "We advanced, filling up space made by the fallen, and when we had gotten about 50 yards from the enemy our lines wavered, caused by filling up the space, and it seemed that our thin lines were destined to complete annihilation."[32] Daniel A. Tompkins, also of Company K, 14th South Carolina, gives his account of this galling attack: "Company K went into action, as stated above, with 39 men, rank and file. At the 'charge bayonets' the enemy were behind a rock fence, and we could hear their officers distinctly encouraging their men to hold their fire, until the command to fire was given. They obeyed their command implicitly, and rose to their feet and took as deliberate aim as if they were on dress parade, and to show you how accurate their aim was, 34 out of our 39 men fell at the first fire of the enemy." Nonetheless, the Civil War historian Steven Newton contends that the Iron Brigade "died as a coherent brigade in this intense battle. The 26th North Carolina nearly decimated the 24th Michigan and the 7th Wisconsin faced multiple foes and was 'cut up by superior numbers.'"[33]

Col. George McFarland was the commander of the 151st Pennsylvania regiment, which had been raised in central Pennsylvania as a nine-month regiment. George McFarland was born in 1834 and worked on the Susquehanna Canal as a boatman, but ultimately chose teaching as a profession. McFarland was the founder of the McAlisterville Academy in Juniata County, Pennsylvania, a school noted for the preparation of future educators. As an adamant supporter of the Union, he raised a unit of volunteers, which became Company D of the 151st. The regiment had over one hundred teachers in its ranks and so was called the "Schoolteachers Regiment." Gettysburg would be its first real test of battle readiness.[34]

Colonel McFarland, in his report on the final ninety minutes of the Battle of Gettysburg on July 1, states that he realized he was unsupported, and ordered the regiment to fall back to the breastworks, from which it had advanced after his intense struggle with Pettigrew's brigade. McFarland writes he found portions of the Iron Brigade, the 20th New York, and the 121st and 142nd Pennsylvania regiments on his left. Some of General Gamble's dismounted cavalry (the 3rd Indiana) were also part of this force firing from McMillan woods. "The cavalrymen were no match for the veteran infantry regiments and Gamble ordered them back to their horses, to mount and retire to Cemetery Ridge."[35] The Confederates were rapidly increasing in number and had almost gained control of his left flank.

McFarland ends by describing events after 4:00 P.M.: "The enemy [Perrin's brigade] had increased and was now rapidly forming on my left. All support had left both flanks and were already well to the rear." McFarland ordered a withdrawal and concludes, "Then stopping perhaps 20 paces from the seminary, I turned, and stooping down, examined the condition of the enemy in front. At that instant, 4:20 P.M., I was hit by flank

6. Gettysburg: More Than a Battle

fire in both legs at the same instant, which caused the amputation of my right leg...."[36] On July 2, the 151st Pennsylvania had eight officers and 123 men left from the total of twenty-one officers and 446 men the day before. Perrin had sought and driven McFarland through the town of Gettysburg to the foot of Cemetery Hill after an intense battle, which had also resulted in the loss of a staggering number of men in Perrin's brigade. In an address after the war, Colonel McFarland said, "Perrin's brigade with Scales ... attacked us fiercely, the Fourteenth South Carolina, Colonel Brown, in our immediate front. For ten or more minutes we successfully contested the position breaking its lines in front from our better position behind the entrenchment and the trees in the grove.... But in a second attempt made soon after he gained our left flank moving in single file double quick."[37]

McGowan's brigade, led by Colonel Perrin, is ranked as one of the ten best regiments in the Confederate Army, and the Iron Brigade is ranked as the second-best regiment in the Union Army.[38] Thus, this exchange between Colonel Perrin and the Iron Brigade and Biddle's Brigade ranks as no ordinary battle, but rather a shootout between two heavyweights. Sadly, the three brigades buried many exceptional soldiers on that July day in 1863.

Perrin, in his description of the last ninety minutes of the Battle of Gettysburg on July 1, states that he discovered in the heat of the battle and the hail of bullets that he was without any support on the left or right. Scales had stopped his forward motion to return fire, about 200 yards back, Lane was not in sight — and the 14th South Carolina was under enfilading fire. Some historical accounts blame Gen. Dorsey Pender, commander of the Light Division, for Lane's inaction. Lane overlapped the I Corps' left by at least one-quarter mile, but his advance stalled when he came into a skirmish with Gamble's Union cavalry. Lane went into a cavalry action deployment, which, in essence, took him out of action. Had Pender acted to prevent this move by Lane, or corrected it in some way, Cemetery Hill might have been taken by the Confederates, which assuredly would have greatly affected the outcome of the battle. Pender's inexperience as a division commander was a crucial factor at this stage of the Battle of Gettysburg.[39]

Perrin directed the 1st South Carolina to oblique right to avoid enemy fire from a breastwork, and then to charge front to the left and attack. With this motion, the enemy was routed, which resulted in the movement of the enemy's artillery (30 pieces) to the rear. Perrin, during this rapid course of events, then ordered the 12th and 13th South Carolina regiments to oblique to the right, and charge the enemy. The two regiments rushed up to the crest of the hill and the stone fence, driving the Union troops before them. The 12th South Carolina gained the fence area with enfilading fire, and the 13th South Carolina, coming up the hill, drove the Federals down the hill on the opposite slope west of Gettysburg. When Perrin realized the enemy was in disarray, he then reunited the four regiments for pursuit.[40] As one reads the accounts of the Union and Confederate commanders concerning the battle on July 1, the thought immediately comes to mind: how did the Army of Northern Virginia lose the Battle of Gettysburg?

Colonel Perrin continues: "Finding the two regiments [1st & 14th South Carolina] now reduced to less than half the number with which they entered the battle, and the men much exhausted, I ordered them back from the town, to await the Twelfth and Thirteenth, and sent a small detachment through the town to take such prisoners as the enemy had left in retreat. It was after the recall of these two regiments that the brigade of Brigadier-General Ramseur filed through Gettysburg from the direction of my left."[41] This statement, to some degree, puts to rest the controversy as to which Confederate regiment or brigade was first to enter the town of Gettysburg. Skirmishers of the 1st and 14th South Carolina, led by Captain T.P. Alston, pushed into the town of Gettysburg with their flags unfurled. The 1st South Carolina entered on Chambersburg Street and proclaimed that the flag of the 1st South Carolina was the "first Confederate banner raised in Gettysburg."[42] The 3rd Alabama, commanded by Col. Cullen A. Battle, laid claim to this honor also. Captain W.H. May asserted that the July 1 battle at Gettysburg was "the most murderous" he saw in the war, and "the regiment [3rd Alabama] was the first to enter the streets of Gettysburg."[43] The 3rd Alabama was part of O'Neal's brigade, Rodes's division, II Corps. Col. Battle's regiment somehow was separated from O'Neal's brigade at the time of the Oak Hill attack. The 3rd Alabama passed near General Ramseur's brigade and Ramseur asked Colonel (later general) Battle to join his attack, whereupon the 3rd Alabama then moved with Ramseur. Thus, Battle was with Ramseur when Ramseur's brigade entered on Perrin's left, after the 1st and 14th had been recalled by Perrin from Gettysburg.[44] One can easily see how Captain May of the 3rd Alabama could have reached the conclusion that he did, since he did not see any other Confederate troops at that time.

6. Gettysburg: More Than a Battle

What thoughts did Col. Chapman Biddle of the 1st Brigade, 3rd Division, I Corps have concerning the July 1 battle at Gettysburg? The following comments are but a sample taken from an address given to the Historical Society of Pennsylvania on March 8, 1880. Concerning the outcome at Gettysburg: "There is no question as to what a combined attack on Cemetery Hill, made within an hour ... would have been successful ... unquestionably the *great mistake of the battle* was the failure to follow through the town and attack them [Union troops] before they could reform on Cemetery Hill." Concerning the scope of the battle: "The area of the field upon which the most important operations of the 1st of July took place scarcely exceeds two miles." Concerning the length and importance of the battle: "The July 1 battle, the actual fighting was only about seven hours."[45]

The battle on July 2 was radically different from that of July 1. The actual fighting did not commence until somewhere between 12 and 1 P.M. and continued until nightfall. The two armies engaged in furious combat, and while July 1 was mainly taken up with the III Corps in the forefront of the battle, July 2 was focused on the endeavors of Ewell and Longstreet. The delayed start of the day's action was due to the two generals positioning and aligning their two Corps for battle. Longstreet was on the right, Hill in the center, and Ewell on the left.[46] General Meade arrived in Gettysburg at about 1 P.M. and established his headquarters at the Leister House on Taneytown Road, to rear of the line of the II Corps. All or parts of the I, II, III, V, VI, XI, and XII Corps were now present at Gettysburg as the battle was about to get underway, and upon arrival, Meade made an inspection of his army and made plans for the upcoming battle, which was already in progress.[47]

Pender's division readied for battle on a hot and muggy July 2 on Seminary Ridge, stretching from the theological seminary on their left to Gen. Richard H. Anderson's division on their right. In the afternoon, Pender was conferring with his chief of staff, Maj. Joseph Englehard, when cannon fire erupted nearby. General Pender immediately moved to survey the situation, as few Union troops were in the immediate area. Pender felt a sharp pain as a shell fragment placed a large gash in his thigh, so severe that he was forced to leave the field, and General Lane took command of the division. Lane made no move to advance the division, and consequently, Generals Rodes and Early of Ewell's Corps did not advance as was planned, since they were supposed to follow Pender's advance. This inaction may have determined the outcome of the July 2 battle. More importantly, the Army of Northern Virginia lost a brilliant young officer. Pender was not very popular with the troops in Colonel Perrin's brigade, but while at Gettysburg his reputation improved greatly and the brigade felt genuine affection and appreciation for General Pender.[48]

The second day of fighting at Gettysburg was one of a "lot of smoke, but very little heat," as the old expression goes, a day that little or nothing was accomplished for the Confederate Army. General Hill displayed scant little leadership and handled his responsibilities poorly, especially his relationship with General Longstreet. The second day of battle was a sequence of miscalculations and blunders on the part of the Confederate high command, and General Lee was not immune from this situation either. He could have altered any aspect of the battle scene by simply ordering a change. General Hill greeted Stuart's officers on July 2, late in the evening, after which Lee came out and spoke to Hill saying, "All is well, General. Everything is well."[49] In truth, it was not. Lee was physically not himself at Gettysburg. He suffered from diarrhea and demonstrated signs of a recurring coronary problem. In addition, he had been without his ever-present eyes, Stuart's cavalry. George Townsend, a notable English newspaper reporter of the day who was allowed to travel for a time with the Confederate Army on a burial detail, gives his impressions of Stuart: "Stuart entered into a familiar conversation with the party.... He described the Confederate uniform to me, and laughed over some reminiscences of his raid around McClellan's army.... Stuart exhibited what is known in America as 'airiness,' and evidently loved to talk of his prowess. He related trifling occurrences [involving a northern general] and Stuart might have been a plain farmer jaunting home from market."[50] Stuart's absence betrayed Lee's ability to command his army as he had in recent battles; yet, he was responsible for the failures of his subordinates.[51] Stuart's "airiness" and boastfulness, while making for a colorful personality, offered no needed reconnaissance to Lee during the most important battle of the war.

Colonel Perrin and his brigade remained, relatively speaking, in the same position they occupied at the end of the day on July 1, at the foot of Cemetery Ridge. Longstreet's Corps had arrived and had taken a position on the right of the army, and there were various exchanges of fire on both the right and left of the army, but Perrin's brigade and Pender's division were not involved. The brigade sharpshooters were in position and were under fire, but not constant fire. Capt. William Haskell, in command of

6. Gettysburg: More Than a Battle

the brigade sharpshooters, was killed on July 2 by Union skirmishers. It seemed to many of the men in the III Corps that the army was in preparation for a ground battle on Friday, July 3, and they were correct. Both armies secured their positions and continued to work on breastworks and other aspects of protection from the impending battle.[52] From about 10 P.M. July 2 until about 3 P.M. on July 3, the brigades commanded by Perrin and Thomas were under a degree of fire because of their location nearest Cemetery Ridge. On July 3, the ground attack occurred. Col. Joseph Brown, commanding the 14th South Carolina, describes the attack:

> Not the Confederate army but only 14,000 Confederates fought in the charge on the last day. These comprised Pickett's three brigades, of Longstreet's Corps, with 4,000 or 5,000 men, and seven brigades of A.P. Hill's Corps, namely, Heth's four brigades commanded by General Pettigrew, Lane's and Scales' brigades commanded by General Trimble, and Wilcox's brigade, making altogether probably nine thousand men — Pettigrew's, Archer's, Davis', and Scales' brigades having lost heavily on July 1.
>
> When the long lines of artillery and musketry fire suddenly burst upon them in front, obliquely, and enfilading, about half were killed, wounded, or captured; the other half were compelled to retreat. Neither the Federals nor the Confederate army knew whether the result was decisive or whether Lee would attack again on the next day.[53]

Readers may perhaps be wondering why this attack is usually referred to as Pickett's Charge when in fact Pickett's Division made up less than 40 percent of the Confederate troops who took part in the attack. It seems that since General Lee was unsure about the two generals from Pender's division, he substituted General Trimble to lead the two brigades from Pender's division. Longstreet opposed the attack, while Hill wanted to commit the entire III Corps to the attack. Lee refused Hill's offer and Longstreet was given overall control of the attack force in an unsuccessful effort to gain his support. Pickett was Longstreet's entry into the attack — hence the name Pickett's Charge.[54] No matter the name of the attack, it was an absolute failure and a suicidal last-ditch effort to salvage some measure of success.

One of the two leading authorities on the first day's battle at Gettysburg, the historian David G. Martin, points out a number of major miscalculations or mistakes made by the Confederates which led to their failure to take advantage of the day's military supremacy and successes. The first failure concerns General Pendleton's failure to open artillery fire on Cemetery Hill and renew the battle on his own authority. Since Pendleton was the chief artillery officer it was his duty to make such decisions. A second major mistake was General Hill's request to be passed over in the pursuit of the enemy on Cemetery Hill. Hill complained that the III Corps was exhausted from the day's extensive and intensive fighting. Gen. Ed Thomas's brigade had been held in reserve and was rested and ready. Also, Gen. Robert Anderson's division was nearby, had already encamped, and could have easily been a part of the attack on Cemetery Hill. Much more will be discussed concerning General Anderson's role in the July 1 battle shortly. For now, the failure to use available troops in an attack on Cemetery Hill late in the day on July 1 would prove to be a monumental third mistake. Indecisive suggestions passed to subordinate officers by General Lee as an order was the fourth major faux pas of July 1. The now-famous "suggestion" to General Ewell to "carry the hill [Cemetery Hill] occupied by the enemy if you find it practical," simply left too much unsaid.[55] With an officer such as Longstreet or Jackson, this technique would have worked well, but with less experienced or less aggressive officers it was too perilous.

The other of the two major authorities on the first day's battle at Gettysburg is the historian Edwin B. Coddington. Both Coddington and Martin speak to Hill's lack of activity in the late hours of July 1 when he was asked to assault Cemetery Hill, but Coddington offers a different logic as to why Hill has never really been cited as part of the failure to take action on seizing Cemetery Hill. General Lee was present during the entire day on Seminary Ridge and could have made any changes he desired. To criticize Hill would indirectly be a criticism of Lee and no military authority or anyone else of that period or a hundred years afterwards would dare to think of such action.[56] Coddington asserts that the Confederate assault lost its momentum *after* the Federal troops were forced to withdraw into Gettysburg. While the confines of the town's streets slowed the retreat toward Cemetery Hill considerably, and led to the capture of many Union troops, it also delayed Confederate ability to pursue retreating troops for the exact same reason. Add this factor to a long-drawn-out battle from early morning until late afternoon and disorganization sets in and dims one's sense of purpose. Coddington states, "Responsibility for the failure of the Confederates to make an all-out assault on Cemetery Hill on July 1 must rest with Lee."[57]

By 5:30 P.M. on July 1, the battle of Gettysburg was lost to the Confederacy and both Martin and Coddington seem to concur that in Lee's

6. Gettysburg: More Than a Battle

view, the battle on July 1 ended sometime around 5 P.M. Capt. Louis G. Young, in his article "Pettigrew's Brigade at Gettysburg," confirms that Lee instructed Gen. Richard H. Anderson to bivouac his division that was located a scant three miles from Gettysburg, and ready to enter the battle. Captain Young states that General Anderson related this information to him after the war, and he further explains that Anderson rode to Gettysburg to confirm that this in fact was what General Lee intended. Lee, according to Anderson, said that Anderson's division was the only reserve he had available, since the remainder of his army had not yet arrived and that he, Lee, was ignorant of the exact force he faced at that point. With a division of nearly 7,000 fresh troops available, Lee obviously felt the battle on July 1, concerning Cemetery Hill and/or Culp's Hill was at an end.[58] Doubtless, this action allowed the Union to immediately rush in additional troops. Moreover, even if Captain Young's statement is not true, General Lee did not order General Anderson's division to move to Gettysburg to attack the Union troops on Cemetery Ridge because he felt the battle was at a end until July 2. In a letter published by the *National Tribune*, a New York newspaper, General Meade wrote in 1876 that General Ewell informed him after the war that General Lee refused his request to take Culp's Hill, which overlooked Cemetery Hill, and was unoccupied at the time. A second request was also denied. Culp's Hill could have been instrumental in routing the Union Army off Cemetery Ridge. Meade stated that Ewell said Lee's refusal came about because, with Slocum's Union troops coming up, General Lee thought that most of the Federal army was on the ground at that point, which was about 4 P.M.[59] This is additional proof which confirms Coddington's statement as to who is accountable for the Confederate failure at Gettysburg.

General Isaac Trimble graduated from West Point in 1822 and was one of several commanders in the failed assault on Cemetery Hill on July 3. General Trimble offered his judgment as to the failure of the Confederates at Gettysburg in a 1917 article in *The Confederate Veteran*. He enumerates a number of reasons, beginning with Stuart's absence at the battle's first day, and continuing his outline of reasons with Ewell's not moving directly on Gettysburg early on the first day; Confederate failure to follow up the first day's successes; the failure to attack at daybreak on July 2; the lack of concerted attacks on July 2, especially Rodes's failure to sustain Early's attack that night; Longstreet's failure to reach the battlefield early on July 2; even though he was only three miles away; Longstreet's failure to attack

Drawing depicting the Union Army organizing materials in readiness for battle at Gettysburg in July 1863 (courtesy Dover Publications).

with vengeance on July 3; failure to occupy Culp's Hill on July 1, which could have provided a position to have driven the Federals from Cemetery Hill; and error in the July 3 attack, which should have been a concentration of two corps against the Union left instead of attacking a line six miles long. General Trimble also states that only a small portion of the Confederate army, three divisions, took part in the July 3 attack, and these three divisions all attacked only the Union's left center.[60]

Lt. J.F.J. Caldwell of the 1st South Carolina gives a vivid account of the final charge of the Confederate army on July 3:

> Out they marched, banners flying, arms glittering in the sun, crashing over the wheat field, breasting the storm of fire that met them.... The whole federal line wavered and swayed. Victory hung upon a hair. At that moment of ecstatic doubt, standing upon the threshold of that awful region where they must either conquer or be swallowed up, the division paused! What madness! That settled their fate. The tide of enthusiasm, once checked, could not be revived.[61]

The veteran soldiers of the Army of Northern Virginia had never been asked to engage in such an attack. Many of the soldiers simply ran into

6. Gettysburg: More Than a Battle

the enemy, some tried to escape, and many were killed or disabled. There was no pursuit by the Union troops. Unfortunately, as Caldwell informed future readers of his work, "the battle of Gettysburg was irretrievably lost."

A vexing question about this attack lingers until this day: Why did Lee select Longstreet to direct the attack? Longstreet had been sullen and antagonistic during the entire two previous days and vehemently opposed the charge on Cemetery Hill, while Hill had expressed a strong desire for his corps to take part in the attack. Lee made no effort to formulate the details of the attack, but left that to Longstreet and Hill. Longstreet refused to make the proper arrangements and Hill felt he could not, since he concluded Longstreet was in charge of the assault. Thus, no real arrangements were made and the assault was haphazard from the outset. Late evening on July 3, Lee informed Hill that he would lead the retreat, and plans were made late into the night. Hill listened and said little, but how could he speak up after losing 7,600 men killed, wounded, and missing?[62] McGowan's brigade, led by Colonel Perrin, had lost 647 men in the same three categories.[63]

By this time, Gen. Dorsey Pender was in his final days on this earth. Pender died at age twenty-nine, in Staunton, Virginia. An interesting comment was made about General Pender by Dr. Spencer Welch, the surgeon in McGowan's brigade: "Wilcox is the major-general appointed over us, but he cannot surpass General Pender, who commanded us at Gettysburg. Pender was an officer evidently superior even to Hill. He was as brave as a lion and seemed to love danger."[64] General Pender's death occurred on July 18 due to an infection of his wound after amputation of his leg. This loss, plus that of Capt. William T. Haskell, commanding the brigade sharpshooters, was indeed a severe blow to Colonel Perrin and the brigade.

The question immediately arose as to who should replace General Pender. Of the original or longstanding brigade commanders in the Light Division, Gen. Edward Thomas was senior brigadier. General Lee described how meritorious and deserving of promotion General Thomas was, but asserted that his promotion as division commander "might create dissatisfaction" among the two North Carolina brigades and the South Carolina brigade. Therefore, Gen. Cadmus Wilcox, a North Carolinian and a good friend of Hill's from West Point, received the promotion. On the face of it, this seems a stretch of fact since Wilcox was at that time in command of a brigade of Alabama troops. If this was the real reason, then the entire Army of North Virginia probably needed to be revamped to place commanders only with troops from their own states. No doubt, Wilcox was a fine soldier, but not a first-rate military thinker, so he probably was no better qualified than General Thomas, and it's unlikely that troops from the Carolinas would have resented General Thomas's promotion.[65]

On the night of July 4, the Army of Northern Virginia began the trek back to Virginia in a heavy rainstorm. The roads were deep in mud, yet the march was driven and no rest was had until the morning of July 5 near Fairfield. General Hill's III Corps was in reasonably good spirits, seemingly realizing that they would be able to fight another day. On July 7, the III Corps reached Hagerstown, where General Hill ordered earthworks formed and battle lines drawn, as Federal troops were about a mile in front of the corps. Unfortunately, Confederate supply trains had made a rapid exit from Gettysburg on July 4 toward Williamsport, Maryland, about fifty miles from Gettysburg. Federal cavalry had intercepted some of the supply trains south of Greencastle, Pennsylvania; prisoners were taken and supplies were lost, but finally the trains drove off the cavalry and they arrived in Williamsport. Another Federal cavalry force advanced on the trains at Williamsport, and the Potomac was too swift and high due to the rain of July 4 and 5 for the trains to cross into Virginia, except by ferry. The trains made it into a low region, protected by high hills between Williamsport and the river, but yet far away from the army. General Pleasonton's Federal cavalry made an attack line toward Williamsport, and the existing Confederate cavalry at Williamsport was woefully inadequate to meet the attack, so the quartermaster was called upon to supply men to ward off the Federal cavalry. The makeshift army of infantry and quartermaster's forces were able to survive the attack. General Imboden, in command of the supply trains, called it the "Battle of the Teamsters."[66]

A pontoon bridge was completed at Falling Waters, and when the river was somewhat less turbulent and lower for fording at Williamsport, the army left Hagerstown. The rain was even worse than at Gettysburg on the night of July 5 and mud was up to knee deep. The III Corps crossed the Potomac on the pontoon bridge at Falling Waters while the I and II Corps forded the river at Williamsport. Heth's division, which also embraced Pender's division, since no new appointment had been officially made, was at the end of corps and thus moved aside while the wagon trains, about a mile and a half ahead, crossed. Due to extreme conditions and a long march, most of the troops fell asleep immediately. The division was rudely awakened by Federal cavalry and was caught with their ammu-

6. Gettysburg: More Than a Battle

nition wet, and their weapons unloaded and generally gummed up with mud. The cavalry first attacked Pettigrew's brigade. Colonel Perrin's brigade was about fifty yards behind General Pettigrew's brigade. Pettigrew was killed in the attack and Hill gave the order to fall back across the river, which was done in good order. The attack was a total surprise, and some, including Dr. Welch, felt that either General Hill or General Heth should have been court-martialed for neglect of duty.[67] Lt. J.J. Caldwell states that Col. Perrin's brigade lost more prisoners at this battle than at any other battle of the entire war, but offers no criticism about the lax conditions that allowed this attack to occur. The division was marched across the pontoon bridge, with Colonel Perrin's brigade covering the retreat.[68]

General James Johnston Pettigrew was born on July 4, 1818, in Tyrrell County, North Carolina, at the family's home "Bonarva." In 1843 he enrolled at the University of North Carolina at age fifteen and graduated first in his class in 1847, not yet nineteen years old. He became an assistant professor at the Naval Observatory in Washington, D.C., and in six months he left the position, moved to Charleston, and engaged in law and politics. At the war's beginning he had little military training and he thus joined Hampton's Legion as a private. He made his way to Virginia, and ultimately in July of 1861 took command of the 22nd North Carolina. At age 33, the newly promoted colonel wanted action, and actually refused, for a time, a brigadier's commission. General Pettigrew was severely wounded at Seven Pines, and was taken prisoner, and was presumed dead. He returned to duty on the North Carolina coast in 1863, returning to Virginia in May of 1863 as part of General Heth's division. Pettigrew took command of the division when Heth was wounded and was the anchor of the Confederate left line in the famous Pickett's Charge. He continued to command Heth's division until his death on July 17.[69]

As ordered, Hill's Corps departed at 5 A.M. from the Martinsburg, Virginia, area after the return from Gettysburg and after crossing the Potomac into Virginia. The corps camped for two days in the Bunker Hill area, some twelve miles from Winchester, on Mill Creek. During this time there were no contests with the Union troops, and thus on Monday, July 20, the corps marched down the turnpike to Winchester and a few miles beyond before bivouacking for the night. On July 21, the army passed Kernstown, crossed the Shenandoah on pontoons, and encamped west of Front Royal for the night. The corps passed through Front Royal several days later, crossed the Blue Ridge at Chester Gap and bivouacked at Flint

Hill. After the corps passed Gaines' Cross Roads, skirmishers were sent out as a precaution against Federal cavalry attacks, and artillery fire was encountered near the Thornton River, although no damage was done. Some rifle fire also occurred, and it was suspected that Whitworth rifles were used, since no Federal troops were seen. The Whitworth rifle is a .45 caliber muzzle-loading rifle with a range of 1,800 yards, or slightly over one mile, and was a prized weapon for sharpshooters in both armies. Later, at the Battle of Spotsylvania Courthouse, General Sedgwick, a Union Corps commander, was killed with a Whitworth rifle.[70]

After crossing the Hazel River, the army bivouacked for several days and later passed within a few miles of Culpeper Court House. After several days there, the encampment was moved a mile or so, where it remained for about a week. On August 1, intelligence reported that Federal cavalry had attacked the Confederate cavalry picket, driven them in and followed them to the area where the 14th South Carolina was camped. The 14th South Carolina formed a battle line and the attackers were quickly driven away with no killed or wounded reported.[71]

During this week-long interlude between battles, Colonel Perrin composed a very important letter to Governor Milledge Luke Bonham concerning the battle that had taken place on July 1, 1863, at Gettysburg. In this letter Perrin explains that he took command of the brigade on June 5 due to General McGowan's wounds and was still in command on July 29. He mentions Colonel Hamilton's illness and that Hamilton ranked him. He continues by giving the movements of the army from June 28, giving details of the I and II Corps positions. He gives General Heth's position and gives details already discussed concerning the positions of Lane and Scales, the regiments of McGowan's brigade, and the entrance of the 1st South Carolina into the town of Gettysburg. He then states that General Pender told him to gather the brigade for rest, adding "He had sent for General Richard Anderson's division, supposing as I supposed of course that Anderson was not off. But neither Anderson nor his division was anywhere to be found. The enemy during this eventful time was taking their new position at Cemetery Hill which afterwards baffled all our efforts to take."[72] Perrin continues to stress that the enemy that had just been defeated and the artillery that could have been taken was used against his brigade. Perrin then uses italics and declares, "His failure to be up was the cause of the failure of the campaign. I know he had camped some miles in our rear that night preceding the battle, but I know not why. It may have been General Hill's fault & it may have been the fault of Anderson himself."[73]

General Anderson's biographer contests this statement by Perrin, saying, "Soon after daylight of July 1, Anderson's Division was moved to Cashtown, reaching there early in the afternoon, and resting for an hour moved on to Gettysburg. Reaching near that point, they were placed in a position in reserve, recently vacated by Pender's Division."[74] Perrin continues, asserting, "Had our forces been where it could have united rapidly the 20,000 Yankees that were there in the morning would have been devoured in twenty minutes."[75] He also makes the same statement made by the majority of the Confederate officers that Stuart's absence was a major contributing factor in the Confederate defeat at Gettysburg.

Colonel Perrin continues his letter with a discussion of the brigade's position on July 2 and 3, the army's retreat, and General Pettigrew's death, mentioning that the brigade was the cover for the crossing of the army over the Potomac. No less an authority than Edwin Coddington states, "Apparently no one but Perrin noticed any shortcomings in his [Anderson's] performance on July 1, and it never became a subject of discussion after the battle." Coddington seems to feel that the account discussed earlier, whereby Anderson related after the war to Capt. Louis G. Young that Lee ordered his division to remain in camp as a reserve unit, is somewhat suspect.[76] David Martin, a second noted authority on the July 1 battle at Gettysburg, holds the same view and relates the account of Capt. Louis G. Young concerning General Anderson's statements about the battle.[77]

An older account of this battle and exactly who or what is to blame for the Confederate failure to capitalize on victory at Seminary Ridge is that of William W. Hassler, who offers the following:

> Hill, who with Lee had been watching the action from the West Side of Willoughby Run, now rode slowly with his staff over the bitterly won ground to the Seminary on the outskirts of the town. He lamented the absence of cavalry with which to press the pursuit and gain information concerning the enemy's numbers and dispositions.... "My own two divisions, exhausted by some six hours hard fighting — prudence led me to be content with what had been gained...." These two divisions bivouacked in the positions won, and Anderson, who had just come up, was also bivouacked some two miles in rear of the battleground.... Hill's critics accused him of recklessly precipitating a battle which Lee desired to avoid then failing to press a routed enemy.[78]

General Abner M. Perrin, C.S.A.

Hassler does denote that Hill used adequate control over his desire to "jump into battle impulsively." There is no direct blame placed upon Lee, but Hassler does denote that critics held Lee accountable for not pursuing the Federals at Seminary Ridge to prevent them from taking a position on Cemetery Ridge. Historian Hassler, also an outstanding Gettysburg authority, makes no mention of Anderson past page twenty-nine in his work of 155 pages and takes no note of Anderson's absence late in the day of July 1.[79]

General Anderson played a significant role in the July 1 battle at Gettysburg, and for this reason, additional information on General Anderson might be of interest to the reader. Richard Heron Anderson was born in 1821 at Statesburg, near Sumter, South Carolina. Anderson graduated from West Point in 1842, in a class that included Longstreet, McLaws, and D.H. Hill. He served with General Braxton Bragg in Florida in 1861, and was also present at the firing on Fort Sumter. In 1862 he was given a brigade command in Longstreet's division. On July 14, 1862, he was promoted to major general for his service in the Seven Days' Battles and given a division formerly held by General Benjamin Huger. Anderson became part of the Army of Northern Virginia during the Battle of Second Manassas. He suffered a thigh wound at Sharpsburg, but returned to duty in time for the Battle of Fredericksburg. He became somewhat of a favorite of Lee, and was considered as a corps commander after the reorganization of the army into three corps. He served at Gettysburg in Hill's III Corps, and later served as commander of the I Corps when Longstreet was injured at the Wilderness. Anderson survived the war and died in 1879.[80]

In his report filed after the Gettysburg campaign, General Anderson states the following: "Soon after daylight on July 1, in accordance with the commands of the lieutenant general, the division moved from Fayetteville in the direction of Cashtown. Arrived at the latter place **early** in the afternoon, and halted for further orders." Anderson claims he then waited about an hour at Cashtown, and orders then came from General Hill to proceed to Gettysburg and occupy the position in the battle line that was just vacated by Pender's division. General Anderson continues, saying that his division remained in the position previously occupied by Pender's division until the morning of July 2.[81] General William Mahone, a brigade commander in General Anderson's division, makes no pretense and says, "The operations of this brigade in the battle of Gettysburg, Pa., may be summed up in a few remarks. The brigade took no special or active part

6. Gettysburg: More Than a Battle

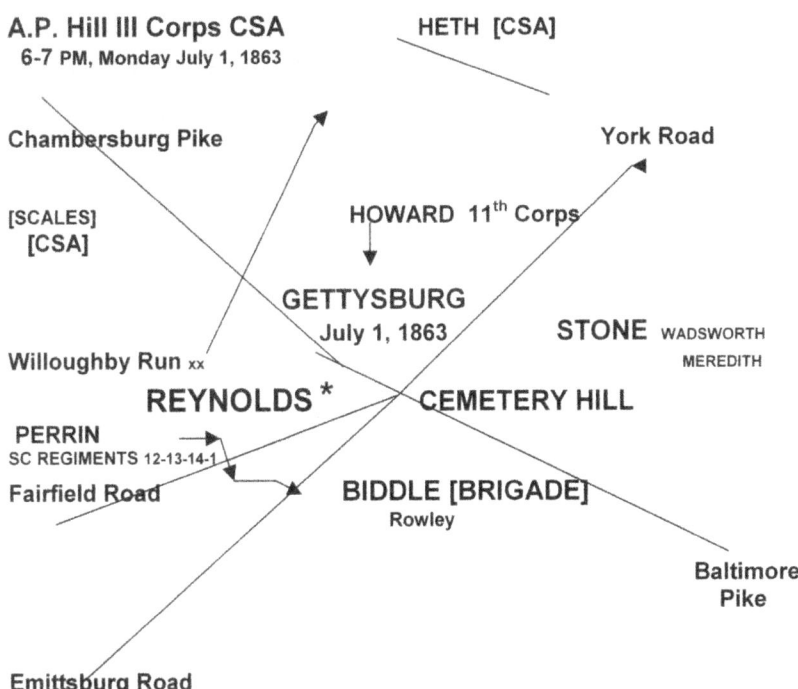

Chart of the battle at Gettysburg, showing Perrin's position at 6 P.M. on July 1, 1863, from *Battles and Leaders*. General Perrin and his brigade made way toward the city of Gettysburg on the afternoon of July 1. By 6 P.M. the 1st South Carolina Regiment entered the city of Gettysburg raising the flag of the 1st Regiment in the city's main area. This was the first Confederate brigade and the first regiment to enter the city. Perrin's brigade fought a furious battle with General Biddle's Pennsylvanians, but with great effort and the loss of many gallant men, they were able to prevail. The 11th Corps of the Union Army was driven through the city, and General O.O. Howard, commander of the 11th Corps, was disgraced as a result. Gen. Reynolds was killed early in the day on July 1, which greatly hurt the Union effort in the battle. Reynolds was one of the Union's finest commanding officers.

in the actions of that battle beyond that which fell to the lot of its line of skirmishers."[82]

As has been said previously, General Anderson is blameless in this situation. Colonel Perrin was exactly on target with his suspicions about why Anderson's division of 7,000 fresh troops was not immediately sent into the battle to prevent the Union Army's occupation of Cemetery Ridge. There was ample time to continue the fight, which could have conjecturably ended the battle in quite a different fashion. All of that aside, Perrin was correct in all of his assertions, and seemingly he was the only battle participant who took note of General Anderson's absence. Every possible explanation has been used to divert attention away from the real reason for Anderson's absence, some of which are: Ewell did not do his job and take Culp's Hill and drive the Federals away before they took command of Cemetery Ridge; Stuart was off somewhere, doing nobody knows what; Hill refused to send in his corps again because they were exhausted; General Lee was sick and "not himself"; Longstreet was late and congested the roads; and at least half a dozen other excuses are frequently offered. Yet, the fact is that Lee and Hill observed the battle all day, close up. They were aware of where General Anderson's division was located, and when it arrived in Gettysburg. Even if the information supplied by Capt. Louis Young concerning General Anderson's statements about why he took no active role in the July 1 battle is rumor, false, or an outright lie, it matters not. General Lee could have sent Anderson's division into the battle and he chose not to do so. As Coddington, Martin, and others have attested, the blame gravitates rapidly toward General Lee. Colonel Perrin simply did not have complete information when he wrote his letter to Governor Luke Bonham in July of 1863 and placed the fault upon General Anderson rather than General Lee. No general in the history of this nation has ever done as much as General Lee with the situation, the supplies, money, manpower, and any other factor one might select to include. His success was phenomenal in every aspect of war, whether dealing with troop movement, generals, and tactics, but in this situation, at about 5 P.M. on July 1, 1863, he was mistaken in his assessment of the best use of General Anderson's division, and it was costly.

The first day of the battle of Gettysburg has received little attention, while most of the print space has gone to the final day of the battle and the famous charge by General Pickett. But careful consideration immediately leads one to conclude that the battle was lost on July 1, between 4 and 6 P.M. Nothing was accomplished by the final charge, and it reminds one somewhat of Sherman's frontal attack at the Battle of Kenesaw, Georgia, in 1864. Had the Army of Northern Virginia left Gettysburg on July 1, much more would have been accomplished, especially the psychological threat of a recurrence of the intrusion of Confederate troops into the so-called safe areas inside the northern states.

In early August, the division made its way toward Orange Court

6. Gettysburg: More Than a Battle

House and there set up camp for a period of time. The troops rested and tended to things which had been long neglected, such as letter writing, clothing repair, weapon maintenance, and so forth. The health of the army seemed good, food was plentiful, and the religious spirit ran exceptionally high. Many division and brigade members returned to service from illness, wounds, and other factors, plus a few fresh recruits joined the ranks. By this time, McGowan's brigade was becoming accustomed to General Wilcox and his expectations for the division and the individual brigades.

This also was a critical time in the military career of Col. Abner M. Perrin. Three very significant letters are contained in Colonel Perrin's military service record from this period. The first of the three letters was written by the regimental commanders explaining that Colonel Hamilton, absent since June 5, had returned and had again assumed command of the brigade in General McGowan's absence. The letter continues by explaining that while they held Colonel Hamilton in respect, "Experience has taught us that his incompetence and unfitness to command, even in camp, but especially in active campaign or battle, and consider it an act of justice to the brave men we command.... To give us a different commander." The letter continues, "We therefore respectfully petition the General Commanding to recommend the promotion of Col. A. Perrin 14th SC to Brigadier General, assigned to command this brigade during the absence of General McGowan for active duty."[83]

A second letter was written by the Assistant Adjutant General Maj. Joseph A. Engelhard and addressed to Capt. A.C. Haskell, the Assistant Adjutant General of McGowan's brigade. This letter explains the great confidence and fondness that Gen. Dorsey Pender held for Colonel Perrin. Engelhard states, "I am confident from the frequent conversations held with General Pender previous to and as well after July 1 that had he lived to have written the official reports of the engagement he would have not only complimented Col. Perrin in the highest levels, but would have undoubtedly recommended him for promotion."[84]

The third letter was written by General A.P. Hill to General Lee and dated August 28, 1863. It seems that the letters made their way up the chain of command all the way to General Lee. General Hill's letter is far and away the least respectful to Colonel Hamilton. General Hill's letter explains that Hamilton has returned and desires to assume command of the brigade on September 4. Hill states that McGowan's brigade is "one of the finest fighting brigades in the army." He continues, "From causes both known and unknown, Col. Hamilton is most obnoxious to the whole brigade, and I am constrained to believe that under his command, the strength of the army will be less by the brigade." Hill continues to explain that McGowan is out of service, and will be for some time. Hill writes in conclusion, "Col. Perrin at present commands the brigade, is an admirable officer and possess the entire confidence of his officers and men. Can we not preserve this condition of things without Col Hamilton? Can he not be detailed in some special duty? Say as comd. of conscripts in So Ca. in place of Col. Preston ... I consider it a matter of some importance."[85]

Col. David Hamilton was born in 1816; it is, however, unclear as to whether he was born in Virginia or South Carolina. Hamilton attended the University of Virginia, later took part in the Mexican War, and served as a United States Marshal after the war. At the outbreak of the war, Hamilton was given a lieutenant colonel's commission in Gregg's brigade in July of 1861, and was promoted to colonel in December of 1861. In late August of 1863, Hamilton was "permanently detached" from the 1st South Carolina Regiment and assigned to duty on the South Carolina coast. Colonel Hamilton officially resigned from the army on January 4, 1864, but left the army probably much earlier. The assistant adjutant general of McGowan's Brigade, Capt. A.C. Haskell, is quoted as saying, "The Brigade had no confidence in him, for he had never shown any capacity." Colonel Hamilton's son, David Jr., was a major in the 13th North Carolina, serving on General Ripley's staff and later, for a time, in the 1st SC regiment.[86]

The brigade historian, Lt. J.J. Caldwell, writes that Colonel Hamilton resigned in November, after commanding a brigade on the South Carolina coast. Caldwell states, "Colonel Hamilton was a gallant officer, an excellent disciplinarian, and a careful manager of troops, an honorable and accomplished gentleman."[87] In addition Lt. Caldwell expressed the view that the 1st South Carolina greatly regretted the loss of the colonel.

Colonel Abner Perrin was promoted to brigadier rank from September 10, 1863, and was temporarily assigned to command McGowan's Brigade in the absence of General McGowan.[88] It would seem that General Hill succeeded in persuading General Lee to arrange placements of officers according to Hill's desires. However it occurred, General Perrin deserved the promotion and doubtless the majority of officers in the Light Division, if asked, would have agreed with his promotion to brigadier general.

A statement made by William Swinton, a reporter with the *New York Times*, concerning the Confederate army's ability and determination seems

6. Gettysburg: More Than a Battle

> ## Perrin's Brigade Monument at Gettysburg
>
> There are approximately sixty-four brigade monuments on the Gettysburg Battlefield to honor both armies for their courage and bloodshed.
>
> C.S.A.
> ARMY OF NORTHERN VIRGINIA
> HILL'S CORPS PENDER'S DIVISION
> PERRIN'S BRIGADE
> 1st Rifles 12th 13th 14th Regiments and 1st Provisional South Carolina Infantry
>
> July 1. Crossed Willoughby Run about 3:30 P.M. with its left in Reynolds Woods and advancing relieved Heth's line. Took a prominent part in the struggle by which the Union forces were dislodged from Seminary Ridge and pursuing them into town captured many prisoners. The Rifle Regiment was on duty as train guard and not in the battle of this day.
>
> July 2. Supported artillery south of Fairfield Road. At 6 P.M. advanced a battalion of Sharpshooters which skirmished with Union outposts until dark. At 10 P.M. took position on Ramseur's right in the Long Lane leading from the town to the Bliss House and Barn.
>
> July 3. In the same position and constantly engaged in skirmishing.
>
> July 4. After night withdrew and began the march to Hagerstown.
>
> Present about 1600 Killed 100 Wounded 477 Total 577
>
> Artist/Founder: Albert Russell & Sons of Newburyport, Massachusetts

somehow appropriate. While rampant with imponderably detrimental decisions on the part of the Confederate high command, and regardless of one's view on this battle, no army has ever given more to a cause than the Confederate army at Gettysburg. Swinton, what would be identified today as "an imbedded reporter" with the Army of the Potomac, wrote: "When we take into account the quality of the men, the loss was irreparable; for the thirty thousand, put *hors de combat* at Gettysburg were the very flower and *elite* of that incomparable Southern infantry which, tempered by two years of battle and habituated to victory, equalled any soldiers that ever followed the eagles to conquest."[89]

Near the end of September, a small cavalry engagement occurred at

Liberty Mills on the Rapidan River, and the Light Division was assigned duty to aid the cavalry. The division actually saw no action, with the exception of Lane's brigade, which did come under shelling. The entire engagement took about three days, after which time the division moved its encampment closer to the Rapidan River to a place called Cave's Ford. The Light Division remained in this location until October 4, when it united with the entire III Corps, now located in the same place. The I Corps, commanded by General Longstreet, was in Georgia or Tennessee assisting General Braxton Bragg's Army of Tennessee, with the exception of Pickett's Division, which was sent to the Richmond area for defense of the city.[90]

About October 11, the corps began a march toward Madison Court House. After passing through Madison, the corps crossed the Robinson River, and following a minor cavalry skirmish, crossed the Hazel River. On October 12, the III Corps passed near Culpeper Court House and came into contact with Federal troops, who immediately withdrew, leaving supplies behind. The march continued toward the Rappahannock River, with a stop in Amissville. Around October 12, A.P. Hill's command crossed the North Fork of the Rappahannock and marched toward Warrenton. No doubt, Hill correctly assumed that another battle was near at hand, which was always the case.

CHAPTER 7

From the Mine Run Campaign to the Wilderness

On October 14, at about 5:30 P.M., McGowan's brigade, under the command of General Perrin, came near to Bristoe Station and at that point the sound of artillery fire and small arms was audible. Shortly the message came that Heth's division had come into contact with the Union forces. In addition, Early's division of Ewell's Corps was approaching on the right of Perrin's brigade, and skirmishers were put out to alert and connect with Early's division. At this point, the hostilities increased, and Wilcox's division was placed in a countermarch formation so that it went from left to right. Anderson's division then moved forward, and then Wilcox's division followed. A railroad embankment protected the Federals, but the Confederates had to make their approach across open and level ground. Consequently, as Perrin's men made their approach, they met troops from Heth's division, and ultimately Cooke's brigade, many of whom were in dire condition.[1]

Perrin's brigade was formed on the right so as to be in line with the enemy, facing them along the railroad on a bushy hill without trees, which commanded the country in their front. The brigade was in two lines, and while battle seemed inevitable, it never occurred. The brigade remained in place for the remainder of the day and into the night. At some point during the night, the Union troops withdrew toward Manassas Junction, about ten miles distant.

Meade's army had been encamped north of the Culpeper area, and two army corps were present near the Rapidan River. General Lee hoped to force Meade to retreat, and then attack the Federals as they moved toward Washington. Lee reasoned that the Warrenton Road was not only his best, but also his only option, and thus moved the army forward; as stated earlier, Hill's Corps was already in the Warrenton area. The Confederate III Corps entered Culpeper on October 11, and to their surprise, no Union troops were to be found. Lee and Ewell reached Warrenton on October 13 in the early afternoon, and Hill arrived near dark. It was the general feeling among the men in the ranks that this was their chance to destroy Meade in total.[2]

Hill moved his corps over old and familiar ground. The corps moved toward Auburn Mills and then to Greenwich, where they actually found campfires still burning and the material possessions of the departed Union troops scattered about everywhere. Overwhelmed with desire to find and destroy the Federal troops immediately, Hill headed toward Bristoe Station. As the III Corps neared Bristoe Station, General Hill noticed Union troops moving toward Manassas Junction, and he noted that they were crossing Broad Run, which slowed their movement as they crossed the ford. Broad Run was a stream above Bristoe Station that ran north to south, and Hill came in from the west. The decision was made to send Heth's division and create as much confusion as possible; thus Heth was ordered to send in three of his brigades and hold one in reserve. In addition, Poague's artillery battery was ordered to open fire on the Union forces.

General Hill was so overpowered with the potential gains he could accomplish at this time that he completely disregarded the fact that he also had two additional divisions ready for action. Hill made several rapid choices before making a complete assessment of the battle scene. The brigades of Cooke and Kirkland in Heth's division were placed in grave danger of crossfire from Gen. G.K. Warren's II Corps, which was undetected by Hill in his rush to attack. Hence, three divisions in Warren's II Corps simply waited for two brigades in Heth's division to get into position for the disaster to take place.[3] In addition to an already bad scene, Hill left McIntosh's artillery unit unprotected; it was overrun by Federal troops, resulting in the loss of two guns. The Confederate III Corps lost over 1,300 men in this forty-minute battle. From General Anderson's report, it seems that the Federal artillery had been placed to enfilade the road leading to the railroad embankment, trapping any Confederate troops attempting to pursue them — in short, a well-thought-out trap.[4]

Dr. Spencer Welch of the 13th South Carolina regiment had this to say about the Bristoe Station engagement: "Two North Carolina brigades became engaged with the enemy late one afternoon near Bristoe station,

7. From the Mine Run Campaign to the Wilderness

and our side got rather the worst of it. It was all due to the miserable management of General Hill or General Heth, or possibly both of them." Col. John C. Haskell, an artillery commander in the III Corps, said of the battle: "Bristoe Station was a most unfortunate blunder, as it cost us a good many men and we lost large stores which would have been valuable to us. It could have been easily avoided too.... I never heard who was responsible for it. General Lee was present, but he never took the army into his confidence, less than ever after a disaster."[5] General Hill seems to have paid too much attention to the III Corps of the Federal Army and failed to see that the II Corps was in position to attack his two brigades as well.

The Bristoe Station engagement was another in a long series of post–Gettysburg pursuits by the Union forces. Meade was hoping to wrap up the Confederate Army, and the Confederate Army equally and fervently desired to destroy Meade and his army, as each side had sought to do during the Gettysburg Campaign.

The morning of October 15 was taken up with moving the encampment back a mile or so and cooking rations. Rain fell most of the day, accompanied by rumors that General Stuart was in hot pursuit of vast numbers of enemy stragglers who were discarding their weapons and other gear. Federal units were in fact losing many men to capture and other assorted problems. Perrin's brigade assumed that an attempt would be made to pursue Meade's army, but it was not to be. Instead, a march back toward the Rappahannock was undertaken, well into the night and under very adverse conditions, including mud, rain, and hunger. The march resumed on the morning of the 16th, and when the Warrenton Junction was reached, the corps began the destruction of the railroad.[6] Throughout the next few days the area fell under extreme rains, and on October 17, the railroad work was completed. October 18 was on Sunday and the corps did no physical work, but instead had religious services and was allowed much-needed rest. The following day, Monday, the army crossed the Rappahannock near the railroad and established encampment south of the river, where the brigade remained with no engagements until November 1.

The 1st South Carolina and the 12th Georgia regiments were sent out into the Blue Ridge Mountains to round up deserters and conscripts. The two regiments returned with nearly 200 men, some of whom were released as too young, in bad health, with family emergencies, or for other reasons;

nevertheless, in a real sense this was a pleasant outing for the two brigades. In the Blue Ridge many men joined the Federal army as a last resort to avoid service in the Confederate Army; they were referred to as "Lincoln's Loyalists," "galvanized Yankees," and other less respectful names.[7]

Meade was under pressure to launch an attack before winter set in, and on November 7, Gen. John Sedgwick's corps attacked Ewell at Rappahannock Station, taking 2,000 prisoners in a southward plunge. Lee was somewhat at a loss to determine what the Federals planned to do, but events of the weather, human factors, and Confederate vigilance ended the threat until spring.[8]

Lee determined that Meade was content to hold any action against the Confederates in abeyance until spring, and for this reason, Lee decided to generate action of his own. On November 27, Perrin and the brigade began a march, passing through Orange Court House, in a movement toward Fredericksburg in extremely bitter weather. In the afternoon of the 27th, cannon fire was noted as Gen. Edward Johnson's division of Ewell's Corps engaged the Union forces. The combat was short-lived and Perrin's troops bivouacked near Mine Run. On the night of November 30, General Lee held a high-level council and it was decided that Hill's Corps would make a night movement, set up on Meade's left, and attack at dawn. Anderson and Wilcox got their divisions in order and into position and spent a bitter cold night waiting for sunrise. As the sun came up on December 1, the corps rushed forward and found only the debris of a departed army. Afterwards the III Corps took some 200 prisoners. From this "battle that never was," the army returned to their winter quarters, with the full realization that the campaigns and engagements of the fall of 1863 were of no real consequence in terms of winning the war.[9]

Because of the cold, little militarily was expected of the troops, with the exception of picket duty, which was a necessity. The pickets were spread out from Cave's Ford to Barnett's Ford on the Rapidan. Later this was expanded from Bradford's Ford to Cave's Ford, and required five companies, with each company required to cut and haul logs for the five miles of plank road from Orange Court House to Liberty Mills on the Rapidan River. The other two corps hauled broken stone to use on the streets of the town.[10]

Furloughs were now allowed, and in fact increased to as many as eight per one hundred men during a given period, but a leave to South Carolina was a maximum of twenty-one days. Taking travel into account, this left

7. From the Mine Run Campaign to the Wilderness

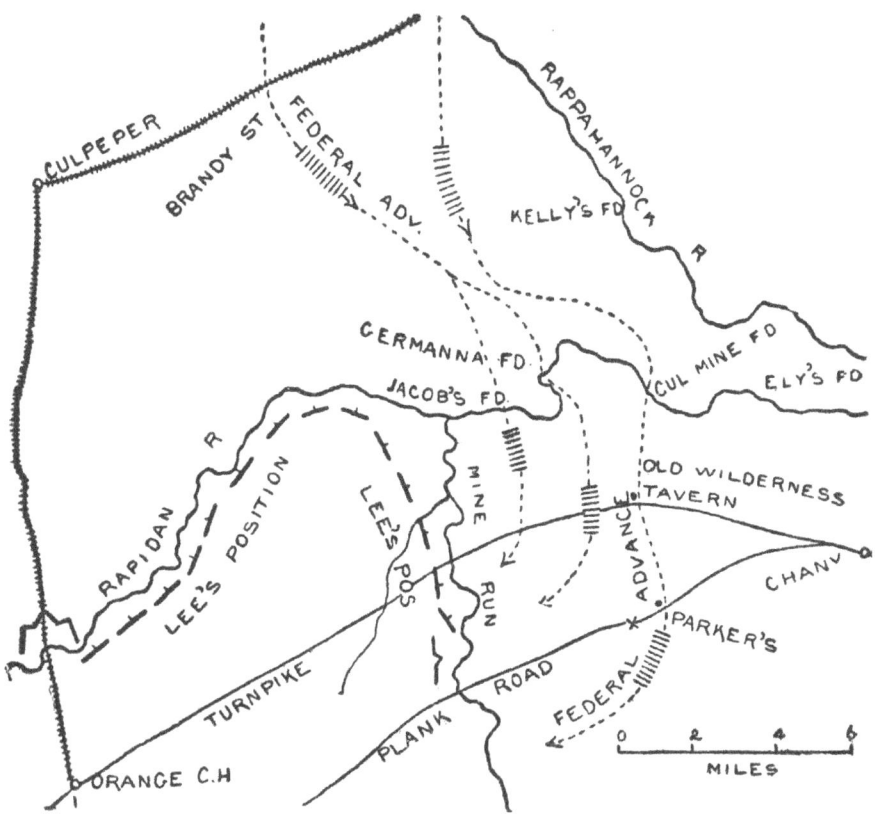

Map of the Mine Run battle area in November of 1863 (Florida Center for Instructional Technology).

little time with friends and family. During this winter period, the brigade camp was moved because of a shortage of wood, less than a mile up river. The health of the army was as good as could have been expected due to exactness concerning simple rules of cleanliness. Food was passable, but lacked protein, and clothing was abhorrent — too little, and what was available was inferior. Food and clothing sent from home were especially welcomed, as is true in any military conflict.

A rather unpleasant task was dealt with during this time — the task of dealing with deserters. The 12th South Carolina had two deserters tried and convicted by court-martial and sentenced to death. General Perrin made an effort to save them and advised his various regiments to send petitions for a pardon for the two soldiers, which meant much in light of the reputation of the brigade for its service. General Perrin personally carried the petitions to General Lee, who allowed a respite for the two convicted men. General Lee commuted the sentence to a term of imprisonment in Richmond, although (and somewhat puzzling) in a nearby brigade, ten soldiers were shot for the same offense.[11]

In early February, General McGowan returned to the brigade, and even though not completely recovered, he was able to function during this inactive period of the war. Thus, as a result of General Wilcox's promotion to major general and his assignment to division command, Gen. Abner Perrin was given command of General Wilcox's former brigade on February 4, 1864. This must have been a bittersweet promotion for General Perrin in that he had served with McGowan's brigade since the Seven Days' Battles and had acted as the brigade commander for a segment of that time.[12]

How did a soldier such as Col. Abner M. Perrin, or for that matter, any individual, become a brigadier general in the Confederate or the Union Army? Agreement will not be universal on this matter, but it usually came about in one of three or four ways. First, if a candidate was a graduate of the United States Military Academy and had any estimable qualities and an air of probity, his chances were better than average of ultimately gaining that esteemed rank. Also, if he was a graduate of a known and valued military college, such as Virginia Military Institute or the Citadel, he was only marginally less desirable than a graduate of West Point. A second avenue of attaining the rank of brigadier was via political appointment from the president, or intercession by a powerful individual near the president who might be able to intervene on one's behalf. Examples of this type general might be Banks, Logan, McClernand, and Butler. Some of this group became creditable leaders, but many were vastly sub-par soldiers. A third way of entrance into this elite group could be attained by a private soldier who made his way through the ranks. General Nathan B. Forrest and Ambrose R. Wright are the supreme models of this approach in the Confederate Army; both men became highly successful leaders in the Army of Tennessee and the Army of Northern Virginia. A final pathway to a brigadier's star was previous experience or a field promotion, and this best describes General Perrin's advancement to that level of leadership. His conduct and performance at Gettysburg and the accolades within battle reports concerning his leadership and judgment assured his promotion at some point to the rank of brigadier. Also, in another example, Jefferson Davis

7. From the Mine Run Campaign to the Wilderness

promoted Gen. Dorsey Pender onsite at the Battle of the Seven Days from colonel to brigadier.

Wilcox's former brigade was in Gen. Robert H. Anderson's division of Gen. A.P. Hill's III Corps. Anderson had previously been in Longstreet's I Corps, but after the reorganization of the army, his division became part of the III Corps. It is somewhat ironic that General Perrin fell under the direct command of General Anderson in light of his remarks and feelings about how he perceived General Anderson's role and his seeming inaction at Gettysburg. The new brigade was made up of all Alabama troops: 8th, 9th, 10th, 11th, and 14th Alabama regiments. Some of the prominent officers of this brigade were Col. Y.C. Royston and Col. Hilary Herbert of the 8th Alabama; Col. Samuel Henry of the 9th Alabama; Gen. William H. Forney of the 10th Alabama; Cols. J.C.C. Sanders and George E. Tayloe of the 11th Alabama; and Col. Lucius Pinkard of the 14th Alabama. As fate would have it, General Perrin would never have time to become fully acquainted with these officers.[13] A short biographical introduction to some of these field officers is worthwhile for an understanding of General Perrin's new command.

Col. George E. Tayloe resided in Big Lick, Virginia, before the war, and was a graduate of the Virginia Military Institute. Tayloe was wounded in the Seven Days' Battle, but survived and returned to Virginia after the war.[14]

Gen. William H. Forney was born in Lincolnton, North Carolina, and moved with his family to Alabama in 1835. Forney served in the Alabama legislature and was a lieutenant in the Mexican War. General Forney was severely wounded at the Battle of Williamsburg and was taken prisoner. After his release he took command of the 10th Alabama at the Battle of Chancellorsville, where he was again wounded. At Gettysburg he received three wounds; he was again taken prisoner and not released until April of 1864, only to be placed in detention at Fort Delaware on June 15, 1864. After his release, Forney took command of the brigade formerly held by General Perrin in February of 1865. After the war, Forney served in the United States Congress from 1875 until 1893.[15]

General John C.C. Sanders was born in Tuscaloosa, Alabama (other sources states his birthplace as Lowndesville, South Carolina), and was a student at the University of Alabama when the war began. He raised Company C, "The Confederate Guards," as part of the 11th Alabama regiment. Sanders suffered several wounds, one at the Seven Days' Battles and another at Gettysburg. When Gen. Cadmus Wilcox took command of the Light Division, Sanders was the senior colonel and would have been brigade commander, but he had not physically recovered to take command. Thus, General Perrin took command of the brigade. Sanders was promoted to brigadier in June of 1864, the third youngest brigadier in the Confederate Army. Sanders was fatally wounded at the Battle of Second Deep Bottom in August 1864.[16]

General Perrin's selection to assume command of General Wilcox's former brigade came with some severe sequential calamities. If General Forney or General Sanders had been available for service, Gen. Abner Perrin would most likely have received command of another brigade in different circumstances, and he might have survived the war. However, as Union Gen. Joshua Chamberlain said, "There is no promise of life in peace, and no decree of death in war."

The inactive period of the past few months was about to come to an end for the III Corps. The order was given to send back all surplus baggage and be ready to move at any time. The men in the ranks felt that General Lee was confident and would continue a defensive posture, using all means to deny the Union forces entry into Richmond. The private soldiers seemed to feel that Richmond could not be taken as long as they survived as a fighting force.[17]

General Hill was not, and had not been well for some time, and could barely function. Prostatitis was an ongoing illness with Hill and limited his ability to carry out the duties of a corps commander; in fact, he was forced to give up his command for a time in March. Lee was also not in the best of health and Longstreet had recently returned from Tennessee embittered about his lack of success at Knoxville. In short, the high command of the Army of Northern Virginia did not have the same outlook and attitude that it had enjoyed at Gettysburg. The situation that was developing in May of 1864 for the Army of Northern Virginia seemed to lend itself to Shakespeare's advice, "Defer no time, delays have dangerous ends."[18]

On May 2, Lee, Longstreet, Hill, and Ewell had a discussion about the events at hand on top of Clark's Mountain. Lee had contemplated this situation previously and stated he felt that the Union attack would come against the Confederate right over the Rapidan River via Ely's or Germanna Ford. Gen. U.S. Grant was also involved in similar planning activities. In his *Personal Memoirs,* after reviewing the nip and tuck of the two armies since 1861, Grant then states: "So here was a standoff. The campaign now begun was destined to result in heavier losses, to both armies, in a given time, than any previously suffered; but the carnage was to be limited to a single year, and to accomplish all that had been anticipated or desired at the beginning in that time. We had to have hard fighting to achieve this."[19]

Grant's immersion into the Virginia campaign would actuate a whole set of new problems for the Army of Northern Virginia. Grant was a different cynosure, a westerner from a family of modest means, unlike the Lees, who were one of Virginia's foremost families. Thus, he was estranged or separated from the "Virginia mentality." Grant did not view Lee as invincible or "protected by the war muses," and he seemed to feel that his goal should not be to destroy the Army of Northern Virginia but rather to *contain* it.

The campaign launched by Grant has come to be known as the Overland Campaign. Grant's objective seems to have been to try to force Lee to abandon his usual technique of maintaining a strong position, and then to somehow implant the Army of the Potomac between Lee and his lines of communications. To accomplish this, Grant intended to start from Culpeper, but then the campaign seems to have developed a life of its own, which probably was not what Grant intended. From Culpeper the campaign moved to the Wilderness, then to Spotsylvania, to the North Anna River, and then on to Cold Harbor. The Overland Campaign took about thirty days, from May 3 until about June 7, if one concurs with the view that the Overland Campaign included the battles beginning with the Wilderness and ending with Cold Harbor. Grant's commanders were more or less the same throughout this campaign: Hancock, II Corps; Warren, V Corps; Segwick, VI Corps (until his death on May 9, 1864); and Burnside, IX Corps. Lee would establish his headquarters behind Mine Run at the Rapidan River, Lee's battle line. May 12 would be the crucial date of this campaign, even though the war would continue for about another ten months. When the ability of the two armies to replenish their manpower and military supplies is examined, it is evident as to why the Confederacy could not contain Grant and why the end was near.

General Lee was dilatory in consigning his corps to specific locations. The III Corps was camped at Orange Court House; a full twenty-five miles distant, Ewell's Corps was encamped ten miles closer to the Wilderness but more dispersed; and Longstreet was over *forty miles* away from where Lee felt Grant might attack. And to add an additional negative to

General Abner M. Perrin, C.S.A.

this upcoming campaign, the manpower odds would be stacked in Grant's favor nearly two to one. Grant states that he felt Lee discovered early on the morning of May 4 that the Army of the Potomac was moving, but did not know until past noon exactly on what roads the army was traveling. Grant also alleged that he was aware of exactly where each of the corps commanders in Lee's army was located and by what roads they would move across to attack him — a decided advantage.[20]

Lee established his headquarters at Orange Court House, which gave him the use of two good roads, the Orange Court House Road, the more southerly of the two, and the Orange Turnpike. Both of these roads ran nearly parallel to the Wilderness and both roads came into contact with the road from Germanna Ford in the Wilderness. The use of this location as a headquarters gave Lee a definite advantage in the placement of his troops.

At 9 A.M. on Wednesday, May 4, the signal officer on Clark's Mountain sent the news that blue uniforms were in sight on Lee's right. The III Corps headed eastward on the Orange Plank Road toward Chancellorsville. Heth's division, followed by Wilcox (minus Anderson's division, which Hill left at Rapidan Heights as a rear guard to follow the next day), led the march. Ewell

Drawing illustrating a sniper in position at the Battle of the Wilderness, exemplifying the method used to end the life of Union Gen. John Sedgwick on May 9, 1864 (courtesy Dover Publications).

7. From the Mine Run Campaign to the Wilderness

was parallel and to the left of Hill's Corps and traveled along the Orange Turnpike. Ewell was urged and instructed by Lee to avoid, if possible, a general engagement until Longstreet arrived from Gordonsville. He was ordered to gauge and regulate his march with that of Hill's Corps. General Lee hoped to engage the Federal forces in the dense growth of the Wilderness, which would disguise his smaller army and also limit Grant's use of his superior ordnance forces. Hill proceeded to Parker's store and was engaged by dismounted cavalry, which was ultimately driven back to Brock Road after a brisk encounter.[21]

A very accurate description of the area around the Orange Plank Road and the Orange Turnpike is presented in a May 1864 edition of the *Charleston Mercury*:

> The surrounding country is very appropriately called the Wilderness, the people being ignorant, the soil destitute of fertility, the supply of water scant, the ground broken and covered with a dense and almost impenetrable growth of stunted bushes, pines, and black jacks. It is a blasted region, adjoining the district known as the "poison fields of Orange," and producing but little for subsistence for either man or beast. So thick are the woods in some places that it is impossible to distinguish a man, even in the absence of verdure, at a distance of fifty paces.[22]

The *Mercury* goes on to say, "It would be difficult to select a more unfavorable ground for a battle between to great armies." A line drawn from Fredericksburg through Chancellorsville to Orange Court House describes the battle area, which was at right angles to this line.

One can only wonder what was occurring to General Perrin as this great battle was about to begin. This was the first significant battle in which Perrin was in command of a brigade now known as Perrin's Brigade; no longer was Perrin commanding McGowan's Brigade. He had new regimental colonels to deal with, and a brigade which was accustomed to General Wilcox's way of doing things. And he was now under the direct command of General Anderson, a general for which he had little regard because of what he incorrectly saw as General Anderson's failure to support him at Cemetery Ridge at Gettysburg late in the day on July 1, 1863.

To give the reader a sense of the battle's location, Ewell's II Corps was moving from the southwest toward the northeast and would shortly come into conflict with Sedgwick's VI Corps and Warren's V Corps as they moved in the opposite direction on the Orange Turnpike. Hill's III Corps met Hancock's II Corps as it traveled off the Brock Road onto the Orange

Plank Road and then moved from the northeast to the southwest. General Lee's headquarters was located at the Widow Tapp's farm near Orange Plank Road, northeast of Parker's Store. General Grant's headquarters was located near the crossing of the Germanna Plank Road and the Orange Turnpike. The area at the crossing of Orange Plank Road and Brock Road saw much of the action of the Battle of the Wilderness. General Warren was moving toward Parker's Store as Hancock was headed to Shady Grove Church, and during the interim period, General Meade established his headquarters at the Old Wilderness Tavern.[23] This campaign was an attempt by General Grant in his new command to place the Army of the Potomac between Lee's Army of Northern Virginia and Richmond.

Grant was a new factor in this area of the war, and in this phase of the war. He was an unknown quantity, and Lee and his generals had first to gauge his intentions, his valor, and his determination to carry out his plans. Charles Dana, an emissary of Secretary of War Stanton, who traveled by day with Grant, had this to say about the general: "Grant was an uncommon fellow, the most honest and most disinterested man I ever knew, with a temper that nothing could disturb, and judgment that was judicial in its comprehensiveness and wisdom. Not a great man, except morally; not an original or brilliant man, but sincere, thoughtful, deep, and gifted with courage which never faltered."[24]

In addition, this was a perilous time for the Army of Northern Virginia. The war had depleted, to one extent or another, many of the resources of the Confederacy, as evidenced in a statement by Lt. William C. Nelson of the 17th Mississippi: "I will give you our bill of fare, breakfast, a piece of cornbread ... a piece of meat 2 inches square, and a cup of coffee.... [W]hen we eat hearty dinners, we dine on meat and bread without the coffee...."[25] One must but wonder that if the officers had this meager ration, what must have been the diet of the men in the ranks?

As the battle neared, the Union brought five corps, with fifteen divisions (forty brigades) of infantry; three divisions (six brigades) of cavalry; and finally 242 guns to bear on the Army of Northern Virginia. The Confederates had four corps, nine divisions (forty brigades) of infantry, three divisions (seven brigades) of cavalry, and 224 guns with which to defend themselves. The Union total force was 105,000, and the Confederate total force was 69,000 at the beginning of the campaign (Pickett's division came up at the end of May).[26] The opening clash on May 5 occurred about noon between General Griffin's division of Warren's V Corps and Ewell's

7. From the Mine Run Campaign to the Wilderness

II Corps. Ewell was repulsed but countercharged, repulsing the V Corps, and both corps made later attacks. A few miles south, two divisions of Hill's III Corps, Wilcox and Heth, met Getty's division advancing from Brock Road with Hancock's II Corps ready to attack.

General Perrin remained at Orange Court House as part of the rear guard of General Anderson's division. Perrin's Alabama brigade broke camp and left Orange Court House on May 5 at around 2 P.M. and traveled the Orange Plank Road toward the Widerness. The brigade arrived at Vediersville at about 8 P.M. on May 5, a few miles from the battle site. The brigades of Mahone and Davis were part of Longstreet's attack on the Union left on May 6 in an attempt to drive it back to Brock Road. The attack was a complete success: the Federals were caught somewhat by surprise, not having expected Longstreet to arrive in time to take part in an attack or a defense, and were driven across the railroad cut and on to Brock Road with heavy losses. Grant was banking on the hope that Longstreet would be too late to save Hill's III Corps, and he had ordered a 4:30 A.M. attack by General Hancock. Hancock's II Corps had been in battle since 5 A.M., the adjusted attack time, when Longstreet's I Corps and two brigades of Anderson's Division of the III Corps, at about 11 A.M., attacked Hancock's II Corps with accelerated dispatch. Colonel Haskell, in his *Memoirs*, made this observation of Longstreet on May 6 at the Wilderness: "Longstreet rode up and down the lines, encouraging, exhorting, and steadying the men, with an effect on them that no other leader I ever saw had on his troops."[27] Longstreet was severely wounded by a musket shot to the shoulder, from which the ball traveled upward, causing great injury to his throat. His division protégé, Gen. Micah Jenkins, was mortally wounded by friendly fire from Mahone's brigade on May 6, 1864.[28]

Gen. James Wadsworth was able, after he engineered a reorganization of the Union forces, to assume command of all troops north of the Orange Plank Road. General Rice's brigade and what remained of the V Corps that he originally commanded were put in as the first line of battle, and the commands of Webb and Stevenson were placed as second-line defense. After the morning "blitz," Hancock and Wadsworth were attempting to sort out the command's next moves, while Longstreet was planning his next attack on the Union line. Since the early morning attack had been frontal, little attention had been paid to the left flank. The Confederates had located an unfinished railroad, and this was used for the attack discussed above at about 11 A.M. As General Kershaw's division of Longstreet's

I Corps moved to make the flanking attack, General Field, reinforced by General Perrin's brigade and the brigade of General Perry, moved to extend the line of attack to the north side of the Orange Plank Road.

General Wadsworth struck back with major force, pushing hard the left side of the Confederate line. General Perrin's brigade waited behind their entrenchments and Perrin told his men, "Hold your fire until you see the whites of their eyes." (This order has been cited by at least twenty different individuals in Perrin's brigade.) Meanwhile, Wadsworth had commandeered the 20th Massachusetts and ordered Lt. Colonel Macy, the regimental commander, to attack. Colonel Macy stalled in protest, stating that the useless deaths would be to no avail. Wadsworth, in fury, took command of the regiment and prepared to lead the charge. Lt. Colonel Macy then ordered the charge and was the first to suffer injury as the attack progressed. The command of the regiment then fell upon Major Abbot, a very promising young officer. Abbot led the charge with courage and conviction, but was killed in the process. General Perrin's brigade then sent a killing blast that stalled the 20th in their tracks. In the furious action that was taking place, General Wadsworth lost control of his horse as he turned to move away from the galling fire. His aide, Lieutenant Rogers, attempted to help the general regain control of the horse, but it was too late to avoid the head wound which took the general's life.

An alternate account of this incident places the 37th Massachusetts, the 56th Pennsylvania, and the 76th New York regiments as part of the attack on General Perrin's Alabama brigade.[29] A number of accounts disagree as to which Confederate command actually killed Wadsworth. Lt. Morris Schaff, who was present at the battle scene, states that a member of General Perrin's brigade killed Wadsworth. Wadsworth's biographer, Mahood, also gives several other possibilities: a member of Mahone's brigade, a member of Gen. Nathaniel Harris's Mississippi brigade, or one of General Kershaw's division troopers, any of which could be correct.[30] Gen. Alexander Webb offers his account of the fiasco created by General Wadsworth: "General Wadsworth had given to me the most astonishing and bewildering order, which was to leave the twelve regiments under my command at his disposal, and go to the left and find four regiments, and stop the retreat of those troops of the left of our line who were flying to Brock Road." General Webb goes on to explain the already discussed situation concerning the 20th Massachusetts and concludes his remarks concerning General Wadsworth by saying, "My line was broken by Field, and

7. From the Mine Run Campaign to the Wilderness

swept off as by a whirlwind. Birney's line, as a consequence, was broken to pieces, and back on Brock Road went the troops."[31]

With the death of General Wadsworth it now became imperative that General Burnside quickly come to the aid of Hancock and the II Corps because Hancock needed additional support on his right. Hancock intended to begin his attack at about 8:30 A.M., and the news of Wadsworth's death arrived at Grant's headquarters at about that time. Burnside was ordered to desist his movement toward Parker's Store and immediately move his thrust against the Confederate left, which was opposing General Birney's attack on the Orange Plank Road. Burnside diverted Potter's division, Hartranft's brigade, and Wilcox's division and made his way toward Hancock's corps, a distance of two miles, arriving five hours later, at 2 P.M. Grant was agitated to the extreme.

General Mahone was already on Birney's left, and it was not looking good for Birney's attack. Colonel Perry, commanding Gen. Evander Law's Alabama brigade and holding the left of Field's battle line, was attacked by Burnside about 2 P.M. General Perrin's brigade and the Alabama brigade of Colonel Perry, plus the Florida brigade of General E. Perry, forced Burnside to retreat. Burnside ordered up two brigades and twelve regiments (mostly New England troops) and used them to oppose the Confederate line. Most of these men from the twelve brigades were raw recruits and quickly withdrew when they came into contact with Perrin and the two Perrys' veteran brigades. Colonel Hartranft with four Michigan regiments and one New York (109th) and one Pennsylvania (51st) regiment made a second attempt. Success was quick, but short: Potter's troop folded and Hartranft's raw troops were in total panic and General Burnside withdrew. Private John Smith Lewis of the 16th Mississippi, Wilkinson Rifles, had this comment in his diary for May 7, 1864: "The woods are full of the dead on both sides. The Yanks have lost fully 4 to our one left dead in the field. After sleeping an hour on the Plank Road after daylight we moved to the left and built breastworks. Here we waited the advance of the enemy. They didn't come, though they charged in dense masses just to our left against Perrin's Ala Brigade, and were repulsed with little difficulty."[32]

Private Wilbur Fisk of the 2nd Vermont gives this very dynamic account of the retreat of the Union left as a result of the attack on May 6 by the Confederates. The 2nd Vermont was a part of the VI Corps and was fighting with the II Corps under General Hancock during this three-day battle: "There was considerable disorder and confusion in our hasty retreat, and the regiment was more or less broken up. There was no chance for us when the left gave way except to run or be taken prisoner. We were between two fires and the enemy had every advantage. The road was to be the rallying point in case of disaster. The disaster came, and every man that had good legs was in duty bound to use them."[33] To make a bad situation impossible, Hancock's breastworks of timber caught fire, and the Union troops were attempting to fight the flames and maintain their position under Confederate fire at the same time. Hancock attempted to rally his troops as best he could, but Confederates made their way up to and on top of the breastworks, placing battle flags atop the works. One can envision Wilbur Fisk's description of the overthrow of the Union left, the fires and the battle scene, but can hardly imagine the intensity of the situation.

It has been suggested by Edward Steere, one of the leading authorities on the Battle of the Wilderness, that Lee intended to make an all-out offensive assault on Grant at the Wilderness, similar to Gaines' Mill, Malvern Hill, and Chancellorsville on May 3, or Pickett's Charge on Cemetery Hill. The frontal attack on Hancock was the focus of this offensive, and General Perrin's Alabama brigade was to be a part of this attack, along with the brigades of Heth, Field, Kershaw, Perry, E. Perry, two brigades of Wilcox's division, and Wright's brigade. Steere states that along with Malvern Hill and Cemetery Ridge, the Wilderness assault on Hancock's center must go down as one of Lee's tactical failures. Steere continues his observations of the Battle of the Wilderness asserting: "It therefore seems reasonable ... to regard the movement from May 5 to June 18 in a vast semi-circle around the Confederate Capital ... really constituting a single battle in the modern sense of the term. In this light, it should be most logically designated as the Battle of Virginia."[34] Steere concludes his analysis of the battle with a very insightful comment which has been alluded to in many historical works both directly and indirectly: "Lee, in short, fought in the Wilderness for the same reason that had determined his decision to fight at Fredericksburg in December 1862 and at Chancellorsville in May of 1863, namely to hold the river line as the military frontier of Virginia."[35]

Gordon Rhea also makes several sterling points about the Battle of the Wilderness. First, had Grant been of the same caliber as the previous commanders of the Army of the Potomac, doubtless the Union forces would have been defeated. This would have possibly determined the elec-

7. From the Mine Run Campaign to the Wilderness

tion of 1864 and it could have ended in Lincoln's defeat. Thus, Grant saved Lincoln's presidency and possibly won the war. Secondly, Rhea states clearly, "For the South, the battle of the Wilderness was the beginning of the end," without doubt an accurate statement.[36] The final year of the war would be an attempt by General Lee to maintain this river line, which would ultimately be traversed by Grant and the Union Army.

One might ask the question: what was the significance of this battle? According to Gen. Alexander Webb, a division commander in the II Corps of the Army of the Potomac, it denoted a lack of leadership identification:

> The 6th of May was the last day of the battle of the Wilderness. Ewell had most effectually stopped the forward movement of the right wing of Meade's army, and Hill and Longstreet defeated our left under Hancock. The fact is that the whole of the left was disorganized. From Hancock down through Birney and Gibbon, each general commanded something not strictly in his command. Hancock had "the left," Gibbon "the left of Hancock," Birney had his own and Mott's divisions, and Wadsworth had Webb and Stevenson. The troops of these three division commanders were without proper leaders.[37]

General Grant would ultimately fix the leadership identification problem, and that would change the course and outcome of the war.

The Honorable George Clark of Waco, Texas, a member of Perrin's brigade gives an account of the battle as it was ending:

> On the next morning [May 7] about ten o'clock the enemy advanced upon us, but were easily and quickly repulsed, as the movement was made to discover our position. Here we remained all the day of May 7, and after dark we were moved about a mile to the right. The next morning [May 8] a detachment was sent forward to ascertain the whereabouts of the enemy, and failing to discover their lines, the march was resumed toward Spotsylvania C.H., where we arrived on May 9, and took our position on the right.

Clark continues saying that Ewell made an attack on the enemy in Perrin's front, and that the brigade took part in the attack, sweeping the Federals back to their original lines.[38]

Only now was General Lee beginning to understand that Grant was a completely new entity, a general quite different from any faced by his army in the past. The overland route to Richmond had been attempted five times — by McDowell in 1861, by Pope and Burnside in 1862, by Hooker and Meade in 1863 — and each effort had failed. In 1864, Grant again tried it and again failed. After six weeks of the most difficult fighting of the entire war, and the loss of around 55,000 men, close to the total number of Lee's entire army, Grant finally made it to the James River. Notwithstanding all of these factors, if Lee had made better use of Longstreet's Corps and not allowed his corps to be over forty miles away from the battle scene, Hancock might have been cut off and neutralized. This might have offered a very different outcome to the Battle of the Wilderness.[39]

Little did Abner Perrin realize that he was less than one week from his entrance into eternity. Had General Perrin survived Spotsylvania, in all likelihood he would have been promoted to major general and would have been placed in command of a division in the Army of Northern Virginia. This outcome was not to be, and it is impossible to estimate how he would have conducted himself in that position.

CHAPTER 8

Perrin's Brigade

The five Alabama regiments under the command of General Perrin had previously served under the leadership of Gen. Cadmus Wilcox. This brigade was exceptional in several areas. The 8th Alabama was the first Confederate regiment to sign up "for the war," meaning the entire regiment to the man reenlisted to serve for the duration of the war. In addition, the brigade had been involved in every major battle fought by the Army of Northern Virginia, and a number of the brigade members were present for the surrender at Appomattox. It would be no exaggeration to make the claim that this brigade was about as good as any in the Confederate Army. Thus, General Perrin took command of an experienced and notable brigade on February 5, 1864. The brigade contained five regiments rather than four, which was the more common number for most Confederate brigades. While the brigade was made up of men from many counties in Alabama as well as other Confederate states, the members of the brigade seemed to have come more frequently from counties in middle and middle-western sections of Alabama. An attempt has been made in this survey to present a selection of soldiers from each of the five regiments with the rank of colonel or below and a brief sketch, if known, of their lives. The soldiers contained in this listing are discussed by regiment and rank, and only individuals who served with General Perrin, as far as is known, as their brigade commander are included.

Col. Young L. Royston was born in Perry County, Alabama, and after graduation from the University of Alabama he opened a law practice in Selma, Alabama. Colonel Royston served in the 8th regiment, was wounded at Frayser's Farm and Salem Church, and retired from Confederate service in November of 1864. Royston was one of the tallest men in the Confederate army at six feet and seven and one-half inches.[1]

Colonel Hillary A. Herbert was born in South Carolina but spent most of his life in Greenville, Alabama. He attended both the University of Alabama and the University of Virginia. Colonel Herbert served in the 8th regiment, was wounded at the Wilderness, and retired from Confederate service in November of 1864. After the war he served in the U.S. Congress from 1877 until 1893, and as Secretary of the Navy from 1893 until 1897. He died in 1919 in Tampa, Florida.[2]

Lt. Col. John P. Emrich was born in Germany and worked as a mechanic in Mobile after coming to the United States. Colonel Emrich served in the 8th regiment and was wounded at Gaines' Mill and Petersburg. After the war he returned to Mobile, where he later died.[3]

Major Duke Nall was born in Perry County, Alabama, in 1830 and was a planter before the war. Major Nall served in the 8th regiment, was wounded at Frayser's Farm, and later received a mortal wound at the Wilderness. He was transferred to Augusta, Georgia, for treatment at Blackie Hospital, where he died in November of 1864. Major Nall is buried in Magnolia Cemetery in Augusta, Georgia.[4]

Capt. D.F. Floyd served as an Adjutant in the 8th Alabama and after the war was elected to the Alabama House of Representatives in 1876.[5]

As was the case in other states, many members of the same family often joined the Confederate (or Union) Army as a group. This was the case with the Fuller family of Alabama. The following five men were all private soldiers from the Fuller family who joined the 8th Alabama regiment: Company A, John T. Fuller; Company K, George W., Jesse S., James M., and Richard P.T. Fuller. In addition, Lt. B.J. Fuller was the only officer-grade soldier in this exceptional family of soldiers. Another family also supplied two members to the 8th Alabama: Daniel H. DeBardelaben, born in 1845, died in 1909; and Arthur M. DeBardelaben, born in 1843, died in 1880, with no descendants as he was never married. The DeBardelaben family also contributed members to other Alabama brigades. Both Daniel and Arthur were private soldiers.[6]

Col. Joseph H. King was born in Morgan County, Alabama, and served in the 9th Alabama regiment. Colonel King was wounded in the Seven Days' Battles and again at Gettysburg. Shortly after the war Col. King died in Decatur, Alabama.[7]

Lt. Col. Gaynes C. Smith served in the 9th Alabama regiment. Lt. Col. Smith was born in Giles City, Tennessee, in 1827, and at the time of the Civil War, he lived in Limestone County, Alabama. Smith was taken as a prisoner at the Battle of Gettysburg, but later returned to the war. He survived until 1910.[8]

Major James M. Crow was born in Florence, Alabama, in 1836 and resided in Lauderdale County. He joined the Confederate Army in May of 1861 and was wounded at Gaines' Mill. Major Crow served in the 9th Alabama regiment and at the close of the war moved to Kentucky, where died in 1922.[9]

Henry J. Fusch served as a private soldier in the 9th Alabama regiment and was a member of Company F serving under Capt. T.H. Hobbs at the beginning of the war. He enlisted at Athens, Alabama. The regiment enrolled 259 men, of whom thirty-five were still alive in 1896.[10]

Col. James E. Shelley was born in Tennessee, but moved to Talladega, Alabama, where he became a brick maker. Colonel Shelley served in the 10th Alabama regiment and was wounded at Gaines' Mill, but recovered to fight again. He was killed in action at Spotsylvania in June of 1864, during the Overland Campaign.[11]

Col. William T. Smith was born in Petersburg, Virginia, and later in life moved to St. Clair County, Alabama. Colonel Smith joined the 10th Alabama regiment early in the war and survived the conflict to become a state representative. After service in the Alabama legislature, Smith ultimately retired in Wilsonville, Alabama, and died in 1915.[12]

Col. L.W. Johnson was born in Wilkes County, North Carolina, on October 1, 1832. At the beginning of the war he operated a business in Talladega, Alabama, and joined the Confederate Army in June of 1861. Johnson enlisted in Company E, the Jeff Davis Blues, for the duration of the war, and served in every important engagement of the war in which the 10th Alabama was involved. He was noted for bravery and was a favorite with the men who served with him. Colonel Johnson married Malissa Brown after the war in 1881, and until his death in 1909, resided in Holt, Alabama.[13]

Maj. John W. Woodward was born in Wilkes County, North Carolina, and joined the 10th Alabama regiment of the Confederate army early in the conflict. Woodward sustained a wound in 1862 from which he recovered, and later, in November of 1864, was promoted to the rank of major. After the war, Major Woodward became a businessman in Talladega, Alabama.[14]

Maj. James Truss was a member of a very distinguished Alabama family with roots in eastern Jefferson and St. Clair counties. A city, Trussville, was named for the family. Captain Truss joined the 10th Alabama in June of 1864, at Cropwell, Alabama, and served with honor during the war with the Coosa Valley Blues.[15]

Maj. Lewis W. Johnson served in the 10th Alabama regiment. Born in Wilkes County, North Carolina, Johnson joined the 10th Alabama in 1861. Major Johnson received a severe wound to his foot during the Mine Run Campaign but returned to service. He became a businessman in Talladega, Alabama, following the war and died in 1909.[16]

First Lieutenant Roger Williams joined the Confederate Army in 1861 as a member of Company A of the 10th Alabama and was later elected captain. Williams was kind, respected, and well liked by the men he commanded. Captain Williams married Sarah Phillips in 1865. He moved to Tupelo, Mississippi, and later to Dallas, Texas, where he died in 1907.[17]

Private Marshman W. Byers, born in 1845, was a member of Company B, 10th Alabama regiment. He enlisted in 1862 at Elyton, Alabama, and remained in the army until the war ended, surrendering with his regiment in April of 1865. Private Byers died in 1904 at age fifty-nine.[18]

Cpl. William S. Brown was born in 1840 in Jefferson County, Alabama. He entered military service in June of 1861. Corporal Brown took part in most the battles in Northern Virginia as part of the 10th Alabama regiment. He was severely wounded at Gettysburg on July 2, but survived.[19]

Private Jessee T. Bell was born in 1833 and was twenty-nine years of age when he enlisted and became part of the 10th Alabama regiment. Private Bell survived the war and died at age seventy-four in 1907.[20]

Private Rueben C. Crumly was born in 1845 in Jefferson County, Alabama. Information suggests that Private Crumly lived with his mother or an aunt and that his father was not in the household when he joined the 10th Alabama regiment. Private Crumly was possibly under age for military service, yet this was not unusual, and he may have claimed that he was eighteen rather than sixteen or seventeen years of age.[21]

Private George W. DeShazo enlisted in the 10th Alabama regiment in June of 1861 at Montevallo, Alabama, and served as a wagoner and teamster. Captured at Spotsylvania, Private DeShazo was taken to Point Lookout, Maryland, and ultimately to Elmira, New York, where he died in March of 1865.[22]

Elder Elias B. Hardie was born in South Carolina in 1836. He moved to Georgia at age seventeen, and when he turned twenty-one, he moved

8. Perrin's Brigade

again to Marion, Alabama, to attend Howard College. Hardie enlisted in the Confederate Army and served until surrender at Appomattox. After seven wounds he still continued to serve in robust health. After the war, Hardie married Emily C. Mosely, after which he studied at the Southern Baptist Theological Seminary in Greenville, South Carolina. Hardie died leaving adult children, who were also engaged in ministerial work.[23]

W.W. Draper, also a member of the 10th Alabama, had this to say about the regiment: "The 10th Alabama regiment was the best in the army. This thought, with all the regiments, made the Southern army the best the world ever saw. In our regiment [10th Alabama] we had in Congress at one time after the war four members." Without questions or qualms, this was the belief of most soldiers in the Confederate Army, and soldiers in the Union army held the same view about their regiments.

M.C. Stapp served in the 10th Alabama, eighth company; he spent one week in military training and was deployed to Virginia. Stapp took part in twenty-two battles and served as a regimental color bearer toward the end of the war. Private Stapp was ninety-two years old in the late 1890s.[24]

Col. George E. Tayloe was born in 1838 at Big Lick, Virginia, and graduated from Virginia Military Institute 1858. Colonel Tayloe joined the 11th Alabama regiment in June of 1861. Tayloe survived the war, and in 1865, he commended Sorrel's Brigade at the surrender at Appomattox. The colonel died in 1879 in Orange County, Virginia.[25]

Capt. Zachariah Abney was born in Randolph County, Alabama, in 1835. He attended the University of Alabama and was a practicing lawyer in Selma at the time of the Civil War. Captain Abney joined the 11th Alabama regiment as a private and served in the ranks for over a year before ultimately achieving the rank of captain. This is a commendable accomplishment.[26]

Capt. John B. Rains was born in Virginia and was a resident of Linden, Alabama, at the outbreak of the war. Captain Rains was famous for his attempts to drill the troops and for causing such confusion that another officer had to be called to get them in correct formation again. In the important matters, Rains was a creditable soldier.[27]

Capt. John Prince was from Marengo County, Alabama, and was a member of the 11th Alabama regiment. Captain Prince was involved in the capture and death of the Union General James Wadsworth, after which he took Wadsworth's sword, sash, and field glasses and placed them in the tent of General Perrin, his brigade commander. The tent was burned but Captain Prince was able to retrieve the glasses. They were returned after the war to General Wadsworth's family. Much speculation has occurred as to who killed Wadsworth and the events surrounding his death.[28]

Lt. Frank Mundy was born in England and educated at Oxford University before moving to Eutaw, Alabama. At the outbreak of the war Lieutenant Mundy immediately volunteered for service with the 11th Alabama. He survived the war and surrendered with his regiment at Appomattox. He returned to Eutaw and held public office in his adopted town.[29]

First Lieutenant C. Watlington was a native of Marengo County, Alabama, and served as the Adjutant of the 11th Alabama regiment for a period of time, as well as a line officer. Lt. Watlington replaced Lt. Ashe, who was killed in action.[30]

Private William R. DeShazo joined the 11th Alabama regiment in June of 1861 in Washington, Alabama. Private DeShazo was taken prisoner in August of 1864, but fortunately was quickly exchanged at Point Lookout, Maryland. DeShazo was from Barbour County, Alabama, and is related to George W. DeShazo, who served in the 19th Alabama regiment. The DeShazo family supplied a number of men to Alabama regiments.[31]

Private Albert Rainwater served in the 11th Alabama, Company E. Private Rainwater died in May of 1864, most likely at Spotslyvania. The Rainwater family supplied at least fifteen men to the Confederate Army, four of whom served in the 11th Alabama; but only one, Private Albert Rainwater, served with General Perrin.[32]

Col. James A. Broome was born in LaGrange, Georgia, in 1839. Broome attended Virginia Military Institute and joined the Confederate Army in July of 1861, as part of the 14th Alabama regiment. Colonel Broome witnessed at least two significant events in his life concerning this period in history. He was present at the execution of John Brown on December 2, 1859, and he took part in Pickett's Charge during the Battle of Gettysburg on July 3, 1863. Colonel Broome was wounded at Gettysburg and again at the Wilderness, where he lost a leg; afterwards he returned to civilian life at LaGrange as a farmer and merchant. He died in 1917.[33]

Lt. Col. George W. Taylor was a resident of Milltown, Alabama, when he joined the 14th Alabama regiment in July of 1861 at age twenty-four. Colonel Taylor was wounded at Spotsylvania on May 12, 1864, the most intense day of the long battle. As a result, he could no longer be a part of

8. Perrin's Brigade

the active army, but remained in the Invalid Corps to do whatever he was able to do for the cause.[34]

Capt. Stephen Hodge was a member of Company A, likely from Chambers County, Alabama. He served as company commander of Company A during 1864, with honor.[35]

Capt. T.C. Meadows also was a member of Company A, 14th regiment, Alabama Infantry. He served as company commander of Company A from a point late in 1864 to 1865.[36]

Capt. Simon G. Perry served with Company B, 14th Alabama regiment as company commander, and probably commanded the company at the time of surrender at Appomattox. The original commander, Capt. James S. Williamson, was killed at Frayser's Farm. Captain Perry served for the remainder of the war as company commander of Company B.[37]

Capt. M.L. Barber served as company commander of Company C, 14th Alabama regiment until his retirement in late August of 1864, due to a lingering wound suffered at the Battle of Frayser's Farm. Captain Barber was a competent and notable soldier.[38]

Capt. Joseph S.E. Davis served as commander of Company E, 14th Alabama regiment for much of the war (April 1862–1864). Captain Davis suffered several wounds during the war but remained a highly dedicated officer.[39]

Private William W. Cawthen of Lapine, Alabama, was born in Lancaster County, South Carolina. Private Cawthen joined the 14th Alabama in June of 1861 and was wounded in the Seven Days' Battle on June 27, 1862. He reenlisted again in the 14th in August of 1862, and was wounded again at Fredericksburg, May of 1863. He again reenlisted in the 14th in July of 1863. He remained in the 14th Alabama until the surrender of the army in April of 1865.[40] (The spelling of Private Cawthen's name is Cauthen in South Carolina.)

Walter Emmett Winn was a brigade officer of outstanding ability who served as an *aide de camp* to General Wilcox and assistant adjutant general to General Perrin. Captain Winn was born in Green County, Alabama, in 1833; however, another source cites his birth as Lowndesville, South Carolina. He graduated from the University of Alabama with honors, and also received a law degree. Captain Winn taught school in the Tutwiler School at Green Springs, Alabama, a highly regarded educational institution of that day. In addition he practiced law at Uniontown, Alabama, until 1857, at which time he moved to Demopolis and remained there until the war began. In 1861, he joined the Confederate Army and was commissioned a 1st lieutenant; in 1862 he was promoted to captain in the adjutant general's department. During this time he was a campaign speaker for John C. Breckenridge's bid for the presidency in 1860. Colonel Winn was a member of Company D, 11th Alabama regiment. Winn was wounded at Frayser's Farm, again at Gettysburg, and yet again at Spotsylvania on May 12, 1864. At Petersburg on June 22, Colonel Winn received a mortal wound; he died on July 22,1864, and was buried at Prairieville Episcopal Church cemetery in Marengo County, Alabama. Colonel Winn had family ties to the Pendleton District of South Carolina via his wife's father Goodman Griffin. Perrin's family moved to Alabama before the war began. It is probable that Perrin and Winn had mutual friends and acquaintances in both Alabama and South Carolina.[41]

To be given command of a brigade of experienced and determined soldiers must have been a confidence-building event for Abner Perrin. There were other creditable brigadiers who could have received this assignment, but Perrin was appropriately selected for the command. In fact, he should have received the brigadier promotion in July rather than September of 1863. Even though the official promotion was to rank from September 1863, the command position was actually delayed until 1864. As to who actually commanded this brigade from the point of Wilcox's promotion August 1, 1863, to command the Light Division, until February 5,1864, when General Perrin took command of Wilcox's brigade, is undetermined. Who, if any other officer or officers, received consideration for this position is also unknown.

When thoughtful reflection is given to the fact that this was the third year of the war, and many of the United States Military Academy graduates were either already in command positions or lost to the army by way of death or injury, it strains reason to determine what prevented Perrin's advancement for such an extended time. Yet this seems to have been the pattern in the Confederate Army of 1863, and this failure to take swift action to appoint competent officers to command positions proved to be costly. Abner Perrin and Cadmus Wilcox were both dependable, steady officers and should not have had to guess when or if they would be promoted. In consequence, whoever was available was promoted, and when that officer could not serve, then the next officer, competent or not, took command. In some instances 2nd lieutenants took command of regiments because of the failure or delay to promote competent and dependable officers. It is of interest to note that in 1862, the brigade had 5,000 men, and in June of 1864, the brigade could muster only 628 soldiers. Granted, some were discharged for various reasons and others may have deserted, while some were no-shows for other reasons, but this is an astounding loss of men in a single brigade in two years.[42] One must weigh the options that existed for command positions and the outcome of the selections made to fill these positions as he sees appropriate.

CHAPTER 9

The Final Battle

On Saturday afternoon, May 7, Lee conferred with Hill at the III Corps headquarters in an abandoned farmhouse. During the course of the conference, Hill's staff observed Grant's army moving heavy guns along the run to the right of the Confederate lines. Lee immediately made the decision to order General R.H. Anderson, now commanding the I Corps in Longstreet's absence, to intercept the Union forces at Spotsylvania. General Anderson traveled down Shady Grove Road; General Ewell would then follow Anderson and Hill would take the position of rear guard.[1] Spotsylvania was a sleepy little village, but its importance rested on the fact that it joined the Brock and Fredericksburg Roads, a major crossroads point for commerce and for armies in 1864.

Lee had an excessive number of problems to deal with at this point of the war. He played a more direct role in the management of the army than at any time in the past. Ewell, it seemed, was now somewhat discredited in Lee's eyes because of his performance at the Wilderness a few days before. A.P. Hill was ill and forced to take leave of his corps for a time, and Lee appointed Gen. Jubal Early to command the III Corps in Hill's absence, even though he seems to have had a dislike and a distrust for Early. General Longstreet was unable to command his corps due to his friendly-fire wounds at the Wilderness, and so Gen. Richard H. Anderson was placed in command of the I Corps. Anderson was competent but had never commanded a corps; Lee seems to have been somewhat uneasy about his lack of experience and felt that he might not be up to the task. Finally, Stuart was attempting to contain a Union cavalry force about to raid Richmond. It seems that Lee could have solved his corps command problems with more ratiocination about generals he *could* have appointed to these positions. Seemingly, a number of other pros-

9. The Final Battle

pects were available if he distrusted Early and wondered about Anderson.[2]

About one and a half miles northwest of Spotsylvania Court House, near the intersection of Brock Road and Old Court House Road, the cavalry of Fitzhugh Lee held off the Union troops until Kershaw's brigade of the I Corps arrived on March 8, followed closely by Field's division. The Confederate infantry repulsed the Union V Corps of General Warren at Laurel Hill near the crossing of the Po River, after which both Union and Confederate infantry Corps began construction of entrenchments. The III Corps of General Hill and General Hampton's cavalry blocked Hancock's II Corps on Shady Grove Road, forcing him to connect with the Federal V Corps on their right. The Federal VI Corps of General Sedgwick arrived and began building fortifications on the left of the V Corps, facing eastward. Private Theodore Garrish of Sedgwick's VI Corps offers this account of the encounter between the VI Corps and the Confederates: "At six o'clock in the evening we were again pushed to the front, to assault the enemy's position. The troops were in three lines, our regiment being in the third.... It was hand-to-hand conflict, resembling a mob in its character.... Federal and Confederate would roll on the ground in a death struggle.... And thus the Blue and Gray fought for victory.... The lumberman of the North crossed bayonets with the Southern planters, and both lay down to die together."[3]

There seems to have been some rather intense friction among the Union generals and General Meade. Meade felt that General Sheridan was failing to command his cavalry and that the cavalry was delaying the advance of the infantry. Sheridan claimed that when he reached Spotsylvania Courthouse the infantry had not arrived and he was forced to fall back. The conversation became intense and Sheridan began to lace his replies with expletives. In addition, Warren and Grant had words concerning Grant's orders for Warren to cooperate with Sedgwick. Warren patently refused, and also laced his remarks with expletives. Grant seemed to have sided with Sheridan and Segdwick in these disputes, making it difficult for Meade to command his corps commanders in an already tense situation.[4] Allen Nevins offers this view of Meade: "Although his demeanor was usually icy, frequently he gave way to fierce bursts of temper, with vitriolic speeches that made many officers his enemy. He lacked the sense of conscious power, the imperious will, and the spirit of leadership that has nerved great captains.... He would clearly be a colorless general."[5] Grant seemed unaware that this situation existed and made no effort to correct the problem.

Ewell's II Corps arrived later, about dusk, and began construction of their entrenchment works. Later in the day on the 8th, Kershaw's brigade was again engaged, and General Robinson, commander of the 2nd division of the Union V Corps, was mortally wounded.[6] Also late in the day on the 8th (Saturday) General Ewell's corps arrived and the Union VI made an attack. General Rodes's division of Ewell's corps came in on Kershaw's right, repulsing the attack. At about 1:30 P.M. Hancock was instructed to send a division to support the V and VI Corps, and General Gibbons was sent forward for that purpose. Earlier, at about 11:00 A.M., Hancock had sent General Miles on a reconnaissance toward Corbin's Bridge, and at a distance of one-half mile from the bridge, he was attacked in force. On his return trip to Todd's Tavern (Hancock's headquarters), Miles was again attacked at about 5:30 P.M. by Mahone's brigade, which was making its way toward Spotsylvania Court House. Hancock sent Barlow's brigade to support Miles, who slowly withdrew from his position and returned to Todd's Tavern.[7]

May 9 was more relaxed than the previous day, in that it was more of a preparations day: trenches were dug and other aspects leading to the crucial battles to come were given attention. Spotsylvania would actually be a series of battles of varying intensity that would continue for about nine days. The first two days would be used to determine the opposition's strengths and weaknesses. This would be a battle of brigades and regiments as opposed to divisions and corps. The Confederate command discussed the possibility of an attack, but it was decided that the Federals would likely make an attack soon. The skirmishers of General Field's division were tested by the Federals in the afternoon of the 9th, but no real threat developed. It was decided that Mahone's division (Mahone was now in command of Anderson's division, and Anderson was commanding the I Corps in Longstreet's absence) should fortify the area to the left of Field and contest movement on Shady Grove Road.

Lee hoped to induce Hancock to make a move and trap him between the two Confederate divisions of Mahone and Heth. Thus, Mahone sent General Perrin's Alabama brigade and General Harris's Mississippi brigade to the Block House bridge at about the same time (7:00 P.M.) that Hancock's forces arrived on the opposite bank of the Po River. Mahone began to fortify his position on the high ground a few hundreds yards from the

9. The Final Battle

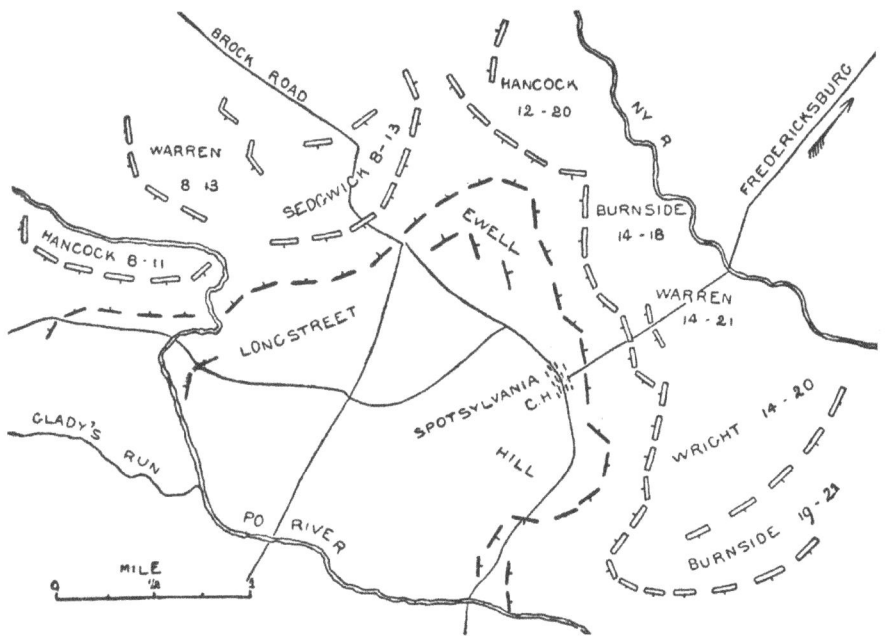

Map showing the general position of the armies at the Battle of Spotsylvania in May of 1864 (Florida Center for Instructional Technology).

bank, and then ordered more forces from Spotsylvania Court House. Perry's Florida brigade soon arrived, completing the same deployment that had worked so well at the Wilderness. General Wright's Georgia brigade was added to bolster the troop level.[8] Hancock faltered and sent word to General Meade, giving him the situation and asking what he should do. Meade held off the attack until morning, leaving Hancock in a desperate position. Heth was then ordered to move across the Po River below Hancock and attack his flank.[9]

Gen. John Sedgwick, who commanded the Union VI Corps, was killed on May 9 by a sharpshooter. General Sedgwick had taken part in the Peninsula Campaign with McClellan; he was wounded at Glendale and received his promotion to major general in the summer of 1862. At Antietam he came into conflict with Stonewall Jackson and was battered around somewhat. His military approach was one of caution, although he was an ardent professional. In February of 1863, he became the commander of the VI Corps, and remained as its commander until his death. Sedgwick

155

General Abner M. Perrin, C.S.A.

was a lifelong bachelor who enjoyed many long sessions of solitaire. General Sedgwick was a stern disciplinarian but was fair and competent, and he used good judgment in the use of his corps. Because of his pleasant demeanor, Sedgwick avoided many of the personal entanglements of others in the Army of the Potomac. General Sedgwick had been cautioned by his command to take care as to how he exposed himself as he went about aligning his men and attending to other details that placed him in open areas. Sedgwick is purported to have said, "They couldn't hit an elephant at this distance." At that instant the crack of a shell was heard to strike the general in the forehead, ending his life.[10] A report concerning General Sedgwick's death has been given by the famous Confederate sharpshooter, Berry Benson, of Hill's III Corps, Wilcox's division. Benson attest, "On that day [May 9] Ben Powell came in from sharpshooting and told us he had killed a Yankee officer. He fired at long range at a group of horsemen whom he recognized as officers. At his shot, one fell from his horse, and the others dismounted and bore him away. That night the enemy's pickets called over to ours that Major General Sedgwick commanding the VI Corps, was killed that day by a sharpshooter."[11] Powell, in a 1907 letter to his wife, claimed he was the sharpshooter who claimed the life of General Sedgwick. Berry Benson, in the *Confederate Veteran* in 1917, supports this claim, as does Major William Dunlop, the commander of the sharpshooter battalion in Hill's III Corps, CSA. Many variables must be satisfied before this claim can be finally declared as fact.[12]

While Hancock was stuck on the wrong side of the Po River, Warren decided to attempt to redeem himself for his less than stellar performance on May 8. He continued to probe Field's battle line for a weak spot to make an attack, and finally to launch his entire corps against Field's division. General Porter Alexander had two days to prepare for this assault and unloaded a blistering artillery attack against Warren's troops. General Perrin's brigade watched as fire roared up and around their works. The brigade teased the Union troops to come forward, but they refused, and wisely so. The attack was called off late in the morning of the 10th, and seemingly nothing was accomplished by General Warren's attempt to attack Field's division. Confederate accounts of the Union V Corps attacks state that they occurred during the entire day and did not completely cease until 7 P.M., when the most intense attacks were made against Anderson and Gregg. Reports indicate that the Union troops of the V Corps actually were able to enter the works, but were immediately killed. Ewell's lines

9. The Final Battle

were also attacked at that hour and Doles's Georgia brigade lines were broken.[13] As late as 10 P.M. a few attacks were made, unsuccessfully, on Field's division, and General Gordon assisted in the defense of Doles's brigade. Gordon states he was instructed by General Ewell to assist Rodes, so Gordon's leading brigade, Johnson's North Carolinians, was immediately formed; ordered to attack, they drove the enemy back with considerable loss.[14] In his diary, Robert Stiles offers this account of the May 10 attacks by the Union forces: "I cannot pretend to identify the separate attacks or to distinguish between them, but there must have been at least a dozen of them.... Toward the close of the day everything seemed to have quieted down. Someone rose up ... cried out ... It's the Yankees. Quicker than I can tell it, our infantry supports ... fairly tore the head of the Federal column to pieces.... [T]hose who were able to do so turned to fly and our infantry were following them over the entrenchment's."[15]

May 10 did not come off as General Grant had expected. His subordinates were not as aggressive as he had hoped; they made unwise decisions, and seemingly underestimated the Confederate will to hold the line established by General Lee. Grant seemed to feel that the "blitz" technique he had used elsewhere would also work equally as well in Virginia. He was mistaken. With the unlimited resources to which he had access, he would prevail, but it would not be quick or easy: the war would continue for another year.

When General Ewell established his battle line, he discovered a long gap between his corps and that of General Hill on the southeast, and the gap covered the east side of Spotsylvania Court House at the Fredericksburg Road. Ewell then attempted to bend the right side of his battle line toward the south forming a salient (an outwardly projecting part of a fortification or line of defense).[16] The gap resembled a "mule shoe" and it actually contained two salients, one at Rodes's right brigade (General Doles's brigade), and the other at General Johnson's center. The two salients are frequently referred to as the West and East Angles. General Grant made a statement about the salient and the importance he assigned to it: "In the reconnaissance made by Mott on the 11th, a salient was discovered. I determined that an assault should be made at that point. Accordingly in the afternoon Hancock was ordered to move his command by the rear of Warren, under cover of night, to Wright's left, and there form it for an assault at four o'clock the next morning."[17]

The day before (May 10) Mott had been indirectly accused of not

General Abner M. Perrin, C.S.A.

supporting Col. Emory Upton's pell-mell attack on what was actually the salient. Upton was willing to cross 200 yards of open field and proclaimed that speed and momentum would allow his attack to push through the West Side of the Muleshoe. Upton assumed that Mott's command would be in support of his attack, but it is questionable if Mott was ever informed as to what his assignment in the attack entailed. General Wright had just taken command of the VI Corps on the death of General Sedgwick and communications were lacking or unclear. The attack looked promising at first, but ultimately fizzled as Confederate reinforcements arrived. Upton rode back to his commander, General Russell, and was allowed to retreat. An account of Upton's bold attack by a member of the 96th Pennsylvania foretold the outcome: "Shortly after 6 P.M. the Union artillery fell silent. At that point, Upton, astride his horse, turned to his strike force, and shattering the serenity of the pine forest shouted, 'Attention battalions! Forward, double quick!' ... I felt my gorge rise, and my stomach and intestines shrink together in a knot.... I fully realized the terrible peril I was to encounter. I looked about in the faces of the boys around me, and they told the tale of expected death."[18]

Grant nonetheless thought so highly of Upton's attack plan on the salient that he ordered Hancock's attack, discussed above, on the May 12. Grant immediately promoted Upton to brigadier, which was approved by Lincoln. As for General Mott, Grant seemed to have had a lack of confidence in his ability, going back to the Wilderness battle. Mott was a Mexican War veteran who had seen no combat in that crisis. Born in New Jersey, General Mott served his entire career in the Army of the Potomac. He was appointed brigadier in September of 1862 and served at Chancellorsville, and was later a division commander in the II Corps. The Spotsylvania fiasco brought about a demotion from division to brigade command, but General Mott was able to regain his division command (3rd Division, II Corps), replacing General Birney after Birney moved to Butler's Army of the James.[19]

May 11 was a rainy day and there was virtually no fighting, but by nightfall, the Federals were beginning to move away from Anderson's division and to the right of Ewell's corps. Observers expected that the move was toward Fredericksburg; General Lee is thought to have concluded that Grant was retreating, and he was determined to make it as difficult as possible. Lee attempted to position the artillery so as to achieve the best position of attack no matter what direction Grant selected as his line of

9. The Final Battle

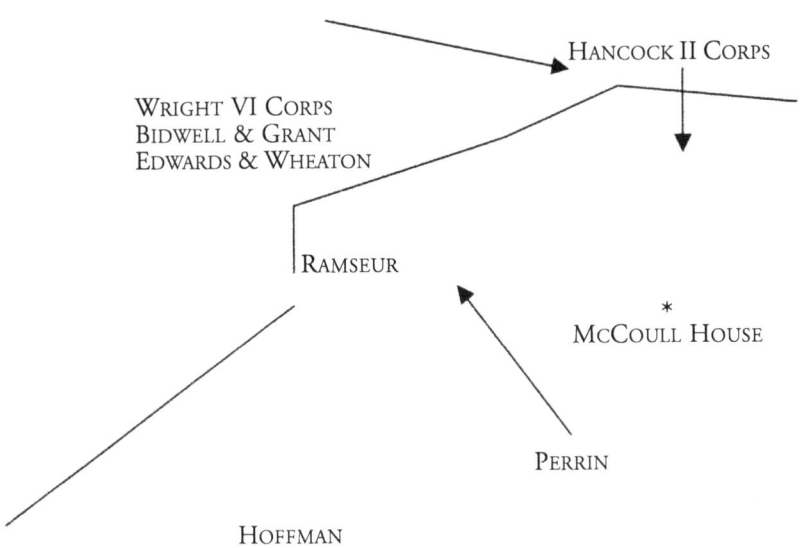

Positions of the armies on May 12, 1864 (author's chart). On May 12, General Grant ordered General Hancock to ready the II Corps for an attack on the "Mule Shoe" held by General Ewell's II Corps. Hancock led some 20,000 troops into battle, and within fifteen minutes poured through the lines held by General Gordon. With assistance of Rhodes's and Early's Divisions, Gordon countered. By late afternoon Hancock had regained his earlier position at the "Bloody Angle" or the Salient. (VI Corps attacked from outside the salient, at the western bend, later known as the "Bloody Angle.") General Abner Perrin's Alabama brigade arrived at about 6:45 A.M. to assist Gordon, leading Early's division, to assist Ramseur; and shortly afterward General Harris's Mississippi brigade arrived to also take part in an effort to regain and support General Ramseur's position at the salient. General Perrin was killed within thirty minutes after he led his brigade into battle against Hancock's II Corps and Wright's VI Corps. General Harris remained at the salient until dawn of May 13.

departure. Unaware that Hancock was aligning his corps for the attack ordered by General Grant at dawn the next day, and with the incorrect impression of Grant's retreat prevailing, General Ewell was ordered to withdraw the artillery, which was in front of General Edward Johnson's division, and return them to Spotsylvania Court House.

Near midnight General Johnson reported that the enemy was massing in his front, and General Long was then ordered to return the artillery by 2:00 A.M. The artillery had been located in the apex of the salient, and General Johnson informed Ewell that he was certain an attack would occur in his front. Johnson ordered several brigades to remain in position and awake throughout the night.[20] General Ewell later stated that different artillery was returned, but unfortunately the returned guns reached the apex of the salient at the time of Hancock's attack. General Lee immediately realized that he had to move toward higher ground, about a mile in the rear of his present location, if the army was to maintain its function. The western side of the salient or "mule shoe" had to be retaken, and soon. Gen. Stephen Ramseur's troops were deployed for this purpose. Ramseur was able to retake a segment of the western area of the salient but additional forces would be required to hold the position.[21]

General Hancock barely had time to complete the details of the attack scheduled to take place at 4:30 A.M., and at 4:35 the order to advance was given. In addition, the rain continued to fall as the troops on both sides prepared themselves for what is considered one of the most contentious and pitiless battles of the war. Ewell's troops attempted to fire their weapons, only to discover that the powder was wet and the weapons would not fire. Barlow's division moved at quick time, moving over the Confederate pickets stationed at the location of the Landrum house, without firing. Birney's division seemed to have had more difficulty making its way through the mud, marsh, and other such obstacles. The two divisions assaulted the Confederate entrenchments with tremendous fury, and received the same intense resistance from the Confederate defenders. Hancock reports that the two divisions attacked the salient at about or near the front of the Landrum house. A disputed number of prisoners were reported taken by Hancock, who placed the number at 4,000. The Confederates accuse Hancock of huge exaggeration as to the numbers of and condition of the dead, the number of prisoners taken, and other reports of the battle statistics. The captives included General Johnson, and Gen. George H. Steuart of Johnson's division.

General Johnson, much like General Perrin, has been somewhat neglected, even though he played a very significant role in the war. Johnson graduated from West Point in 1838, after being forced to repeat his third year. He remained in the army until the outbreak of the Civil War. In March of 1861, he was commissioned a lieutenant colonel in the Confederate Army, and by July was a full colonel and assigned to the Confederate Army of the Northwest. He ultimately led this army, located near the summit of Allegheny Mountain, which may be the origin of his sobriquet, "Allegheny." Johnson often carried a club into battle rather than a musket, which reinforces the claim of his having been very tenacious. The general

9. The Final Battle

also pursued his cousin, Sally "Buck" Preston, also Gen. John Bell Hood's former lady friend, but nonetheless, Johnson died a bachelor. In May of 1863, Johnson was promoted to major general and given command of Jackson's Stonewell Division, in Ewell's Corps. Johnson was considered to act as Longstreet's replacement after the latter's near-fatal wound at the Wilderness, but Hancock's Corps took Johnson captive.

Upon his capture, General Johnson was taken to Hancock's headquarters. With tears in his eyes, he embraced Hancock and stated that he felt that he would be treated justly by his old friend, and that if this situation had to be, then Hancock was the person he felt most comfortable to be captured by.[22] Johnson served a time at Morris Island prisoner of war camp near Charleston as one of the "Immortal 600," prisoners placed in front of Federal guns as human shields. Johnson died in March of 1873.[23]

The attack continued toward Spotsylvania Court House, where the Union troops encountered a second and very formidable line of earthworks that were unknown to Grant and his generals. This defense line and the Confederate reinforcements sent forward contained Hancock's II Corps to the position attained at the early attack.[24] In his report, General Gordon alleges that he ordered Colonel Evans to move his brigade to the McCoull house, and attempted to determine the position of Pegram's brigade so as to also move it to the McCoull house. Evans was then instructed to send in three regiments to determine the Union position and attempt to stop or at least slow the advance of the Union troops until additional reinforcements arrived. The Federals had moved to the right, so Gordon ordered the brigades to form near the Harris house and then attack. The two brigades drove the Federals from the left of Wilcox's division to the salient on General Johnson's line, and about one-fourth of a mile beyond that point. The 13th Virginia of Pegram's brigade recovered a number of the captured guns. The Union forces were able to maintain their control on part of the battle line to the left of the salient.[25] Much of this action of Hancock's forces and the Confederates occurred before 6 A.M.

General Lee quickly determined that more troops were needed at the salient. Once he realized that Grant intended to crush the western side of the salient by bringing in the Union VI Corps of General Wright, he knew that the enemy had to be held at bay until a new defensive line could be constructed. General Mott of Hancock's II Corps aligned with the VI Corps at the salient, and Lee immediately ordered Mahone, now commanding Early's division of the II Corps, to send reinforcements, as his division was located west of the Po River. General Abner Perrin's brigade led the reinforcements across the Po on the way to the salient, and General Harris's Mississippi brigade followed. George Clark, a member of Perrin's brigade, offers the following account of the march toward the area of the salient: "With hurried march the little stream was forded, and the brigade soon reached the scene. The appearances were appalling.... The brigade and others were formed into line promptly, and at once moved forward to attack. Advancing with a rush, the enemy was soon encountered and the rattle of musketry began." Clark continues, stating that the enemy lines were broken, and "in the rush through the woods our line became so mixed that we entered the works [General Johnson's captured works] without regard to organization, but every man for himself. To add to the confusion, the rain poured down in torrents ... during the entire day."[26] The march to the salient was about four miles, which brought them to a clearing around the Harrison house at about 7 A.M.

As General Perrin arrived, he noticed that generals Ewell, Rodes, and Gordon were in deep conversation. General Perrin ordered his brigade to lie down until he could consult the corps commander and division commanders for instructions as to where he should align the brigade. Gordon, in his offhand manner, preempted General Ewell and said, "I'll take the responsibility and order you to charge." During the crisis concerning the salient, Gordon was the moving force and deployed all available troops for a counterattack. The counterattack was gaining ground, and was greatly aided when General Ramseur of Rodes's division brought his brigade to bear on the Federals from the west side of the salient. General Perrin immediately called his brigade to attention and moved his troops forward. The plan was, as mentioned previously, for General Perrin to assist General Ramseur to consolidate his hold on the salient in order to allow the new defense line to be established.[27] The brigade's counterattack was directed toward the western section of the "Bloody Angle," and the 8th Alabama was to be the left side of the brigade. The famed Civil War historian Bruce Catton gives a very succinct account of this area:

> The fighting was worst of all at a place a few hundred yards west of the actual tip of the salient, a place where the trench made a sudden turn, and this spot was known forever after, with an excellent reason, as the Bloody Angle. The trenches were knee-deep in mud and rainwater, wounded men drowning there, dead men falling on top of them. For a final touch, the sol-

9. The Final Battle

diers occasionally had to stop fighting and lift the broken bodies out of the trench so that they themselves could stand there.... The storm of bullets splintered the log breastworks, whipped trees and bushes into fragments, killed and wounded men and then cut up their bodies until they were unrecognizable....[28]

A member of the brigade made the following comments: "Things looked desperate and there was a show of excitement.... Attention rang out and the whole line sprang to its feet. Perrin spurred his horse to the front and the left flank of our regiment and with the accustomed yell, our brigade drove at the enemy with a rushing step. We were being fired on from front, right flank, and rear."[29] General Perrin moved past the McCoull house, where "he reached the second line of works, clearing the McCoull house field of the enemy." As General Perrin's horse attempted to leap over the captured works, he was shot a number of times and died almost immediately. The *Charleston Mercury* reported that General Perrin said, "Carry me back, boys," before he bled to death from the most severe wound he suffered, which was a musket round to the femoral artery.[30] General Perrin's death most likely occurred between 7 and 7:30 A.M.

Three color bearers of the 9th Alabama were shot within seventy-five yards after passing the McCoull house.[31] The troops of General Perrin's brigade waved Confederate flags, indicating they were part of the Army of Northern Virginia, in the hope that they could achieve an easy escape. From this point onward, the activities and movements of Perrin's brigade are essentially unknown. The brigade began to receive fire from their rear, from the Union troops fleeing the attack of Col. John Hoffman's Virginia brigade when Gordon had driven them out in his counterattack. Gen. Cadamus Wilcox gives his account of General Perrin's attack: "Two brigades of Anderson's division [Perrin's and Harris's] and McGowan's brigade of my division were sent to recapture the salient. The first to reach the vicinity of the salient was the Alabama brigade of Perrin. *This was rushed ahead under a terrible fire of musketry*, drove the enemy from the short unfinished line in rear of the salient, and General Perrin fell shot dead.... The Adjutant-General of the brigade, Capt. [later Lt. Col.] Walter E. Winn was wounded near the same place."

Colonel Winn was from Greene County, Alabama, and was thirty-four years old. He had served in the same position under General Wilcox, before Wilcox's promotion to division commander in the III Corps of Gen. A.P. Hill. Colonel Winn had been a teacher and a lawyer in Demopolis,

Alabama. A little over two months after Spotsylvania, on July 22, Colonel Winn received a mortal wound at Petersburg.[32]

As a result of General Perrin's counterattack, and Gordon's counterattack earlier, the Federals were driven from the salient for a brief period, and the Confederate line was saved for a time. For the remainder of May 12, Perrin's brigade was dysfunctional. The brigade members joined the battle with whatever Confederate unit they happened to be near; the 9th Alabama, for example, joined the 13th Virginia, while the 8th Alabama remained near the western sector of the salient. The battle went on into the early hours of the morning of May 13. Private Alfred L. Scott, of the 9th Alabama of Perrin's brigade, made a very insightful remark about the battle near to and around the salient: "The enemy must have been overshooting us wonderfully; for if the bullets had been sweeping closer to the ground as thick as they were through the trees, I don't see how many of us could have gotten through." The *Army and Navy Journal* stated a few days after the battle, "The great battle of the Wilderness was no essential part of Grant's plan. He did not avoid it, but he did not seek it. His plan was to flank the enemy, with or without battle."[33]

Colonel C.C. Sanders of the 11th Alabama assumed command of the brigade, as he was the ranking colonel in the brigade. Before Colonel Sanders assumed command, Colonel Horace King of the 9th Alabama took command of his regiment and that of Capt. William Mordecai's 8th Alabama; they made a fifty-yard charge across a smoke-shrouded area, taking control of their former position. Ultimately, King and Sanders were able to join General Ramseur's position. Perrin's brigade narrowed the odds greatly, but more Confederate troops were needed if any hope existed to maintain their position.[34]

General Nathaniel Harris's Mississippi brigade followed General Perrin's brigade to the Harrison house area. Harris offers some additional details about the battle, asserting that he received instructions from General Rodes to form his brigade on the right of General Ramseur's brigade and recapture the works—in essence, the same order that had been given to General Perrin. Rodes gave Harris a staff officer guide, but the guide deserted him when the firing began. A young soldier of the 10th Alabama (General Perrin's brigade) gave Harris directions to the area of General Ramseur's brigade. General Harris reported that he lost one-third of his command and half of his regimental commanders in this battle and that he kept his command in battle formation for more than twenty hours,

9. The Final Battle

from 7 A.M. on May 12 until 3:30 A.M. May 13.[35] At this time Lee determined that the new line was in place, and he ordered the defenders of the salient to withdraw.

Of additional interest is the statement made by Col. Joseph Brown of the 14th South Carolina Regiment of McGowan's brigade, the former brigade of General Perrin. Colonel Brown asserts that General Ewell refused to give official recognition to any of the Confederate troops from outside his corps who fought with his corps at Spotsylvania. Brown alleges that General Harris requested this recognition for his Mississippi brigade and it was patently refused. This was also the case for McGowan's brigade, as well as Perrin's Alabama brigade, all of which were part of Hill's III Corps.[36] One may draw one's own conclusions as to what this omission has taken from the honor of the many Confederate soldiers who were denied recognition for their service, not the least of whom is General Abner Perrin.

A Union enlisted man serving in the New York 11th Battery had this to say about the effort put forth by the Federals and their results for the Union cause:

> Early on the morning of May 12th the Second Corps carried by assault the Confederate works held by Johnson's division of Ewell's corps, capturing about three thousand five hundred prisoners and thirty guns. Our troops caught the battle-exhausted Confederates asleep in their blankets. The Confederate line was broken. Their army was cut in twain. But it amounted to nothing. As it was, many thousands of enlisted men were killed and wounded in a furious fight which lasted all day, and the next morning we found that the Confederates had fortified a line ... our losses of thousands of brave men resulted in nothing but the capture of twenty guns.[37]

Francis A. Walker made an interesting statement concerning Hancock's command ability at Spotsylvania on May 12: "Hancock presided, stern, strong, and masterful, withdrawing the shattered brigades as their ammunition became exhausted, supplying their places with fresh troops, feeding the fires of battle all day long and far into the night."[38] An unidentified North Carolina soldier spoke bluntly: "The battle of Thursday [May 12] was one of the bloodiest that ever dyed God's footstool with human blood." An unknown Federal officer described the battle thusly: "The horseshoe was a boiling, bubbling and hissing cauldron of death. Clubbed muskets, and bayonets were the modes of fighting for those who had used up their cartridges, and frenzy seemed to possess the yelling, demonic hordes on either side."[39] To fully understand the fury of this battle, an additional benchmark is that the United States gave twenty-three Union soldiers the Medal of Honor for their actions on May 12.[40]

Grant, the military realist, realized that Spotsylvania would not be the place where Lee and the Army of Northern Virginia would surrender. Thus, on May 20, Grant ordered General Hancock to march south to Guinea Station. The remaining part of the army moved toward Guinea Station on May 21, ending a conflict approaching two weeks in duration.

Grant had a different psychological approach to war than that of General Lee. Where Lee had determination, perseverance, and focus to conquer the enemy, Grant's approach was more of a reliance on the moral effect of his maneuvers than on the fighting qualities of his troops, which ultimately gave him success.[41] Yet it must be remembered that General Grant had nearly unlimited troops and resources, and this was certainly not the case with the Confederate Army.

Nonetheless, this battle indicates some shortcomings in the Union command system. The plan was well thought out, but no thought was given to what should be done once the Confederate line was crossed. No troops were on hand to advance, and the whole situation was nearly defused as a result. Grant and Meade did not come to the battle line nor send a delegate to do so and coordinate the army's corps and divisions. Also, Lee's faulty judgment can be detected in his reading of Grant's intentions and in his decision to withdraw the artillery from the "Mule Shoe," which almost led to the demise of the Confederate Army.[42] Estimates vary, but most agree that on May 12, 1864, between 10,000 and 11,000 men died in battle at Spotsylvania.[43] This battle was a doleful situation for both the Union and Confederate armies. Here 27,000 plus men were killed or wounded during a period of less than two weeks, and nothing tangible had been gained by either army. Many historians have compared this battle to Fredericksburg, although one may draw whatever conclusion he might choose about that comparison.

General Abner Perrin's obituary appeared in the *Edgefield Advertiser* on May 25, 1864. General Perrin's death notice was less than half the length of that of his wife, which was posted on December 24, 1862, in the same newspaper. General Perrin was referred to as a "high tone" gentleman and gallant soldier: "Here we have known him long and loved him well, this sad announcement brings a sigh and a tear, and in sorrow we mourn, for one of nature's noblemen has been taken from us forever."[44] One must wonder: if he was "known long and loved well," why did he receive such

9. The Final Battle

a small amount of print space from the *Advertiser*, as little coverage as he had received during the entire course of the war? It brings to mind the oft-quoted words, "A prophet is never honored in his own land." It has been said, "Soldiers are citizens of death's gray land." Spotsylvania must have taken up a fair share of that gray land.

General Ramseur's location seems to have been the site which Generals Perrin and Harris were instructed to locate. Stephen Ramseur was an outstanding young man, much like General Pettigrew, and suffered the same end. He was born in Lincolnton, North Carolina, attended Davidson College at age sixteen, and in 1855 left Davidson to attend the United States Military Academy. Ramseur graduated number fourteen in a class of forty-one in 1860, served until April of 1861, and resigned his commission to join the Confederate Army. Ramseur was appointed captain of the 49th North Carolina, and was promoted to colonel of the 49th North Carolina in April of 1862. He was wounded at the Battle of Malvern Hill, after which he was promoted to brigadier general on November 1, 1862, and assigned a brigade in D.H. Hill's division. General Ramseur took part in all of the major battles of the Army of Northern Virginia, and on October 19, 1864, he was mortally wounded at the Battle of Cedar Creek. Both Union and Confederate doctors attended to General Ramseur at General Philip Sheridan's headquarters, and soldiers in blue, old friends from West Point, took down messages to send to his wife with a lock of the general's hair for the baby he would never see. After hours of suffering, General Stephen Ramseur died on October 20, 1864.[45] His body was returned to Lincolnton for burial at St. Luke's Episcopal Church.

Disposition of the bodies of the dead in warfare is always a problem for the military command, and in the 1860s, it was a monumental problem for a number of reasons. First, the sheer number of dead soldiers; secondly, the rapid pace at which the deaths occurred; and thirdly, preservation of bodies was in its infancy during the Civil War, and the ability to embalm a body in the midst of a war was a new science. The price the government paid ranged from $7 to $50 per embalming, and more in some situations. Shipping a body to a distant location posed another set of problems. Thus, proper care of the dead was a state of affairs difficult for the present-day population to understand. The bodies of dead field officers received greater meticulousness, and greater diligence was paid to the disposal of their remains.

In death as in life, Gen. Abner M. Perrin's remains somehow did not

General Abner M. Perrin, C.S.A.

receive this concerted attention. It seems that after his death on May 12, 1864, General Perrin's remains were not taken to the Confederate cemetery at the courthouse with the other dead. Instead, Perrin and Lieutenant W.H. Micks, of the 11th Alabama, were buried on the farm of Byrd Waller. When the two bodies were recovered in 1903, the farm was owned by Mr. W.W. Micks, and had been the location of a Confederate hospital. Capt. S.J. Quinn, commander of the Maury Camp of Confederate Veterans, and Officer Charles A. Gore unselfishly gave their time to disinter the remains of the two Confederate soldiers. The headboards of the graves were of cedar and the inscriptions were still very legible. The bodies were entombed in the Confederate cemetery in Fredericksburg.

Only by diligent effort did General Perrin's remains find their just and honorable resting place.[46]

A few years later, in 1906, a letter was published in the *Fredericksburg Daily Star* written by Thomas P. Ivy. It is evident from the letter that Mr. Ivy had more than a passing knowledge of the Perrin family. He states that he was acquainted with four of General Perrin's brothers who lived near the state line of Mississippi and Alabama. Mr. Ivy goes on to say that he

Drawing of Gen. Hancock's II Corps of the Union Army of the Potomac attacking the "Mule Shoe" on May 12, 1864 (courtesy Dover Publications).

9. The Final Battle

was born and grew up in Alabama and that Gen. James J. Pettigrew was a personal friend of his family. The general sought and received permission for a family member to raise a company for the Mexican War, and Abner M. Perrin served as a lieutenant in this company. Ivy mentions Perrin's wife's death in 1862, and states that one of General Perrin's sons, Pierce Butler Perrin, was near his age and was known to him. The most interesting single statement mentioned in this letter concerns General Perrin's acquaintance, or maybe more, with a young Virginia lady who searched the area for the grave of General Perrin, clad in mourning clothes, and gave it "tender and sacred care." Ivy's uncle and a younger brother of General Perrin were married to sisters, which also added a bond between the two families. All in all, Thomas Ivy gave insight into the life of Abner Perrin that would have perished save for the publication of his letter.[47]

It seems appropriate to note that the South Carolina chapters of the United Daughters of the Confederacy placed the grave marker on General Perrin's grave in the Confederate Cemetery at Fredericksburg. It appears that the confusion about General Perrin's date of birth may have originated from this grave marker. The gravestone lists his date of birth as February 2, 1827, and this date appears in many of the articles that discuss Perrin's role in the Civil War. As stated earlier in chapter one, Perrin gives his date of birth as 1830, meaning that he was thirty-one years of age when he joined the Confederate Army in June of 1861. The error most likely was due to a mix-up by the stonemason who carved the stone, a type of mistake which is not rare even in the present day.

CHAPTER 10

Bereft of Life and Recognition

General Perrin's remains were not interred with the other dead Confederate soldiers killed at Spotsylvania, nor was any attempt made to transport his body for burial in South Carolina. Granted, in consideration of the time and place, and the situation, this would have been exceedingly difficult. As stated previously, he was buried in near isolation and later moved to the Confederate Cemetery in Fredericksburg. What happened to his property in South Carolina and elsewhere seems to be equally an unknown aspect of his death, other than the facts that appeared in his will, discussed earlier and stated again below.

Strange as it may seem, life continued in the South in much the same way in 1864 as it had in 1854, at least in the legal sense. General Perrin had made arrangements for the settlement of his estate in the event that he did not survive the war. His attorney was Samuel F. Goode of Edgefield, South Carolina. The estate was handled in the usual fashion and filed on July 18, 1864. This in itself is amazingly prompt, since his death was May 12, 1864. William F. Durisal was the Ordinary for the Edgefield District of South Carolina, and on August 1, 1864, Durisal arranged the administration bond of the appraisers. The estate was then inventoried and the date of October 3, 1864, was set for certification of the appraisement of General Perrin's estate. This is not unlike what would occur today after the death of one who has a planned estate and has made prior arrangements. The most striking aspect of this estate settlement is the dispatch with which the lawyer and the court completed the work. It would be atypical even today for an estate the size of Abner Perrin's to be settled within a six-month period.[1] General Perrin's estate contained the usual items, and all of the values assigned and the moneys paid were in Confederate dollars, so one must reduce the amounts by ninety percent or more (an estimate), given the time in the life of the Confederacy. The total estate was valued at $9,000 and contained the following: three slaves valued at $3,200; one piano, $300; household items, $570. The sale of the estate items was substantial — two of the slaves sold for $6,050, and the piano and household items brought $2,120. The debts owed by General Perrin amounted to $8,170. This list of estate items leaves much to the imagination, and one must wonder what happened to the vast property holdings Perrin owned in South Carolina and other Southern states. In addition, nothing is mentioned as to what went with the money after all debts were paid.

General Perrin had two sons, Pierce and Robert, and at some point in time after the beginning of the war, his wife Emily and his sons left South Carolina and took up residence in Bossier City, Louisiana. His son Pierce appears on the U.S. Census records of 1880 in Haughton, Louisiana.[2] Thus one might ask why his sons did not receive title to his property, the remainder of the estate, or any other tangible items of value. Doubtless, Samuel Goode, Perrin's lawyer, was an honest man, and the wartime situation may have prevented the money from being transferred to his children, or maybe Goode was simply unable to locate Perrin's sons. Efforts were made to locate the records of his property in Mississippi, but storms and other acts of nature have destroyed the records.[3] In all probability Emily Perrin and her two sons lived with her mother or other family members until her death in 1862. From that point, Emily's family cared for her sons as best they could. It must have seemed like the world turned upside down for Emily and her sons, and unfortunately Abner Perrin's two sons were ill-prepared for such a life.

Abner Monroe Perrin was a desperately serious individual, and proof of this requires no more than a quick review of his life. Born in 1830, Perrin was a lieutenant in the U.S. Army in 1848, and served in the Mexican War. This was a mere eighteen years after his birth, and he had no military training that can be verified. Also, he was not a military school graduate, not even a college or university graduate, yet he was serving in a war, as an officer, with the likes of Robert E. Lee and U.S. Grant, to mention a few notable individuals. This is not an archetypical event, especially considering the time and place. In addition, he had been *requested* to serve in this position by the likes of future brigadier general and brigade commander Maxcy Gregg, and the then former governor of South Carolina,

Pierce Butler. As a result of his service, he became a close friend of the future South Carolina governor and brigadier general Milledge Luke Bonham.

Since it was imperative that he attend school, the Perrin family selected the Liberty Academy, which was also called the Bethany School. The location of the school was too far to travel to daily as it was located near the edge of what was then the northern boundary of the Edgefield and Abbeville Districts.[4] It is reasonable to assume that Abner Perrin was a boarding student of some description, either at the school if such a facility existed, or with friends or relatives, as many of the other students must also have been required to do. Thus, General Perrin must have gained immense self-confidence and a sense of self-direction early in life as a result of this arrangement for his education. The experience of making decisions and living with the consequences would prove a great assist in the future. And if this was not enough, Perrin studied law and ultimately became a board-certified, practicing lawyer in South Carolina, all in a matter of twenty-two years. Such ability and ego development, unfortunately, often comes with brash and inimical behavior.

An example of this ego-driven and anxiety-laced behavior typical of General Perrin is described in Varina Brown's book, *A Colonel at Gettysburg and Spotsylvania*. As recalled by Capt. H.P. Griffith of the 14th South Carolina, a close friend of Col. Joseph Brown, also of the 14th South Carolina: "Captain Perrin was a man of great ambition and seemed to have no regard for the feelings of any man who crossed his purposes, or in any respect stood in his way. He was of nervous temperament, overbearing and tyrannical at times, but brave to recklessness."[5] These are typical behavioral characteristics of an egocentric personality in that they exhibit behavior that others are expected to follow even though it may be impossible for them to do so.

Another appraisal of Perrin's personality comes from Col. John C. Haskell, a member of General McGowan's staff and a creditable soldier in his own right. Colonel Haskell states in reference to Perrin's performance at Gettysburg: "He dashed through the Pennsylvania Bucktails at Gettysburg, swinging his remnant of a brigade to right and left, and swept from the field an enemy command which had held our troops in check for hours with terrible losses."[6]

Another example of this type of behavior was displayed when General Perrin's Alabama brigade was at rest awaiting orders as to what direction

10. Bereft of Life and Recognition

they should take to locate and assist General Ramseur at the Salient at Sportsylvania. As discussed earlier, General Gordon was in command of Early's division, II Corps of General Ewell, as Early commanded the III Corps in the absence of General A.P. Hill, who was ill. General Perrin's Alabama brigade was in General Richard H. Anderson's division of the III Corps. Gordon temporarily commanded part of Anderson's division at Sportsylvania, which included Perrin's brigade. On the morning of May 12, 1864, General Perrin made way toward the salient. As the brigade came on the scene, General Gordon and other officers were in a discussion about the course of the battle. General Perrin asked what action he should take and who was in command. Gordon, another somewhat egocentric personality, proclaimed he would be responsible and ordered General Perrin's brigade forward. Perrin asked *no questions and did not hesitate*, and ordered his brigade to advance. While he was beyond doubt an exceptionally brave general, still many if not most brigade commanders would have asked for more direction and explanation. This bears out Captain Griffith's observation that General Perrin was brave to recklessness, but he did not expect anything from his men that he was unwilling to do — he led by example.

Another display of General Perrin's captious and disputatious behavior is found in a series of letters written by Sidney Carter of Company A, 14th South Carolina regiment to his brother, in this case unidentified, and his sister, Bet. Sidney was a private soldier seeking a lieutenancy in the 14th South Carolina, Company A. In his letter he relates the following:

> I am induced to write you on business of vital importance and I hope you will give me your immediate attention. I want you to get me up a recommendation of my character and moral standing before I volunteered. Old Perrin refuses to promote me as 1st Lieu. and is going to attack me on every point and will do everything in his power to have me dropped. He has appointed Lieut. Watson to command the Co. over me. I demanded his reason. He answered that I was not fit to command the Co. and one thing I might understand, if I made a case from where I was I would have to work for it. The Co. to a man has signed a petition to him to promote me and say they will stand [me] to the last.[7]

This behavioral disposition is typical of General Perrin, who was a man of resignation and fortitude in terms of how he conducted his life.

Another example of this behavior, yet with an exact opposite outcome, involved the regimental commanders of McGowan's Brigade sending a signed request that General Perrin lead the brigade in the absence of

General McGowan, after his wound, and upon the return of Colonel Hamilton, who was the senior colonel of the brigade. Hamilton, who had taken charge of the brigade after General McGowan was seriously wounded at Chancellorsville, later developed an illness and was unable to command the brigade at Gettysburg. Upon Hamilton's return, regimental commanders sent the aforementioned letter to General Hill, who discussed the situation with General Lee. Both Lee and Hill felt that Hamilton should be transferred to the South Carolina Coastal Defense command, to best serve the interest of the brigade and the Army of Northern Virginia, and this transfer occurred shortly thereafter. Colonel Hamilton ultimately resigned his commission and left the army.

In another incident, General Perrin displayed a feeling of humanity and regard for another person that many felt he did not possess. Captain H.P. Griffith, mentioned earlier, asked Colonel Brown, the regimental commander of the 14th South Carolina, if he might be able to have a leave from his duties to be with his wife, since he had been able to secure a respectable boarding place for her about a mile or so from the campsite of the brigade. Colonel Brown said yes, but Captain Griffith asked if he should also secure the permission of General Perrin. Brown said he felt the general would decline, but left the decision to Griffith. Griffith went to General Perrin and asked for the leave of absence, expecting a negative reply. Before he could finish his request, General Perrin's tone became soft and obliging. He gave Griffith the permission he requested, saying, "Certainly, captain, go and stay with your wife. It is fortunate that you have a wife to come to see you." General Perrin's wife had recently died, and this request apparently struck a tender spot in his psyche. This incident changed Griffith's feelings, which had not been very positive, toward General Perrin when he realized that the general also had compassion toward other individuals.[8]

Perhaps the most unparalleled and mystifying action of Perrin during his entire military career occurred when he intervened in the case of two men in McGowan's brigade, 12th South Carolina, who were scheduled to be executed for desertion. Perrin requested and received letters from officers in the brigade asking for mercy and an alternate sentence for the two soldiers. The letters were received and then presented to General Hill and later to General Lee. The two men were given a commuted sentence and confinement to a prison in Richmond. This seems out of character for a man with a sense of reckless bravery, an act of compassion in an area and

10. Bereft of Life and Recognition

aspect of his life that he viewed as without compromise. Perrin's actions are even more puzzling in view of the fact that ten men in another brigade were executed a few days later for the same offense.

An accurate assessment of Abner Perrin might then be that he was a man of varied dispositions, and the key word is varied. This describes the majority of people, but what distinguished Abner Perrin is that he was able to focus on what was immediately and critically needed. He had the ability to separate the nonessential from the indispensable, but in fairness, he was not always correct.

A prime example of this side of his personality concerns the first day of the Battle of Gettysburg. General Perrin penned a letter to the governor of South Carolina, an old friend, M. Luke Bonham, explaining that if he had been given proper support, the battle could have ended differently. He blamed General Richard Anderson, claiming that General Anderson should have come to his support in his attempt to force the Union troops out of Gettysburg and prevent them from taking Cemetery Ridge, since Anderson's division simply bivouacked a few miles from Gettysburg. While his assumption was possibly correct that support could well have changed the outcome of the battle, he indicted the wrong general. General Anderson was following orders given by General Lee and bears no blame for not moving his division to support General Perrin's brigade. Keep in mind, Abner Perrin was, and always had been, an inordinately serious man, and all who had known General Perrin would probably have declared him to be the most goal-oriented military personality they had encountered. Perrin's goal was to take Gettysburg and destroy the Union forces and drive them from the field of battle. He simply could not understand why other Confederate officials, particularly General Richard Anderson, did not cooperate with him to achieve this goal. His assumption as to why support was not given was a reasonable one on General Perrin's part, and historians to this day are pondering the same question. It is unfortunate that Perrin died never realizing that General Anderson was not the cause of his incomplete success at Gettysburg.

Another element that played a major role in the development of General Perrin's perspective of how one should conduct his life was his extended family. The Perrin family was a very important factor in the growth, well-being, and status of western South Carolina bordering the Savannah River and the Georgia border. General Perrin studied law in the office of Thomas C. Perrin. Thomas Perrin also was a law partner of future General Samuel

McGowan, Abner Perrin's brigade commander for much of the war. In addition, Thomas Perrin played a major role in the wording and preparation of South Carolina's Ordinance of Secession, and his name is prominently placed on the Ordinance. Thomas unquestionably influenced Abner Perrin's views on life and the responsibility that one has for family and home. General Perrin, as did many, if not most men from the South who fought in the Civil War, viewed the war as an invasion of the South, and he was determined to do his utmost to destroy the invaders. Abner Perrin owned slaves, but no evidence has been discovered that Perrin felt the primary reason for the war was the preservation of slavery. Still, this cannot be ruled out since he listed his occupation on the 1860 census as "Planter."

The formative years of Abner Perrin were thus filled with a close-knit group of family, extended family, and friends who all blended into a social fabric that was much like that which existed in many areas of the antebellum South. The Perrin family, both immediate and extended, and friends had great influence both politically and economically, and they used this influence for the good of all concerned. As with any element that holds power and influence, they were aware of the factors that allowed them to hold this influence, and they made a great effort not to disturb the relationship that existed between them and the community at large.

In sum, four factors produced the individual who became Gen. Abner M. Perrin: (1) self-confidence and a sense of self-worth gained early in life; (2) determination to follow self-willed decisions; (3) the ability to focus on the desired goals at hand regardless of any hardships encountered; (4) a close association with a highly skilled, well-educated, and magnetic family and society.

With all of these factors working together to mold his personality, Perrin became a somewhat inscrutable individual. He was misunderstood, labeled a tyrant, and somewhat feared and disliked by men who knew him only at a distance. This may explain why he has not received the acclaim he richly deserves. Few men in the Confederate army who accomplished as much have received as little notoriety as that given to Abner Perrin. Perrin is not included in Wakelyn's *Biographical Dictionary of the Confederacy*, which can be found in any library in the United States. In fairness, others are also excluded, and some are included, which must be viewed as an accidental compliment.[9]

The 14th South Carolina was a part of Gregg's, then McGowan's brigade; it became part of the Army of Northern Virginia, Gen. A.P. Hill's

10. Bereft of Life and Recognition

Light Division, in the spring of 1862, and took part in the Seven Days' battles. Perrin thus was involved, directly or indirectly, in every battle that involved the Light Division until his death in May of 1864. General Perrin was a part of McGowan's Brigade until February 4, 1864, three months and eight days before his death at Spotsylvania. His regiment played a significant role at Gaines' Mill, Second Manassas, Chantilly, Harpers Ferry, Antietam, Fredericksburg and Chancellorsville, and Perrin led the brigade at Gettysburg, where he made a major contribution. His regiment faced the famous Iron Brigade, as well as probably the finest fighting force in the Union Army, Hancock's II Corps, which he encountered for a second time at the Wilderness and Spotsylvania. In none of these battles did General Perrin ever falter, run, hide or attempt to shirk his responsibilities. When his death occurred on May 12 at Spotsylvania, the most admired and respected general in the Confederate Army, Gen. Robert E. Lee, said in his report of the battle, "The brave General Perrin was killed...."[10] General Lee mentions other generals killed or wounded in this battle but only refers to General Perrin as "the brave."

If the history of Wilcox's "old brigade," as it was referred to after General Perrin took command, is researched, the name of Gen. Abner Perrin is notably absent in most accounts. The Alabama Department of Archives and History has little mention of Perrin, yet he led the brigade in two of its most important battles, the Wilderness and Spotsylvania in May of 1864. Yet, not even Confederate soldiers made the connection. A corporal by the name of Robert Gambrell in the 19th Mississippi placed Perrin's brigade in Rodes's division, and yet his regiment fought in the same early morning battle with Perrin's brigade on May 12. Not even historians of that day seem to have been aware of who was in command. One can only ponder in amazement how such a personality and competent general as Abner Perrin could suffer such neglect while other far less notable individuals have received extensive print space.[11] Notwithstanding, a general from Longstreet's Corps, Gen. Evander M. Law, named all three brigade commanders called up to support Gordon's left—Perrin, Harris and McGowan—from Hill's III Corps. Law even mentioned General Junius Daniel's death and discussed General Ramseur's condition.[12] It seems that in life as well as in the Confederate Army, selective memory existed.

Perrin and McGowan's brigade, which he led at Gettysburg, can be said without much speculation to have carried the Confederate attack at Gettysburg on July 1. Had Perrin and the South Carolina regiments and the Rifles faltered, the XI Corps of the Union Army and what was left of the I Corps would not have retreated, and in all likelihood there would have been no second or third day for the Confederate Army at Gettysburg. Few historians have acknowledged this as fact, while many continue to dwell on who was late arriving, who didn't attack when they should have, who was marching to or from where, as well as a number of other issues. And while these issues are important, the particulars of the first day of the battle are overlooked as if they were a warm-up, when in reality, the Confederacy lost the battle of Gettysburg on July 1, 1863. Even if the Confederate Army had withdrawn its forces at the end of the day on July 1, their cause would have been better served and lives would have been saved to fight another day. If the points discussed in the letter Perrin wrote to Governor Bonham (see Chapter Six) are considered, it seems probable that the Union would have been unable to have obtained the high ground, which in fact assured them the victory on July 3. General Perrin had all the factors in sync but he simply aimed the arrow of failure toward the wrong general, yet few historians and military authorities, with a few exceptions, have mentioned this in the intervening years. A notable exception is Col. Chapman Biddle, a brigade commander, and the regimental commander of the 121st Pennsylvania. In his address to the Historical Society of Pennsylvania in 1880, Biddle quotes Swinton, the *New York Times* reporter embedded with the Army of the Potomac: "Never was a pause at the door of victory more fatal to the hopes of a commander. Had the enemy followed up his advantage by seizing the crest of Cemetery Hill or Culp's Hill there would have been no Gettysburg."[13] Biddle continues, "The July 1 battle, the actual fighting was only about seven hours ... in some aspects the most important of the series of conflicts comprehended under the general designation of the battle of Gettysburg."[14] Col. Chapman Biddle's brigade also included the famous New York Ulster Guard, commanded by Col. Theodore Gates, that for a time at Gettysburg opposed McGowan's brigade, led by Col. Abner Perrin.

If one reads the accounts of the Battles of the Wilderness and Spotsylvania, save for a few exceptions, he might wonder if Perrin's brigade participated in either battle. As for Spotsylvania, Perrin's death will be mentioned, but little more, and even less about the five regiments of exceptional Alabama soldiers in Perrin's brigade who experienced extremely high death and injury counts in the battles. At the Wilderness, Perrin's brigade was involved in the battle, which involved the wounding and ultimate

10. Bereft of Life and Recognition

death of General James Wadsworth. That encounter, but little more, is mentioned in most accounts concerning Perrin's brigade and its involvement at the Wilderness in May 1864. General Ewell, the II Corps commander, refused to credit Perrin's brigade. He did mention General Nathaniel Harris's Mississippi brigade, yet gave no details concerning their service with his corps at Spotsylvania's salient.[15] General Harris states in his report of the battle, "I saw none of General Ewell's Command except Ramseur's brigade, which joined me on the left." General Harris concludes his report, "I hope the foregoing facts may prove of some value to General Ewell. I ask of him some acknowledgement, because I believe my command bore the brunt of the fight on that eventful day and I think it is due to the men."[16]

Gen. John Gordon, in his book *Reminiscences of the Civil War*, does not mention Gens. Perrin and Harris, yet in his own words takes responsibility for Perrin's movements at Spotsylvania. In addition, Gordon in his report of the May 12 battle does not mention Perrin or Harris and states only, "Two of the brigades are not now under my command." This refers to the brigades of Harris and McGowan, not Perrin.[17] General McGowan's brigade was also sent into the battle at the salient to shore up Ramseur. General Gordon and a number of other individuals devote much space in their writings explaining how they persuaded General Lee to go to the rear of the army rather than lead it at the Wilderness.[18] This statement is not intended to discredit General Gordon, but simply to bring attention to the fact that Perrin has suffered from the silence of division and corps commanders. Still, one must remember that fame is a primary force driving all of humanity. So it is not surprising for General Gordon to acknowledge that he, acting as General Perrin's division commander even though it was a temporary command arrangement, gave the order for Perrin's brigade to reinforce General Ramseur at the salient on May 12, 1864. Perrin's brigade not only lost its commanding officer, but also many experienced and honorable officers and private soldiers, whose loss is not mentioned in any of the battle reports where one would expect to find such information, save that of Gen. R.E. Lee. Since Perrin was killed, and his division commander was elsewhere, then it seems that Gordon or even Ewell should have included his brigade in their report. Critics might reply that Perrin's efforts were not worthy of mention, or that it was an oversight. Yet if a brigade commander and a general in the Confederate Army has given his life, and many officers and private soldiers in that brigade have given their lives, and their sacrifice doesn't rate a mention, then one must ask what *is* worthy of mention in a battle report? Of the sixty-two Confederate brigade commanders killed in the Civil War, only two died at Spotsylvania, Junius Daniel and Abner Perrin.[19] Ewell should have given some account of Perrin's brigade at Spotsylvania. He did not.

A statement attributed to General Perrin, in which he is supposed to have said, "I'll come out of this battle [Spotsylvania] as a live major general or dead brigadier general," has gained some attention over the years. Premonitions of death were extremely common in the Civil War, and the majority lacked real substance. No doubt Abner Perrin felt he might not survive the Battle of Spotsylvania, as did many other soldiers who took part in that horrific battle. In many such cases when such statements were made the situation might have been, as Shakespeare said, "Tired with all these, for restful death I cry."[20] Men in war who have been subjected to extreme stress, horrible conditions, and a lack of life's basics to just survive, may well have seen death as a reasonable alternative. In truth, it is impossible to evaluate such a statement, or even verify if General Perrin made such a statement.

How can a life lost in war be assessed? General Nathan Bedford Forrest said, "War means fightin' and fightin' means killin'." Napoleon called war "the business of barbarians." Another definition: "War is death's feast." If war is these things, then what is victory? Gordon R. Munnoch defines victory as "what is bought with young men's lives to retrieve the errors of the old." Others have said it is when the conquered mourn. War is fighting, and it is barbaric, and young men are usually the sum total of those who die. General Abner Perrin was young, and he fought and died in a war, which was arguably waged for the benefit of older Southerners, and of Northerners who opposed their views. The Roman Claudius Claudianus said, "Death *levels* all things." Philip Bailey agreed: "Death is the sole *equality* on earth." The *views* of the North and the South were leveled by all of the more than 600,000 deaths in the Civil War, and those whose lives were lost died with a degree of *equality*, old, young, all races, nationalities, and all points of view. The South paid for this war with the loss of such men as General Perrin for at least 125 years, and still even to this day feels the pain. The North actually gained little from this war, regardless of the august and munificent mission they waged.

Was the Civil War worth such a price? Could it not have been avoided with discussion and concessions by both sides, with a view toward the

10. Bereft of Life and Recognition

future? Had this been the case, General Abner Perrin and others like him, in the North as well as the South, might have survived into the twentieth century and maybe would have been addressed as governor or senator, or even president. "There is history in all men's lives, figuring the nature of the times deceased."[21]

Epilogue

Any individual who has ever lived is defined by the events unfolding during his lifetime. The events may be uplifting, upsetting, or unbearable, and anyone who did not live during the time period under consideration cannot begin to understand which of the aforementioned describes how a given individual viewed the episodes, happenings, and exigencies of their life during that period.

The historian of the twenty-first century cannot therefore know what a private soldier of the nineteenth century felt, how he viewed life, or what he thought about the conflict with which he was engaged. Furthermore, neither can one know what Generals Lee, Grant, Sherman, Jackson, Perrin, *et al.* thought about the Civil War, or the role which they were called upon to carry out in that war. At best only an intelligent guess can be surmised. The evidence can be very cloudy and easily misunderstood, and thus, legend becomes fact.

The historian of the twenty-first century must simply determine the actions and accomplishments of the individual he is seeking to identify, interpret, fathom, and distinguish to the world at large. This is a very difficult undertaking and the views of the historian often get in the way of the final assessment. Even when the historian attempts to remain value-neutral, he may feel a sense of anger, compassion, admiration, or any number of other emotions about the individual under consideration.

The life and military career of Gen. Abner M. Perrin offers no exception to any of the above problems. Perrin was a very private man, he died early in life, and little information remains about his life today. His comrades, to the man, offer praise and admiration for his bravery and leadership during the Civil War. As for accomplishments, he was a lieutenant in the United States Army at age eighteen, admitted to the bar to practice law

Epilogue

at age twenty-three, was married and the father of two sons before age thirty. All of this was accomplished without any military training or a college degree. This remarkable career was then finalized with a brigadier general's rank in the Confederate Army at age thirty-three. If this was not enough, Abner Perrin took part in the greatest battle ever fought on the American continent, and played a significant role in that battle.

A household name in South Carolina history and in Civil War legend? One would think that would be the case, but it is not. How could such a man glide under the military history radar for so many years? The answer is complexly simple. Perrin was not a glitzy man; he placed duty before fame, character before self-serving renown, and never allowed ambition to become duty. In addition, Perrin displayed a level of honesty almost unknown in the world today, which probably caused him a degree of grief from time to time. While these qualities are beyond admiration, they do not always land one in the history books. It is the belief of this writer that Gen. Abner Perrin would not view this omission as terribly upsetting.

Appendices

1. Perrin's Remains Located on the Spotsylvania Battlefield

Gen. Perrin of South Carolina and Lieut. Richardson Re-Interred Now Sleep in the Confederate Cemetery in Fredericksburg

Capt. B.J. Quinn, commander of Maury Camp of Confederate Veterans, and Officer Charles A. Gore, a member of the camp on Thursday visited the farm of W.W. Micks, of Spotsylvania county, and disinterred the remains of Gen. Abner M. Perrin, of South Carolina, and Lieut. W.H. Richardson, of company C, 11th Alabama regiment, and brought them here for interment in the Confederate cemetery. This patriotic work has been contemplated for a long time, but it was not convenient until the present.

Mrs. J.N. Barney, who has interested herself in the removal has been in correspondence with the Daughters of the Confederacy in these states, and represents their wishes in the removal of the remains.

Both of these brave soldiers were killed at the Bloody Angle on May 12, 1864, thirty-nine and a half years ago, and buried on Mr. Byrd Waller's farm, now owned by Mr. Micks, where one of our field hospitals was located. Why they were not taken to the Confederate Cemetery at the court house with others, just after the war, is not known. The headboards at their graves were made of cedar, and the inscriptions on them are as distinct as when the letters were first cut, and the boards are well preserved.*

Nothing is known of the war history of Lient. Richardson, but that of Gen. Perrin is highly honorable. He came out as a captain in the 14th South Carolina regiment, and was at the battle of Port Royal Ferry, on the first of January 1862. His regiment was then ordered to Virginia and was placed in

*Published by the *Fredericksburg Daily Star,* Edition of March 13, 1903.

Appendix 1

Gen. Gregg's brigade, and, afterwards, in Gen. McGowan's. He was in the battles around Richmond, at Cedar Run, Second Manassas, Harper's Ferry, Sharpsburg and Fredericksburg, where he was promoted to colonel and commended his regiment at Chancellorsville, and at the last day's engagement was in command of the brigade, which he also commanded at Gettysburg. In his report of this battle, Gen. A.P. Hill says Perrin's brigade took position after position of the enemy, driving them through the town of Gettysburg. After that battle he was placed in command of Wilcox's brigade, and passed through the ordeal of the Wilderness, but at Spotsylvania, on the 12th of May, in the words of the telegram of Gen. R.E. Lee to President Davis, "the brave General Perrin was killed." It was just after Hancock had swept over the Bloody Angle, capturing the larger part of Johnson's division, and A.P. Hill was called upon for reinforcements, that Gen. Perrin came up, leading his brigade through a terribly destructive fire, and fell dead from his horse just as he reached the works.

The remains of the two soldiers were interred in the Confederate Cemetery by the Confederate veterans and daughters of the Confederacy, Dr. J.W. Rosebro, chaplain of Maury Camp, conducting the religious exercises. Harry Bridwell blowing the taps.

Published by the *Fredericksburg Daily Star,* November 13, 1903. Courtesy of Mary Louise Perrin Bailey.

2. Letter of Capt. S.J. Quinn of the 14th Mississippi Regarding Perrin Family

Gen. Abner Perrin
Much of His Splendid History Heretofore Unknown Brought to Light
Monument to Mark Grave

Much interest has been felt in the life and career of Gen. Abner Perrin, of South Carolina, since his remains were disinterred on the Spotsylvania Courthouse battlefield, some two years ago, and placed in the Fredericksbirg Confederate Cemetery, and some time since Mr. Ivy, who is intimate with the Perrin family, undertook the work and has succeeded in securing much of the history of the brave man that will be of great interest to the public. The sketch he furnished shows that Gen. Lee made no mistake in designating him as the brave Perrin.

In addition to placing upon record much of the career of Gen. Perrin, heretofore unknown to the public, it is the intention of his comrades and

2. Letter of Capt. S.J. Quinn of the 14th Mississippi

friends to raise funds to suitably and permanently mark his grave in the Confederate Cemetery, which is still marked by the cedar board that stood sentinel over his remains on the battlefield for nearly forty years, or to raise a monument to his memory in our beautiful cemetery. We hope the latter may be decided upon and that sufficient funds may be raised to accomplish the pious and patriotic work.

The following letter will explain itself:

Captain S.J. Quinn, Fredericksburg, Va., late captain Co. A, 13th Mississippi, Barksdale's Brigade.

My Dear Captain: While my previous visits to Fredericksburg have always brought to my path much that was of interest both to Mrs. Ivy and myself, your chance recital of the finding, two years ago, through the direction of a Yankee visitor, of the graves of Lieut. Richardson of Alabama and of General Perrin, of South Carolina, awoke the sleeping memories of my boyhood. For thirty-eight years, since May 12, 1864, these two graves have escaped notice by individuals or memorial associations. And there they would doubtless have been today if you had not with assistance by others taken them from near the Bloody Angle on the battlefield of Spotsylvania Courthouse and re-interred them in the Confederate Cemetery in Fredericksburg.

But how did these incidents excite my attention? As you know, New Hampshire now claims my State loyalty, though born and reared in Alabama, but Virginia has always seemed a grandmother to me, for it was in the Old Dominion that my father was born. The battle of Fredericksburg, too, I have especially studied and inspected the battle line because my oldest brother was in the battle being a member of the 5th Alabama Batallion, which command took a forward part in the charge down at Hamilton Crossing that saved the day there for the Confederate arms. So, when you told me you had been unable to get in touch with any of the relatives of Gen. Perrin in South Carolina, it came to me at once that I could supply you with information on that point. Although only a boy in those stirring days, my father was able to meet with Jas. J. Pettigrew, a warm friend of the family, and he prevailed upon Gen. Pettigrew to procure for him authority to raise a company for the Mexican War then going on. The company was organized with young Perrin as first lieutenant and sent to Mexico. In the very beginning of the Civil War, the young lieutenant of the Mexican War enlisted as a private. However, he was soon elected lieutenant colonel of his regiment, and later commanded McGowan's South Carolina Brigade during the absence of that officer from wounds. For gallantry and efficiency in the field while serving under General Pender, Col. Perrin was promoted a brigadier general. A few days before he was killed, May 12, 1864, his promotion to Major General had been recommended by Gen. Robert E. Lee, and his commission signed by the Confederate Secretary of War. But this he never knew.

Other facts in his career may be found in the military record of the time, for he was active in the campaigns previously to the spring of 1864. His services are conspicuously referred to in the battles of Chancellorsville, Gettysburg, the Wilderness, and lastly Spotsylvania Court House, where an untimely fate awaited him. As a mark of the confidence that Gen. Lee reposed to him, although from South Carolina, he had just been appointed by Gen. Lee to command of Wilcox's Alabama Brigade. Accompanied by Lieut. W.H. Richardson of the 11th Alabama Regiment, Gen. Perrin, on May 12th, 1864, was going to the support of the troops holding the Bloody Angle. They had just reached the breastworks when both were shot down. General Perrin being only yards in front of his command, waving his sword, and calling back to his men to follow him. Then and there fell the man of whom some still speak as the second Stonewall Jackson of the Army of Northern Virginia.

Gen. Perrin's wife had died some years before. She was Miss Emily Butler, daughter of Gen. Pierce M. Butler, of South Carolina, who himself was killed in the Mexican War, the battle of Cherubusco. Of this marriage there were two sons, both long since died. One of them, Pierce Butler Perrin, was known by the writer and only a few years his senior. Tradition relates softly of another, a daughter of Virginia, who was to have been General Perrin's second life companion. True to her sentiments, when peace had at last come to our distracted country, she, this daughter of Virginia, alone and clad in garments fittingly expressive of the desolate heart within, walked the field of Spotsylvania Court House, searched out the grave and gave it tender and sacred care.

Another feature of special interest to me in this discovery of these two graves might be mentioned here also, for to forestry and the use of wood I have given some study in recent years. If the headboard had been of any other species in the United States that *exist, it would be lost*. Upon examination, after taking the weather and storms for forty years, I find these headboards as sound as they were the day they were driven into the ground, and the inscriptions, evidently cut into the board with a penknife, are also perfectly clear and distinct. Therefore, to the name of the tree known in botany as Juniperous Virginiana I add further, fid, the faithful Virginia red cedar.

But these boards will not last always. Gen. Perrin for his deeds and sacrifices deserves a much more enduring headmark in order that time may not level his grave into forgetfulness. With this purpose in view, I wrote to Bishop Ellison Capers, of Columbia, S.C., and he has promptly taken the matter up. I have also written to friends of the Perrins in Mississippi for the same object. This modest movement I hope will grow into sufficient volume to place funds in your hands properly to care for, to protect and preserve the grave of the "brave General Perrin" to quote the words of Gen. Lee's telegram announcing his death.

3. Perrin Obituary • 4. Perrin Endorsed by McGowan's Brigade

Very Sincerely,
Thomas P. Ivy
Belmont, Jan. 17, 1906
This letter is from the *Fredericksburg Daily Star*, January 20, 1906. Courtesy of Mary Louise Perrin Bailey.

3. PERRIN OBITUARY, MAY 25, 1865, *EDGEFIELD ADVERTISER*

Death of Gen. Abner Perrin

All Edgefield is saddened to learn that this high-toned gentleman and gallant soldier has fallen; that Gen. Perrin, the brave, heroic undaunted Perrin is dead. He fell, we understand in the engagement of the 12th inst., nobly leading his Brigade on to victory and undying renown. Here where we have known him long, and loved him well, this sad announcement brings a sigh and a tear, and in sorrow we mourn, for one of nature's noblemen has been taken from us forever.

None were braver — none more ready or willing to fight in defense of country than he — and none more generously offered themselves a sacrifice in their country's behalf. From the first call to arms — as a Private, a Captain, a Colonel or a General, (which he severally had filled) — none have discharged their duty more faithfully or fearlessly than Gen. Abner Perrin.

At home he was the upright man and the true gentleman; in the army the brave soldier and courteous officer. At home he had won the friendship of everyone; in the army he enjoyed the confidence and esteem of his superiors in rank, and the love and adoration of his men.

Ever bright and glorious will be the memory of Gen. Abner Perrin.

4. COL. ABNER M. PERRIN ENDORSED BY MCGOWAN'S BRIGADE

Camp of McGowan's Brigade
Wilcox Light Division 3rd Army Corps
5 September, 1863

General,
In the absence of Brig General McGowan, prolonged indefinitely by the obstinacy of a wound received at Chancellorsville, placed Col. D.H.

Hamilton 1st S.C.V. for a short time, in command of the Brigade. On the 5th of June, '63 Col. Hamilton absented himself on sick leave, and upon his return on 6 September '63 will resume command of the Brigade, relieving Col. Perrin-14th S.C.V. who conducted the brigade through the late campaign.

While we disclaim any intention to reflect upon Col. Hamilton's high character as a gentleman, or upon his personal courage as an officer, we feel painfully- what experience has taught us, his incompetence and unfitness to command, even in camp but especially in active campaign or in battle, and consider it but an act of justice to the brave men we command, that we should respectfully and earnestly appeal to the General Commanding the army, to give us a different commander, who can claim the confidence and respect of the brigade.

We respectfully represent that the brigade has been most ably and gallantly commanded by Col. Perrin, from the 5th of June up to the present time; that with his skill and conduct upon the Battlefield of Gettysburg, he won the confidence and admiration of the officers and soldiers of the brigade, and that this opinion of him has been sustained and strengthened by his whole course as a Commander. We therefore respectfully petition the General Commanding to recommend the promotion of Col. A. Perrin 14th S.C.V. to be a Brigadier General, assigned to command this Brigade during the unfitness of General McGowan for active duty.

We speak *without hesitation* in saying that Col. Perrin is the choice of the whole Brigade. There is no man from the State who would be preferred before him.

The name of the Field Officer placed with Col. Hamilton's Regiment, 1st S.C.V. will not appear, because from motives of delicacy this message has not been submitted for his action. The name of all the other Field Officers present with the Brigade are signed to the petition.

In support of our opinion of Col. Perrin's merit we *respectfully submit* additionally to this paper, a letter furnished to us by Captain A.C. Haskell, Chief of Staff of the Brigade, addressed to him by Major Jos. H. Engelhard, Chief of Staff of the Division. This letter testifies how deeply impressed was Major General Pender, our late lamented leader, by the ability and gallantry displayed by Col. Perrin.

Other members of General Pender's Staff give the same testimony as to General Pender's repeatedly expressed desire to obtain Col. Perrin's immediate promotion.

We trust that the Commanding General will take into favorable disposition the petition thus presented and pass on.... When he remembers how much the ... and success of any command depends upon the commander.

We have the honor General, to be with much respect,
Your obdt. Servits.
F.E. Harrison, Col. Orr's Rifles S.C.V.
...... Daniels, Lt. Col., Orr's Rifles, S.C.V.
B.T. Brockman, Col., 13th Regiment, S.C.V.
...... Hinnant Lt. Col., 13th Regiment S.C.V.
Joseph Brown, Lt. Col., 14th S.C.V.
E.F. Bookter, Major, Commander 12th Regiment S.C.V.

5. IMPORTANT DATES IN PERRIN'S LIFE

Mexican War Service: Oct 19, 1847–February, 1848
Marriage to Emily Butler: November 25, 1851
Birth of his son, Pierce B. Butler: 1853
Admission to the Bar to practice law: 1854
Birth of his daughter, Julia D.: April 16, 1856
Death of his daughter, Julia D.: July 29, 1857
Birth of his son, Robert: 1859
Joined the Confederate Army: August 10, 1861
Promoted to Captain: September 1861
Death of his wife, Emily: November 25, 1862
Promoted to Major: January 17, 1863
Became regimental Col. of 14th Regiment: January 1863
Promoted to Lt. Col.: February 4, 1863
Promoted to Col.: February 20, 1863
Promoted to Brigadier: September 10, 1863
Became brigade commander of Wilcox's "old brigade": February 5, 1864
Death at age 34 years, 3 months, and 10 days: 7:00 A.M., May 12, 1864

6. PERRIN LETTER TO GOVERNOR BONHAM, JULY 29, 1863

Camp of McGowan's Brigade
Near Culpepper CHV, July 29, 1863

Governor,

I have been intending ever since the trying scene [?] which we have lately, proposed to write you. Considering that some accessing of our operation was due you as the chief magistrate of South Carolina from me as the present representative of a part of the forces from the old state.

Appendices

You perhaps already know I was in command of the brigade during the entire campaign, having taken command before we left Fredericksburg on the 5th of June. The brigade is still under my command until Gen. McGowan returns which may be some weeks and Hamilton, the only Colonel who outranks me being absent on account of ill health.

Of the general movements of the army lately you know as much as I do. This brigade together with the two North Carolina brigades of Gen. Scales, formerly Pender's formerly Branch's, and Gen. Thomas' Georgia brigades compose Maj. Gen. Pender's Light Division, being one of the three divisions constituting Lt. Gen. Hill's Corps.

I do not suppose any army ever marched into an enemy's country with greater confidence in its ability to, and with more reasonable grounds for that confidence, more than the Army of Gen. Lee. The truth is we had too much confidence. Had we been more cautious and circumspect, the results may have been different. Everything went regularly and smoothly until the morning of the 1st inst. On the 28th and 29th of June we, that is to say, our corps lay still a few miles from Chambersburg to the southeast of the town. Gen. Ewell's Corps had passed through to Carlisle, in the direction of Harrisburg. Longstreet was at Chambersburg. I judge from this disposition of our forces that Gen. Lee expected to concentrate his army at Chambersburg give the enemy bother then later in the morning of the 30th we were ordered to march instead of going in the direction of Chambersburg as we expected we took an opposite direction took the nearest road leading through one of the gaps of South Mountain to Gettysburg completed just before night within eight miles of Gettysburg. The next morning about eight o'clock we received orders to march and soon came to the conclusion from the hurried and confused manner of our getting out of camp that the enemy was not far off. It was the turn of our majority to be in the advance that Gen. Heath's division was in our front. We moved down the Gettysburg road slowly and about eleven o'clock the first skirmishing commenced. Gen. Heath formed [a] line of battle and about one o' clock soon became hotly engaged with the enemy moving slowly. Our division formed a line in his surveillance within supporting assistance.

About three o'clock Gen. Pender moved up to me in person and ordered me to move forward when I saw Gen. Scales moving left and saying at the same time that his whole line would move, and that if we came upon Heath's division at a halt fighting, to move on and engage the enemy closely and manage my brigade according to my own judgment....

General Pender said he had sent back for Anderson's Division supposing as I suppose of course that Anderson was not far off. But neither Anderson nor his division was any where to be found. The enemy during this eventful time was taking their new position at Cemetery Hill which baffled all our efforts to take. The very batteries which we had run off & which we saw them take off through Gettysburg were the first to fire a shot from their new position. The very infantry that we had run from the stone walls that surround Gettysburg were the first to form a line of battle in their new location. The first shot fired from them from that position was aimed at my brigade. I suppose you will be curious to know where Anderson was, why he was out of the way at so important [a] juncture. *His failure to be up was the cause of the failure of the campaign.* I knew he camped some miles in our rear that night preceding the battle but I knew not why. It may have been the fault of Anderson himself.

I saw nothing of him until the next day. Longstreet as usual was out of the way and was not seen on the field until the next day. [Powell?] as will always be the case with him was in good time, but he had to attack the enemy in a strong position on his right our left, and was held in check for a long time. The Yankees until very late in the day had only two corps on the field. Reynolds the 1st Corps and I believe the 11th Howard's. We soon eat them up, but if there had been a wide concentration of our army in time these could have been destroyed with little lose to us. As it was we had several divisions hardly used before they could be forced to yield the ground. So you see in this campaign like our Maryland campaign of last summer failed because our army fought the enemy in detail while the war was concentrated. If Gen. Lee had had his whole force at Boonesboro instead of scattered at Hagerstown and other places McClellan never would have known what hit him. So at Gettysburg, had our force been where it could have united rapidly the 20,000 Yankees that were there in the morning would have been destroyed in twenty minutes. The balance would have been an easy task.

These in my opinion are mistakes that were made in the preliminary arrangements for the battle. But the gravest mistake of all but one was the absence of our cavalry after we crossed the Potomac. Instead of Gen. Lee's keeping Stuart reconnoitering all of the roads leading from Washington and elsewhere in the direction of his line of marches soon as he crossed the river he was sent on one of those [futile?] raids about Washington city which resulted in the capture of a few hundred wagons. The only excuse I have been given for not having our army concentrated and our consequent failure to defeat Meade the first day is that our body expected a fight, that Gen. Lee supposed there was only a small force at Gettysburg. Hence you see he was ignorant of the approach and presence of Meade's army. He was completely surprised. His cavalry was miles away and of course was deprived of the only means he had of getting knowledge of the enemy's movements in an emenies country. He was now deprived of their services on the battlefield which would have been of incalculable advantage to us on Wednesday.

Appendices

The opinion seems to prevail that the Yankees fought better and our troops worse than usual at Gettysburg. This I think is a mistake. The Yankees fought creditably to win [shure] and I do not think our army ever fought better. In fact, I saw and heard of more acts of individual heroism than in any former battle. I know as far as our brigade is concerned it never fought as well. It has always done its duty true enough, but in this instance it showed more dash, and fought more desperately and more effectually than ever before. If now stands second to no Brigade in this army. I am proud to say as far as I can learn that South Carolina troops generally in this army stand at the very top of the list.

It is painful to think of many brave men we have lost in this campaign. Of the four color sergeants who went into fight every one was killed. Some of the Regts lost three or four color bearers one after another. The 14th Regiment was nigh out of 28 officers who went into the fight all were killed or wounded but seven. 225 men needed surgical treatment out of about 325 who were engaged in the fight. But this is no worse than the loss in many other regiments.

On Thursday & Friday the 2nd and 3rd our brigade was not engaged as a brigade. We were ordered forward with Ramseur's & Toomb's brigades to verify a position just in front of the Cemetery Hill and about four hundred yards from it from which the Yankee sharpshooters had annoyed our artillerists a great deal. We drove them from the hill with ease, but they made desperate efforts to regain it. They succeeded more in driving our skirmishers back upon the line, but the 14th Regt. was deployed, or rather what was left of it, and charged driving them away. We left the battleground on the night of the 4th arriving after a disagreeable march through the rain and mud we had of it. The enemy made no pursuit. We saw nothing of him until we had been at Hagerstown three [or] four days. We went into line of battle there. They made a vigorous effort to drive in our skirmishers but fail. We remained about seven days at Hagerstown. Slept here again last night in the rain and mud again. The worst I ever spent in my life. Our men had had no bread for three days....

<small>Perrin's original letter is located in the South Caroliniana Library at the University of South Carolina and was transcribed by this writer. The letter was cited with permission. Some abridgment was necessary because of the length of the letter.</small>

Chapter Notes

Chapter 1

1. Perrin Family History, compiled by Mary Perrin Bailey of Alna, ME.
2. http://southcarolina-plantations.com/greenwood/winterseat.html; Perrin History.
3. Margaret Watson, *Greenwood County Sketches* (Greenwood, SC: Attic Press, 1970), pp. 344, 342, 204; Perrin History. There are conflicting sources concerning who established Winterseat and when. One must review the sources cited and decide; also see Sciway.com.
4. Perrin History, p. 1; Watson, p. 344.
5. Watson, p. 344; Perrin History, p. 1.
6. Watson, p. 344.
7. Bobby F. Edwards, *The Making of McCormick County* (Columbia: Department of Archives and History, n.d.), p. 378.
8. Francis B. Simkins, *Pitchfork Ben Tillman: South Carolinian* (Baton Rouge: Louisiana State University Press, 1967), p. 42; Festival of History: Tricentennial of South Carolina, 1970 (this a publication of the state of South Carolina giving a sketch of the important aspects of each county).
9. The Office of the Registrar of the University of South Carolina, upon the request of this writer, found no records of Abner Monroe Perrin ever having attended the University, known as South Carolina College in the 1850s.
10. *Cyclopedia of Eminent and Representative Men of the Carolinas of the Nineteenth Century* (Madison, WI: Brant & Fuller, 1892), p. 209.
11. Paul Begley, archivist at the South Carolina Department of Archives and History, Columbia, stated on January 12, 2007, that Abner Monroe Perrin was enrolled as an attorney in 1854.
12. Mark Crawford, *Encyclopedia of the Mexican War* (Denver: ABS-Clio, 1999), pp. 46, 57; *National Cyclopedia of Biography*, vol. 12, 1903, p. 295; Francis B. Heitman, *Historical Register and Dictionary of the United States Army from Its Organization, September 29, 1789 to March 2, 1903* (Urbana: University of Illinois Press, 1965), p. 784; Perrin History; J.F.J. Caldwell, *The History of a Brigade of South Carolinians First Known as Gregg's and Subsequently as McGowan's Brigade* (Dayton, OH: Morningside Press, 1882; reprint of the 1866 addition), p. 158.
13. Ams 1187/7, courtesy of Rosenbach Museum & Library Collection, Philadelphia, PA, Perrin to Perrin, October 24, 1847.
14. The Abner Perrin Papers are located in the Rare Book, Manuscript, and Special Collections Library, Duke University.
15. Rare book, Manuscript, and Special Collections Library, Duke University.
16. "Milledge Luke Bonham," *Dictionary of American Biography.*
17. Jack A. Meyer, *South Carolina in the Mexican War: A History of the Palmetto Regiment*

Notes — Chapter 2

of Volunteers 1846–1917 (Columbia: South Carolina Department of Archives and History, 1996), p. 84.
18. Crawford, p. 46.
19. Rare book, Manuscript, and Special Collections Library, Duke University; Perrin History.
20. David Wallace, *South Carolina: A Short History 1850–1948* (Columbia: University of South Carolina Press, 1951), pp. 501–502; *Who Was Who in America: Historical Volume 1607–1896* (A.N. Marquis Company, 1967), p. 157.
21. Wallace, p. 502; Miles S. Richards, "Pierce Mason Butler: The South Carolina Years, 1830–1841," *South Carolina Historical Magazine* 87, no. 1 (January 1986): pp. 28–29
22. William Shakespeare, *Othello*, Act 1, scene 3, lines 166–167.
23. *The Spartan* (Spartanburg, South Carolina), December 1, 1851.
24. Perrin History; U.S. Census for South Carolina, Edgefield County, 1850.
25. Edgefield County Archives, deed book HHH, p. 364.
26. Edgefield County Archives, deed book III, p. 67.
27. Edgefield County Archives, deed book III, pp. 101–103.
28. Edgefield County Archives, deed book III, pp. 101–103.
29. *Edgefield Advertiser*, July 29, 1857.
30. Edgefield County Archives, deed book JJJ, p. 558.
31. Edgefield County Archives, deed book, JJJ, p. 554.
32. Edgefield County Archives, deed book JJJ, p. 540.
33. Perrin History, p. 4; U.S. Census, South Carolina, Colleton County, St. Bartholomew District.
34. Wallace, pp. 525–528; Watson, pp. 344–345; Michael Martin and Leonard Gelber, *Dictionary of American History* (Totowa, NJ: Littlefield, Adams, 1965), p. 552; Edward Perrin, gentleman and scholar, a descendant of Thomas Chiles Perrin, who lives in Spartanburg, South Carolina.
35. John W. De Forest, "Charleston Under Arms," *Atlantic Monthly* (April 1861): p. 490.

Chapter 2

1. National Archives, Military Service Records, Confederate Army, for Gen. Abner M. Perrin.
2. John A. Chapman, *History of Edgefield County: From the Earliest Settlement to 1897* (Newberry, SC: Elbert H. Aull, 1897), p. 473; *Dictionary of American Biography*, vol. 6, p. 55; http://persi.heritagequestonline.com/hqowb/library/do/books/results/im.
3. Joseph H. Crute, *Units of the Confederate States Army* (Gaithersburg, MD: Old Soldiers Books, 1987), pp. 247, 248, 258, 259.
4. "James M. Gadberry: Leader of the Famous Minute Men," in *I Know What I Know: Stories of the Confederate Years* (United Daughters of the Confederacy, Cherokee District of South Carolina, 2008), pp. 14–17.
5. Members of the 13th, http://members.aol.com/_ht_a/adj61/page3f.htm.
6. Members of the 13th.
7. Charles H. Busha, "Lieutenant Colonel Joseph J. Norton, Captain Miles Moore Norton and other Officers of the South Carolina Rifles, CSA," *Carolina Herald and Newsletter* (Spring 2006): pp. 21, 25, 26–27.
8. Crute, p. 258.
9. Robert K. Krick, *Lee's Colonels: A Biographical Register of the Field Officers of the Army of Northern Virginia* (Dayton: Morningside, 1992), p. 46.
10. The reader is referred to a letter written by General Gregg to Captain Perrin relating to recruitment in chapter 1.
11. Robert K. Krick, "Maxcy Gregg," in *The Confederate General*, vol. 3 (Hanover, PA:

Notes — Chapter 2

National Historical Society, 1992), pp. 41–43; "Maxcy Gregg," *National Cyclopedia*, pp. 161–162.
  12. Clifford Dowdey, *The Seven Days: The Emergence of Robert E. Lee* (New York: Fairfax Press, 1954), p. 181.
  13. Stewart Sifakis, *Compendium of the Confederate Armies, South Carolina–Georgia* (New York: Facts on File, 1995), p. 88.
  14. *The War of the Rebellion: A Compilation of Official Records of the Union and Confederate Armies* (Washington, D.C.: Government Printing Office, 1889), Series 1, vol. 6, p. 310; hereinafter cited as OR.
  15. OR, Series 1, vol. 6, p. 349.
  16. OR, Series 1, vol. 1, no. 8, p. 26.
  17. OR, Series 1, vol. 6, January 1, 1862, pp. 69–71.
  18. Clay Ouzts, "Maxcy Gregg and His Brigade of South Carolinians at the Battle of Fredericksburg," *South Carolina Historical Magazine* 95, no. 1 (January 1994): p. 6.
  19. Caldwell, pp. 29, 34, 35, 36.
  20. Alexander Webb (former Chief of Staff, Army of the Potomac), *The Peninsula: McClellan's Campaign of 1862* (Edison, NJ: Castle Books, 2002; reprint of the 1881 edition), pp. 18–19, 24.
  21. James I. Robertson, "A.P. Hill," in *The Confederate General*, vol. 3 (Hanover, PA: National Historical Society, 1992), p. 96.
  22. Stephen W. Sears, *George B. McClellan: The Young Napoleon* (New York: Ticknor & Fields, 1988), p. 61.
  23. Dowdey, pp. 152, 153, 154; James I. Robertson, *A.P. Hill: The Story of a Confederate Warrior* (New York: Random House, 1987), pp. 66–67.
  24. Caldwell, pp. 38, 39.
  25. Dowdey, p. 181.
  26. Webb, pp. 126, 127.
  27. Col. G.F.R. Henderson, *Stonewall Jackson and the American Civil War* (New York: Barnes and Noble, 1993), pp. 352, 354.
  28. Caldwell, p. 42; Dowdey, p. 222.
  29. Thomas P. Southwick, *A Duryee Zouave* (Brookneal, VA: Patrick A. Schroeder, 1995), pp. 79–80; Thomas H. Mann, *Fighting with the Eighteenth Massachusetts* (Baton Rouge: Louisiana State University Press, 2000), p. 65. This source contains the information on Gen. George Sykes.
  30. Southwick, p. iv.
  31. Stephen W. Sears, *To the Gates of Richmond: The Peninsula Campaign* (Boston: Houghton Mifflin, 2001), pp. 224, 225.
  32. Spencer G. Welch, M.D., *A Confederate Soldier's Letters to His Wife* (Clearwater, SC: Eastern Digital Resources, 2004), p. 12.
  33. Major E.M. Woodward, *Our Campaigns: The Second Regiment of Pennsylvania Reserve Volunteers* (Shippensburg, PA: Burd Street Press, 1995), p. 94.
  34. Jacob D. Cox, "McClellan's Own Story," *The Nation* (January 20, 1887): p. 57.
  35. Sears, *Richmond*, p. 249.
  36. OR, Series 1, vol. 11/2, p. 856. An account of this action is also detailed in Caldwell, p. 42, and the *Charleston Mercury* of July 26, 1862.
  37. Stephen Sears, "Glendale: Opportunity Squandered," *North and South* 5, no. 1 (December 2001): p. 16.
  38. Sears, "Glendale," p. 17.
  39. Sears, "Glendale," p. 19; also see Gen. Clement A. Evans, ed., *Confederate Military History*, vol. 3, p. 297 for information on General Holmes's role at Glendale.
  40. Sears, "Glendale," p. 19.
  41. OR, Series 1, vol. 11/2, p. 838.
  42. Woodward, pp. 104, 105.
  43. Caldwell, p. 46; Sears, *Richmond*, pp. 303, 304; OR Series 1, vol. 11, p. 870; OR

Series 1, vol. 11/2, pp. 117, 428; E.P. Alexander, "Records of Longstreet's Corps," *Southern Historical Society Papers*, vol. 1, pp. 69–70.
44. Sears, "Glendale," p. 24.
45. George W. Booth, *A Maryland Boy in Lee's Army* (Lincoln: University of Nebraska Press, 2000), p. 50.
46. Sears, *Richmond*, p. 313.
47. Sears, *Richmond*, pp. 317, 318.
48. Woodward, p. 112; Sears, *Richmond*, p. 310. The majority of this geographic description of Malvern Hill comes from the primary source of Major E.M. Woodward of the 2nd Pennsylvania regiment.
49. Southwick, p. 84.
50. The *Columbia Spy*, a Pennsylvania newspaper, reporting from a correspondent of the Boston Journal in the July 12, 1862, edition.
51. Robert E.L. Krick, "No Controlling Hand: Lee at Malvern Hill," *Civil War*, no. 73 (April 1999): p. 41.
52. William Miller, "Prelude: Eight Days to Decision," *Civil War: Official Magazine of the Civil War Society*, no. 73 (April 1999): p. 17.
53. Walter Geer, *Campaigns of the Civil War* (Old Saybrook, CT: Konecky & Konecky, 1926 reprint), p. 119; Gen. Edward Porter Alexander's quote came from his *Military Memoirs of a Confederate* (New York: Scribners, 1907), p. 116.

Chapter 3

1. Caldwell, pp. 51–52.
2. Jeffry D. Wert, "Return to the Killing Ground," *America's Civil War* (July 1991): p. 18.
3. George Alfred Townsend, *Rustics in Rebellion: A Yankee Reporter on the Road to Richmond 1861–65* (Chapel Hill: University of North Carolina Press, 1950), p. 192.
4. Caldwell, p. 53; Wert, "Killing Ground," p. 20.
5. John Langellier, *Second Manassas 1862* (Westport, CT: Praeger, 2004), p. 25.
6. Langellier, p. 29; Caldwell, p. 55.
7. Van R. Willard, *With the Third Wisconsin Badgers* (Mechanicsburg, PA: Stackpole Books, 1999), p. 97; Caldwell, pp. 56–57; David G. Martin, *The Second Bull Run Campaign: July–August 1862* (New York: Da Capo Press, 2001), p. 112.
8. Townsend, pp. 202–203, 206. Townsend's descriptions were based on personal contacts with these three generals over a period of time.
9. Jeffery D. Marshall, ed., *A War of the People: Vermont Civil War Letters* (Hanover, NH: University Press of New England, 1999), p. 103.
10. Caldwell, pp. 61–62; Martin, *Second Bull Run*, p. 166. These two sources supply a very vivid view of the opening of the Battle of Second Manassas/Bull Run.
11. Caldwell, p. 64.
12. Caldwell, p. 64; Martin, *Second Bull Run*, pp. 181, 182; John C. Ropes, *Campaigns of the Civil War: The Army Under Pope* (Edison, NJ: Castle Books, 2002; reprint of the 1881 edition), pp. 106–107; Edward McCrady, Lt. Col., 1st SC regiment, "Address to the Survivors of the 12th SC regiment at Walhalla, SC, in 1884," *Southern Historical Society Papers*, vol. 13, pp. 28, 29, 30; OR, Series 1, Vol. 16, pp. 677–681: Col. Samuel McGowan's report on the Battle of Second Manassas.
13. OR, Series 1, Vol. 16, p. 416. Both quotations came from this page.
14. Berry Benson, *Confederate Scout-Sniper: The Civil War Memoir of Berry Benson* (Athens: University of Georgia Press, 1992 edition), p. 21.
15. Caldwell, p. 65.
16. OR, Series 1, Vol. 16, p. 672.
17. Welch, p. 23. McGowan's wounding is on p. 22.

Notes — Chapter 4

18. Ropes, pp. 144–145.
19. Caldwell, pp. 67, 68; Ropes, pp. 147, 148, 149; David Welker, *Tempest at Ox Hill: The Battle of Chantilly* (New York: Da Capo Press, 2002), pp. 147, 155, 163.
20. Ezra Warner, *Generals in Blue* (Baton Rouge: Louisiana State University Press, 1964), p. 475.
21. Welker, pp. 184, 185, 186.
22. Alexander, *Memoirs*, p. 218.
23. Henderson, pp. 239–240.
24. Caldwell, pp. 69, 70. This account follows the description of the army's progress given in Caldwell's narrative.
25. Van Willard, pp. 43–44; R.L. Murray, *Dedication of the New York State Monument on the Battlefield of Antietam* (Albany: J.B. Lyon, 1923), pp. 99, 101.
26. Caldwell, p. 71 (this is simply a paraphrase of the information Caldwell relates about the infantry's role in this battle); Murray, *New York at Antietam*, p. 101.
27. William W. Hassler, *A.P. Hill: Lee's Forgotten General* (Chapel Hill: University of North Carolina Press, 1962), p. 101.
28. Caldwell, 72; Warner, *Blue*, pp. 556–557.
29. D. Scott Hartwig, "Who Would Not Be a Soldier: The Volunteers of '62 in the Maryland Campaign," in *The Antietam Campaign*, Gary W. Gallagher, ed. (Chapel Hill: University of North Carolina Press, 1999), pp. 162, 163.
30. This information came from the National Park Service at Shepherdstown.
31. Stephen Sears, *Civil War Battlefield Guide, Antietam* (New York: Houghton Mifflin, College Division, 1995), p. 1.
32. OR, Series 1, Vol. 19/1, p. 999; also see Vol. 19/1, p. 982. The statement from the *Confederate Veteran* came from the December 1896 issue, p. 444, from a member of Branch's brigade.
33. Peter Carmichael, "D.R. Jones and A.P. Hill Rescue the Right," *Civil War*, no. 74 (June 1999): pp. 54–59; also see Gallagher, ed., *Antietam Campaign*, pp. 162–163.
34. OR, Series 1, Vol. 19/1, p. 457.
35. OR, Series 1, Vol. 19/1, pp. 982, 990, Col. Samuel McGowan's Report.
36. Bruce Catton, "Crisis at the Antietam," in *The Civil War: The Best of American Heritage*, edited by Stephen Sears (Boston: Houghton Mifflin, 1991), pp. 101–102.
37. Caldwell, p. 82, casualty report is listed on page 83; Benson contains essentially the same information concerning this battle, pp. 29–30.
38. OR, Series 1, Vol. 19/1, p. 982, 990, reports of Gen. A.P. Hill and Col. Samuel McGowan concerning the Battle of Shepherdstown.
39. J. Gregory Acken, ed., *Inside the Army of the Potomac: The Civil War Experience of Captain Francis Adams Donaldson* (Mechanicsburg, PA: Stackpole Books, 1998), p. 133.
40. "Battle of Shepherdstown: September 19–20, 1862" (Washington, D.C.: United States Government Printing Office, 2001); Mark A. Snell, "The 118th (Corn Exchange) Pennsylvania Regiment at the Battle of Shepherdstown," *Civil War Regiments* 6, no. 2, pp. 129, 131.

Chapter 4

1. Caldwell, p. 88.
2. Acken, p. 162.
3. *New York Times*, December 17, 1862. Report on the Battle of Fredericksburg.
4. Robert Wooster, *The Civil War 100* (Secaucus, NY: Citadel Press Book, 1998), pp. 137, 138.
5. Edward Stackpole, *Drama on the Rappahannock: The Fredericksburg Campaign* (New York: Bonanza Books, 1957), pp. 65–66.
6. Stackpole, p. 140.

Notes — Chapter 4

7. Richard W. Stewart, ed., *American Military History: The United States Army and the Forging of a Nation, 1775–1917*, vol. 1 (Washington, D.C.: Center of Military History, U.S. Army, 2005), p. 233; Francis W. Palfrey, *Campaigns of the Civil War: The Antietam and Fredericksburg* (Edison, NJ: Castle Books, 2002; reprint of the 1882 edition), vol. 5, p. 138.
8. Palfrey, p. 141.
9. Caldwell, pp. 89, 90–91; Ouzts; Hassler, *A.P. Hill*, pp. 118–119.
10. Caldwell, pp. 90, 91.
11. Hassler, *A.P. Hill*, p. 119.
12. Richard A. Sauers, *Meade: Victor of Gettysburg* (Washington, D.C.: Brassey's, 2003), pp. 4–5.
13. Warner, *Blue*, p. 256 (General Jackson); Roger D. Hunt, *Colonels in Blue: Union Army Colonels of the Civil War* (Mechanicsburg, PA: Stackpole Books, 2007), p. 108 (Colonel Magilton), p. 151 (Colonel Sinclair).
14. Donald C. Pfanz, "Behind the Lines: The Struggle for Prospect Hill," *Fredericksburg Star*, May 26, 2001, part 18; A. Wilson Green, "The Battle of Fredericksburg," http://americancivilwar.com/statepic/va/fredericksburg/fredhist.html.
15. OR, Series 1, Vol. 21, pp. 512, 513.
16. OR, Series 1, Vol. 21, p. 454.
17. Henry S. Seages, *Battle of Fredericksburg*, a paper written in Detroit, Mich. On March 2, 1899, printed and supplied by the Michigan Commandery Loyal Legion, Vernor Building, Detroit, Mich.
18. OR, Series 1, Vol. 21, p. 523.
19. Evans, "South Carolina," vol. 5, p. 171.
20. Robertson, *General A.P. Hill*, p. 165.
21. Benson, p. 33.
22. Caldwell, p. 92; Hassler, *A.P. Hill*, pp. 121–122; Woodward, pp. 182–186, for the Union account of the battle; Sauers, pp. 36–37, a brief but excellent account of Meade's role in the battle; Stackpole, *Drama*, pp. 184, 188.
23. Pfanz, "Behind the Lines."
24. Maxcy Gregg Papers, South Caroliniana Library, University of South Carolina, Columbia. Two letters from this collection are used to support these accounts, written to Gen. Maxcy Gregg's sisters: one written by the Rev. Monroe Anderson, Chaplain of the 12th Regiment, and the other signed "Persona," regarding Gen. A.P. Hill's visit. See also Dr. Hunter McGuire, "Gen. Thomas J. Jackson: Reminiscences," *Southern Historical Society Papers* 19, p. 309; Ouzts, p. 25; Daniel E. Sutherland, *Fredericksburg and Chancellorsville: The Dare Mark Campaign* (Lincoln: University of Nebraska Press, 1998), pp. 46, 49.
25. *Richmond Examiner* 16, no. 242 (December 16, 1862); *Charleston Mercury* 81, no. 11 (December 15, 1862).
26. J.H. Moore, "With Jackson at Hamilton Crossing," in *Battles & Leaders of the Civil War*, Clarence C. Buel and Robert J. Johnson, eds. (New York: The Century Company, 1887), vol. 3, p. 141; OR, Series 1, Vol. 21, p. 635 (corps killed, wounded, and captured/missing report from General Jackson).
27. James Longstreet, *From Manassas to Appomattox: Memoirs of the Civil War in America* (New York: Mallard Press, 1991), p. 299.
28. "Battle of Fredericksburg: Days after the Battle." http://members.aol.com/Imjarl/civwar/after.html.
29. Gen. Rush C. Hawkins, "Why Burnside Did Renew the Attack at Fredericksburg," in *Battles and Leaders*, vol. 3, p. 127.
30. Pfanz, "Behind the Lines," part 31, August 25, 2001.
31. Frank A. O'Reilly, "Battle of Fredericksburg: Lee's Incomplete Victory," *America's Civil War* (November 2001): p. 37; Frank A. O'Reilly, "The Real Battle of Fredericksburg: Stonewall Jackson, Prospect Hill, and the Slaughter Pen," *Blue & Gray* 25, no. 5 (2009), pp. 6–39.

Notes—Chapter 5

32. Survivors' Association, *History of the 121st Regiment Pennsylvania Volunteers* (Harrisburg, PA: 1869–1871), vol. 1, p. 669.
33. *Edgefield Advertiser*, December 24, 1862; also see Chapter 1, which discusses the family history given by Mrs. Louise Bailey of Alna, ME.
34. Nancy S. Anderson and Robert Anderson, *The Generals: Ulysses S. Grant and Robert E. Lee* (New York: Vintage Books, 1987), p. 341. Several other sources are cited by the Andersons for this account.

Chapter 5

1. Service record for Gen. Abner Monroe Perrin, National Archives; Caldwell, p. 108.
2. John S. Bowman, ed., *Who Was Who in the Civil War* (Emmaus, PA: JG Press, 2002), p. 107.
3. Townsend, p. 149.
4. *Battles and Leaders*, vol. 3, p. 218; Ernest Furgurson, *Chancellorsville 1863: The Souls of the Brave* (New York: Vintage Books, 1993), p. 65n.
5. OR, Vol. 21, Series 1, pp. 1058, 1065, 1066.
6. Abner Doubleday, *Chancellorsville and Gettysburg* (Edison, NJ: Castle Books, 2002; reprint of the 1882 edition), p. 5.
7. Caldwell, pp. 109, 110.
8. William C. Davis, ed., *The Confederate General* (Hanover, PA: National Historical Society, 1991), vol. 1, pp. 37, 38; Ezra Warner, *Generals in Gray* (Baton Rouge: Louisiana State University Press, 1989), p. 11.
9. Davis, *Confederate General*, vol. 4, pp. 17, 19; Warner, *Gray*, p. 173; *Confederate Veteran* 2, p. 150.
10. Davis, *Confederate General*, vol. 5, pp. 10, 11; Warner, *Gray*, p. 233.
11. Davis, *Confederate General*, vol. 6, pp. 45, 46; Warner, *Gray*, p. 305; Stewart Sifakis, *Who Was Who in the Confederacy* (New York: Facts on File, 1989), p. 279.
12. Stephen W. Sears, *Chancellorsville* (New York: Houghton Mifflin, 1996), pp. 231, 238, 239; Robert K. Krick, "Lee's Greatest Victory," *Civil War: American Heritage*, pp. 131, 132.
13. OR, Vol. 25/1, Series 1, p. 798 (report of Gen. R.E. Lee); Robert K. Krick, *Battlefield Guide* (New York: Houghton Mifflin, no date given), pp. 1 and 2 of a 2-page guide.
14. Wooster, pp. 161, 162.
15. James Peabody, "The Battle of Chancellorsville," in *From Freeman's Ford to Bentonville: The 61st Ohio Volunteer Infantry*, Robert G. Carron, ed. (Shippensburg, PA: Burd Street Press, 1998), p. 45.
16. OR, Vol. 25/1, Series 1, pp. 798, 799.
17. Col. G.N. Saussy, in an article printed in the *Chattanooga Sunday Times*, May 4, 1913, "Chancellorsville: Fiftieth Anniversary," p. 13.
18. OR, Vol. 25/1, Series 1, p. 442; also see A. Milburn Petty, *History of the 37th Regiment, New York Volunteers* (New York: Irish American Historical Society, 1937), p. 119.
19. William H. Powell, ed., *Officers of the Army and Navy Who Served in the Civil War* (Philadelphia: L.R. Hamersly, 1893), p. 210.
20. OR, Vol. 25/1, Series 1, p. 907.
21. OR, Vol. 25/1, Series 1, p. 711; also see Furguson, pp. 223, 225.
22. David G. Martin, *The Chancellorsville Campaign: March–May, 1863* (Conshohocken, PA: Combined Books, 1991), pp. 175–176; for losses, also see Martin, pp. 152–153, for a very good account of Hazel Grove; also see Sears, *Chancellorsville*, p. 333, for Ruger's losses.
23. OR, Vol. 25/1, Series 1, Col. Quincy, p. 714; Lt. Col. Price, p. 419; Capt. Beardsley, p. 716; Col. Francine, p. 478.
24. "Second Massachusetts Infantry at Chancellorsville, VA: The Battle." www.Geocities.com/Pentagon/2126/chancebattle.html?

Notes — Chapter 6

25. Milo M. Quaife, ed., *The Civil War Letters of General Alpheus S. Williams* (Lincoln: University of Nebraska Press, 1996), pp. 3, 6.
26. OR, Vol. 25/1, Series 1, p. 908.
27. OR, Vol. 25/1, Series 1, p. 908.
28. OR, Vol. 25/1, Series 1, p. 903.
29. Welch, pp. 48–49. For a more detailed account of Col. Oliver Edwards's life, see Ann Shugart, ed., *I Know What I Know: Stories of the Confederate Years*, vol. 2 (Cherokee District, SC: United Daughters of the Confederacy, 2009), p. 68.
30. David G. McIntosh, "The Campaign of Chancellorsville," *Southern Society Historical Papers* 40 (September 1915): pp. 44–45.
31. *Battles and Leaders*, vol. 3, p. 218.
32. Stephen Sears, "In Defense of Fighting Joe Hooker," in *Civil War Generals in Defeat*, edited by Steven E. Woodworth (Lawrence: University of Kansas Press, 1999), pp. 134, 135.
33. Col. Theodore A. Dodge, "Battle of Chancellorsville," *Southern Historical Society Papers* 14, pp. 291–292.
34. Hunter McGuire and George Christian, *The Confederate Cause and Conduct in the War Between the States* (Richmond: L.H. Jenkins, 1907), p. 228.
35. Robertson, *General A.P. Hill*.
36. Hassler, *A.P. Hill*, p. 144.
37. Saussy, pp. 15, 16.

Chapter 6

1. Edgar Lee Masters, "Unknown Soldiers," *Treasury of American Poetry* (New York: Barnes & Noble, 1978), p. 326.
2. Caldwell, pp. 125, 126, 127.
3. Caldwell, pp. 128, 129.
4. Caldwell, p. 131.
5. Hassler, *A.P. Hill*, pp. 150–151; Caldwell, pp. 133–134; Robertson, *General A.P. Hill*. See the map on p. 202 for an excellent guide to the III Corps' route into Pennsylvania; also pp. 201, 203.
6. Welch, pp. 55–56.
7. Hassler, *A.P. Hill*, p. 149.
8. Joseph T. Glatthaar, "The Common Soldier's Gettysburg Campaign," in *The Gettysburg Nobody Knows*, Gabor S. Boritt, ed. (New York: Oxford University Press, 1997), pp. 8, 11, 29.
9. Warner, *Blue*, p. 53.
10. R.L. Murray, *New York's Officers at Gettysburg* (Wolcott, NY: Benedum Books, 2003), pp. 30–31.
11. Warner, *Blue*, p. 165.
12. Edward G. Longacre, *General John Buford: A Military Biography* (New York: Da Capo, 2003), p. 180.
13. OR, Series 1, Vol. 27/2, p. 637.
14. OR, Vol. 27/3, p. 923.
15. Major General Sir Frederick Maurice, *Robert E. Lee: The Soldier* (New York: Bonanza Books, 1925), p. 202.
16. Longacre, *Buford*, pp. 182 (map), 188, 191; OR, Series 1, Vol. 25/2, p. 637.
17. Warren W. Hassler, *Crisis at the Crossroads: The First Day at Gettysburg* (Gettysburg: Stan Clark Military Books, 1991), p. 55.
18. OR, Series I, Vol. 25/1, p. 924.
19. Maurice, p. 204.
20. OR, Series 1, Vol. 27/1, pp. 924, 925.
21. OR, Series 1, Vol. 27/2, p. 637.

Notes — Chapter 6

22. Warner, *Blue*, pp. 396–97; Stewart Sifakis, *Who Was Who in the Union Army* (New York: Facts on File, 1988), p. 331.
23. Longacre, *Buford*, p. 185.
24. Theodore Gates, *The Ulster Guard and the War of the Rebellion* (New York: B.H. Tyrrel, 1879), p. 436.
25. Murray, *New York's Officers*, pp. 104, 105; Warner, *Blue*, pp. 532, 533; Sifakis, *Union*, p. 432.
26. OR, Series 1, Vol. 27/2, p. 660.
27. B.F. Brown, "Some Recollections of Gettysburg," *Confederate Veteran* 31 (1923): p. 51.
28. Varina Davis Brown, *A Colonel at Gettysburg and Spotsylvania: The Life of Colonel Joseph Newton Brown* (Columbia, SC: The State Company, 1931), pp. 78, 79.
29. Warner, *Blue*, pp. 319, 320; Steven H. Newton, *McPherson's Ridge* (New York: Da Capo Press, 2002), p. 36.
30. Kevin E. O'Brien, "Give Them Another Volley, Boys: Biddle's Brigade Defends the Union Left on July 1, 1863," *Gettysburg Magazine*, no. 19 (December 1998); also see R.B. Dawes, "A Gallant Officer," *Milwaukee Sunday Telegraph*, February 3, 1884.
31. James Hemphill Maclay, Letters, http//www.civilwararchives.comLETTERS/james2.htm (Maclay was a soldier in the 1st Pennsylvania Light, Battery B, Col. Charles Wainwright's Artillery Brigade); Seward R. Osborne, *Holding the Left at Gettysburg: The 20th New York State Militia on July 1, 1863* (Hightstown, NJ: Longstreet House, 1990), p. 15; Gates, p. 444.
32. Rufus Harling, *At Gettysburg: Recollections and Reminiscences, 1861–1865* (SC Division of the United Daughters of the Confederacy, 1990), vol. 1.
33. Daniel A. Tompkins, "List of Important Battles in Which Co. K Participated," *Charlotte Observer*, 1897; Newton, p. 98.
34. O'Brien, p. 38; see also Michael Dreese, *An Imperishable Fame: The Civil War Experience of George Fisher McFarland* (Mifflintown, PA: Juniata County Historical Society, 1997), pp. 5–9.
35. Harry W. Pfanz, *Gettysburg: The First Day* (Chapel Hill: University of North Carolina, 2001), p. 318.
36. OR, Series 1, Vol. 27/1, p. 328.
37. Brown, *Colonel at Gettysburg*, p. 91.
38. Editors of the Combined Books, *The Civil War Book of Lists* (Edison, NJ: Castle Books, 2004), p. 9.
39. Christian G. Samito, "Patriot by Nature, Christian by Faith: Major General William Dorsey Pender, CSA," *North Carolina Historical Review* 76, no. 2 (April 1999): pp. 194–195.
40. John Purifoy, "The Myth of the Confederate Hollow Square at Gettysburg," *Confederate Veteran* 33 (1928): p. 54.
41. OR Series 1, Vol. 27/2, p. 663.
42. Caldwell, p. 140; also see David G. Martin, *Gettysburg July 1* (New York: Da Capo Press, 1995), p. 419 (Martin gives the name of Captain Alston but Caldwell only notes the event); Brown, *Colonel at Gettysburg*, p. 83.
43. Brandon H. Beck, ed., *Third Alabama: The Civil War Memoir of Brigadier General Cullen A. Battle* (Tuscaloosa: University of Alabama Press, 2000), p. 103.
44. Martin, *Gettysburg*, p. 251.
45. Chapman Biddle, *The First Day of the Battle of Gettysburg: An Address Delivered Before the Historical Society of Pennsylvania, on the 8th of March, 1880* (Philadelphia: J.B. Lippincott, 1880), pp. 22, 25, 48.
46. Welch, p. 65.
47. W.C. Storrick, *Gettysburg: Battle and Battlefield* (New York: Barnes & Noble, 1993), pp. 45, 46.
48. Caldwell, p. 102.

Notes — Chapter 6

49. Robertson, *General A.P. Hill*, p. 220.
50. Townsend, pp. 241–242.
51. Robertson, *General A.P. Hill*, p. 220.
52. Caldwell, pp. 141, 142.
53. Brown, *Colonel at Gettysburg*, pp. 234–235.
54. Robertson, *General A.P. Hill*, p. 221.
55. Martin, *Gettysburg*, pp. 499–504. Martin gives vivid explanations concerning each of these factors leading to a failure to take advantage of the July 1 successes.
56. Edwin B. Coddington, *The Gettysburg Campaign: A Study in Command* (New York: Simon & Schuster, 1968), p. 318.
57. Coddington, p. 320.
58. Louis G. Young, "Pettigrew's Brigade at Gettysburg," *North Carolina Regiments* 5, p. 121n.
59. Gen. George Meade, "The Battle of Gettysburg: What General Ewell Wished to Do," *National Tribune*, January 7, 1882.
60. Isaac Trimble, "Gettysburg: General Trimble's Account," *Confederate Veteran* 25 (1917): p. 212.
61. Caldwell, p. 143.
62. Robertson, *General A.P. Hill*, p. 224.
63. Caldwell, p. 144.
64. Welch, p. 71.
65. Jeffry Wert, "Edward Lloyd Thomas," in *Confederate General*, vol. 6, p. 45; Robertson, *General A.P. Hill*, p. 230.
66. Caldwell, pp. 147, 148.
67. Welch, pp. 68–69.
68. Caldwell, pp. 150–151; Welch, pp. 68–69.
69. Robert E.L. Krick, "James Johnson Pettigrew," in *The Confederate General* (Harrisburg, PA: National Historical Society, 1991), vol. 5, pp. 24–25; John T. McCall, "7th Tennessee: Battle of Falling Waters," *The Confederate Veteran* (September 1898): p. 406; *Macmillan Compendium: The Confederacy* (New York: Simon & Schuster, 1993), p. 815.
70. Caldwell, p. 153; also see Berry Benson, "How General Sedgwick Was Killed," *Confederate Veteran* (March 1918), p. 115.
71. Caldwell, p. 155.
72. Col. Abner Perrin's letter to Governor Milledge Luke Bonham of South Carolina, July 29, 1863. The original copy of the letter is in the South Caroliniana Library, University of South Carolina, Columbia. This information is from the transcribed edition of the letter printed in the *Mississippi Valley Historical Review* 24 (1937–38): pp. 519–524. The writer has copies of both letters, having transcribed the University of South Carolina copy for as much accuracy as possible.
73. Perrin's letter, p. 523 (the Mississippi Valley Historical Society copy).
74. C. Irvine Walker, *The Life of Lieutenant General Richard Heron Anderson of the Confederate States Army* (Charleston: Art Publishing, 1917), p. 143.
75. Perrin's letter, p. 524.
76. Coddington, p. 317.
77. Martin, *Gettysburg*, pp. 502–503.
78. Hassler, *A.P. Hill*, pp. 156, 157.
79. Hassler, *Crisis*, p. 29.
80. *Macmillan Compendium*, p. 35; also see Richard H. Anderson, *Dictionary of American Biography*, p. 272.
81. OR, Series 1, Vol. 27/2, p. 613.
82. OR, Series 1, Vol. 27/2.
83. Service record of Gen. Abner Perrin, secured from the National Archives.
84. Service Record.
85. Service Record.

86. Krick, *Lee's Colonels*, pp. 174, 176.
87. Caldwell, p. 158.
88. OR, Series 1, Vol. 29/2, p. 740.
89. William Swinton, *Decisive Battles of the Civil War* (New York: Promontory Press, 1986), p. 354.
90. Caldwell, p. 159.

Chapter 7

1. Caldwell, p. 160.
2. Robertson, *General A. P. Hill*, p. 233.
3. Robertson, *General A.P. Hill*, p. 236; Hassler, *A.P. Hill*, pp. 175-177.
4. OR, 1887, Series 1, Vol. 29, p. 429.
5. Welch, p. 78; Gilbert E. Govan and James W. Livingood, eds., *The Haskell Memoirs: The Personal Narrative of a Confederate Officer* (New York: G.P. Putnam's Sons, 1960), p. 62.
6. Caldwell, p. 161.
7. Caldwell, p. 162; also see Richard N. Current, *Lincoln's Loyalists* (New York: Oxford University Press, 1992), p. 61, for an account of the Southerners in the western Carolinas and eastern Tennessee who refused Confederate service.
8. Robertson, *General A.P. Hill*, p. 262.
9. Robertson, *General A.P. Hill*, p. 244; Caldwell, p. 166.
10. Caldwell, p. 168.
11. Caldwell, p. 169.
12. Service Record.
13. *Battles and Leaders*, vol. 3, p. 439.
14. Krick, *Lee's Colonels*, p. 191 (Herbert), 328 (Royston), 367 (Tayloe).
15. Richard J. Sommers, "William Henry Forney," in *Confederate General*, vol. 2, pp. 136-137.
16. *Confederate General*, vol. 5, pp. 126-127.
17. Welch, p. 90.
18. Robertson, *General A.P. Hill*, p. 250; Shakespeare, *Henry VI, Part 1*, 3.ii.
19. Ulysses Simpson Grant, *Personal Memoirs of U.S. Grant* (New York: Dover Publications, 1995), p. 297.
20. Grant, p. 304; also see Michael C.C. Adams, *Fighting for Defeat: Union Military Failure in the East 1861-1865* (Lincoln: University of Nebraska Press, 1992), p. 158, for Grant as a different cynosure.
21. Grant, p. 303.
22. "The Battle of the Wilderness: A letter from P.W.A.," *Charleston Mercury*, May 25, 1864.
23. OR, Series 1, Vol. 36/1, p. 539.
24. Anderson & Anderson, pp. 375-376.
25. The William C. Nelson Letters, Archives and Special Collections, J.D. Williams Library, University of Mississippi.
26. Geer, pp. 330-331.
27. Haskell, p. 63.
28. OR, Series 1, Vol. 36/2, p. 960; also see Robertson, *General A.P. Hill*, p. 267.
29. Eric C. Mink, "The Death, Retrieval, and Remembrance of Brigadier General James S. Wadsworth in the Battle of the Wilderness," *Civil War Regiments: A Journal of the American Civil War* 6, no. 4, p. 94; Wayne Mahood, *General Wadsworth: The Life and Times of General James S. Wadsworth* (New York: Da Capo, 2003), p. 248; Edward Steere, *The Wilderness Campaign: The Meeting of Grant and Lee* (Mechanicsburg, PA: Stackpole Books, 2001), pp. 399-400.

Notes — Chapter 8

30. Mahood, p. 248
31. Gen. Alexander Webb, "Through the Wilderness," *Battles and Leaders*, vol. 4, pp. 159–160.
32. Private John South Lewis, *The Diary of John Lewis, 16th Mississippi, Wilkinson Rifles*, McCain Library & Archives Collection, University of Southern Mississippi.
33. Emil and Ruth Rosenblatt, eds., *Hard Marching Every Day: The Civil War Letters of Private Wilbur Fisk, 1861–1865* (Lawrence: University of Kansas Press, 1992), p. 217.
34. Steere, pp. 422, 459.
35. Steere, p. 461.
36. Gordon Rhea, "The Battle of the Wilderness and its Place in the Civil War," *Civil War Regiments* 6, no. 4 (1999): p. 20.
37. Webb, pp. 159, 160.
38. George Clark, "From the Rapidan to Petersburg," *Confederate Veteran* (June 1910), p. 294.
39. Geer, pp. 341, 343.

Chapter 8

1. Krick, *Lee's Colonels*, p. 328; Alabama Department of Archives and History, Montgomery, Alabama; "Yancey at Syracuse," *New York Times*, August 3, 1883.
2. Krick, *Lee's Colonels*, p. 191; Alabama Department of Archives and History.
3. Krick, *Lee's Colonels*, p. 130; Alabama Department of Archives and History.
4. Krick, *Lee's Colonels*, p. 287; Alabama Department of Archives and History; Mr. Glenn Griffin of Northport, Alabama.
5. Franklin L. Riley, ed., *Mississippi Historical Review*, vol. 13 (Oxford: University of Mississippi Press, 1913).
6. Fuller Family, Alabama Department of Archives and History; DeBardelaben Family, Alabama Department of Archives and History; http://www.mindspring.com/~debard/bardeleben/DanielH.htm.
7. Krick, *Lee's Colonels*, pp. 224–225; Alabama Department of Archives and History; "Military Records: Civil War Service Records," ancestry.com, Disc #2.
8. Krick, *Lee's Colonels*, p. 351; Alabama Department of Archives and History.
9. Krick, *Lee's Colonels*, p. 105; Alabama Department of Archives and History.
10. "Reunion of Company F, 9th Alabama," *Confederate Veteran* (November 1896).
11. Krick, *Lee's Colonels*, p. 341; Alabama Department of Archives and History; "Military Records," Disc #3.
12. Krick, *Lee's Colonels*, pp. 345–346; Alabama Department of Archives and History; "Military Records," Disc #3.
13. *Confederate Veteran* (June 1910): p. 294.
14. Alabama Department of Archives and Records; "Military Records," Disc #3.
15. "Military Records," Disc #3; http://home.earthlink.net/~larsrbl/CW/10ALIinfgh-page.htm.
16. "Military Records," Disc #3; Alabama Department of Archives and Records.
17. "Military Records," Disc #3; *Confederate Veteran* (November 1908), p. 589.
18. Hueytown Historical Society; "Military Records," Disc #2.
19. Hueytown Historical Society; "Military Records," Disc #1.
20. Hueytown Historical Society; "Military Records," Disc #1.
21. Hueytown Historical Society; "Military Records," Disc #1.
22. DeShazo, http://www.geocities.com/Heartland/Valley/3220/militarydeshazos.html? 20089; "Military Records," Disc #3; Alabama Department of Archives and History.
23. *Confederate Veteran* (September 1906): p. 417.
24. *Confederate Veteran* (June 1908): p. 260; "Military Records," Disc #3; Private Stapp is also discussed in Confederate Veteran (June 1908).

25. "Military Records," Disc #3; Alabama Department of Archives and History; Krick, *Lee's Colonels*, p. 367.
26. Alabama Department of Archives and History; "Military Records," Disc #1.
27. N.B. Hogan, *Confederate Veteran* (February 1896), p. 50; "Military Records," Disc #3.
28. "Meeting Again at Albany," *New York Times*, January 14, 1880; "Military Records," Disc #3.
29. G.H. Cole (Commander of Camp Sanders, Eutaw, Alabama), *Confederate Veteran* (September 1897): p. 481.
30. Arthur Wyllie, *Confederate Officers* (printed on demand, 2007), p. 537.
31. DeShazo.
32. http://chronography.com/rainwater/civilwar.html#AL.
33. "Military Records," Disc #3; Krick, *Lee's Colonels*, p. 70.
34. Alabama Department of Archives and Records; Krick, *Lee's Colonels*, p. 368.
35. "Military Records," Disc #1; Alabama Department of Archives and Records.
36. Alabama Department of Archives and Records.
37. Alabama Department of Archives and Records.
38. Alabama Department of Archives and Records.
39. Alabama Department of Archives and Records.
40. http://www.geocities.com/Heartland/River/1757/Confedsoldiers.html.
41. Joel D. Jones, "At 8 o'clock, organ pealed forth Mendelssohn's Famous Wedding March," *Democrat Reporter* (Linden, Alabama), January 10, 2002 (reprinted from December 1938); Robert E.L. Krick, *Staff Officers in Gray: A Biographical Register of Staff Officers in the Army of Northern Virginia* (Chapel Hill: University of North Carolina Press, 2003), p. 307; Ms. Betty Hannah, Gallion, Alabama.
42. Capt. George Clark, Assistant Adjutant, Wilcox's Old Brigade (General Perrin's brigade until May 12, 1864), *Confederate Veteran* (January 1906), p. 24.

Chapter 9

1. Hassler, *A.P. Hill*, p. 197.
2. Douglas S. Freeman, *Lee's Lieutenants: A Study in Command* (New York: Scribners, 1998; one-volume abridgement by Stephen Sears), pp. 695–98.
3. Burke Davis, *Gray Fox: Robert E. Lee and the Civil War* (New York: Fairfax, 1956), pp. 297–98.
4. Gordon C. Rhea, *The Battle for Spotsylvania Court House and the Road to Yellow Tavern, May 7–12, 1864* (Baton Rouge: Louisiana State University Press, 1997), p. 73. Rhea quotes James H. Wilson from his work, *Under the Old Flag*, vol. 1.
5. Brooks D. Simpson, *Ulysses S. Grant: Triumph over Adversity, 1822–1865* (New York: Houghton Mifflin, 2000), pp. 303–304; Allen Nevins's appraisal comes from Allen Nevins, *War for the Union: 1863–1864*, vol. 3, *The Organized War* (New York: Konecky & Konecky, 1971), p. 96.
6. Brown, *Colonel at Gettysburg*, p. 246; "War News," *Daily South Carolinian*, Columbia, SC, May 20, 1864.
7. OR, Series 1, Vol. 36/1, pp. 329, 1056, 541, 1071; also see R.L. Murray, *In Memoriam Francis C. Barlow: 1834–1896* (Albany: J.B. Lyon, 1923; reprint, Wolcott, NY: Benedum Books, 2003), pp. 98–99.
8. David M. Jordan, *Winfield Scott Hancock: A Soldier's Life* (Bloomington: University of Indiana Press, 1988), p. 127; also see Rhea, *Spotsylvania*, p. 113.
9. OR, Series 1, Vol. 36/1, p. 1057.
10. Sifakis, *Union*, pp. 359–360.
11. OR, Series 1, Vol. 36/1, p. 541; Benson, p. 68; Rhea, *Spotsylvania*, pp. 113, 114; also Fred L. Ray, "The Killing of Uncle John," *Civil War Times* 45, no. 4, pp. 29, 32.

Notes — Chapter 9

12. Ray, p. 32.
13. Rhea, *Spotsylvania*, p. 130; OR, Series 1, Vol. 36/1, pp. 1057, 1058.
14. OR, Series 1, Vol. 36/1, p. 1078.
15. Davis, *Gray Fox*, p. 302.
16. Brown, *Colonel at Gettysburg*, p. 246.
17. Grant, p. 322.
18. David A. Ward, "Of Battlefields and Bitter Feuds," *Civil War Regiments* 3, no. 3 (1993).
19. Upton's attack information is from Curtis D. Crockett, "The Union's Bloody Miscue at Spotsylvania's Muleshoe," *America's Civil War* (January 2008): pp. 28, 29; General Mott's biographical information is from Warner, *Blue*, p. 338.
20. OR, Series 1, Vol. 36/1, p. 1072 (General Ewell's report); OR Vol. 36/1, p. 1080 (General Johnson's report).
21. Gordon C. Rhea, "Mule Shoe Redemption," *America's Civil War* (May 2004): p. 48.
22. OR, Series 1, Vol. 36, pp. 358–359.
23. Eddie Woodward, "Invisible Ed," *Civil War Times* 43, no. 4 (October 2004): pp. 20, 21, 22, 25.
24. OR, Series 1, Vol. 36/1, pp. 335–336 (General Hancock's report).
25. OR, Series 1, Vol. 36/1, p. 1079.
26. Clark, p. 382.
27. Rhea, *Spotsylvania*, p. 268. Gordon also includes General Lee in this conversational meeting.
28. Bruce Catton, *Grant Takes Command* (Edison, NJ: Castle Books, 2000), p. 228.
29. Noah Andre Trudeau, *Bloody Roads South: The Wilderness to Cold Harbor, May–June 1864* (New York: Little, Brown, 1989), p. 179. The quotation is from an unidentified member of Perrin's brigade, and is not cited by the author.
30. *Charleston Mercury*, June 9, 1864.
31. William D. Matter, *If It Takes All Summer: The Battle of Spotsylvania* (Chapel Hill: University of North Carolina, 1988), p. 206.
32. General Cadamus Wilcox, "Four Years With General Lee," *Southern Historical Society Papers* 6, 1878, p. 75; Colonel Winn's information comes from Krick, *Staff Officers in Gray*, p. 307.
33. http://www.spotsylvania140th.com/historySCOTT.html; *The Army and Navy Journal* was quoted in Catton, *Grant Takes Command*, p. 236.
34. Rhea, *Spotsylvania*, p. 269; also see John Cannan, *Bloody Angle: Hancock's Assault on the Mule Shoe Salient, May 12, 1864* (New York: Da Capo Press, 2002), p. 106.
35. OR, Series 1, Vol. 36/1, p. 1092.
36. Col. Joseph N. Brown, "The Battle of the Bloody Angle," an address given to the Robert E. Lee Chapter of the Daughters of the Confederacy in November 1900, p. 8.
37. Frank Wilkeson, *Turned Inside Out: Recollections of a Private Soldier in the Army of the Potomac* (Lincoln: University of Nebraska Press, 1997; reprint of the 1887 edition), pp. 86–87.
38. Francis Walker, *General Hancock* (New York: D. Appleton, 1894), pp. 201–202.
39. https://www.nps.gov/frsp/wshist.htm.
40. OR, Series 1, Vol. 36, pp. 1020–1021.
41. Geer, p. 345.
42. Gordon Rhea, "The Overland Campaign of 1864," *North and South* 7, no. 4 (June 2004): p. 21.
43. O.O. Howard, O.O. Howard Papers, Bowdoin College Library. The National Park Service and the Library of Congress estimates that 30,000 men were killed and wounded at Spotsylvania; see americancivilwar.com for information on these numbers.
44. "Death of Gen. Abner Perrin," *Edgefield Advertiser*, May 25, 1864.
45. Gary W. Gallagher, "Stephen D. Ramseur," in *Confederate General*, vol. 5, pp. 74–75.

46. *Fredericksburg Daily Star,* March 13, 1903 (this copy courtesy of Mary Perrin Bailey).
47. *Fredericksburg Daily Star,* January 20, 1906.

Chapter 10

1. Edgefield County Archives & Records, Box 87, pkg. 3475, Estate Records of Abner Monroe Perrin, 1864.
2. Courtesy of Mary Louise Perrin Bailey of Alna, ME, for her research of the Perrin family.
3. Telephone conversation with the clerk of court in Neshoba County, city of Philadelphia, Mississippi, by this writer on April 24, 2008.
4. Map of the Edgefield District, surveyed by Thomas Anderson in 1825 for the Mills' Atlas.
5. Brown, *Colonel at Gettysburg,* p. 53.
6. Haskell, p. 57.
7. Bessie M. Lane, ed. *Dear Bet: The Carter Letters, 1861–1863* (Greenville, SC: Keys, 1979).
8. Brown, *Colonel at Gettysburg,* p. 60.
9. Jon L. Wakelyn, *Biographical Dictionary of the Confederacy* (Westport, CT: Greenwood Press, 1977).
10. OR, Series 1, Vol. 36/2, p. 993.
11. Robert Gambrell, "Fighting at Spotsylvania C.H.," *Confederate Veteran* (May 1909): p. 225.
12. D.I. Hembrix, "That Bloody Angle Battle," *Confederate Veteran* (September 1909), p. 438.
13. Biddle.
14. Biddle.
15. OR, Series 1, Vol. 35/1, p. 1073.
16. OR, Series 1, Vol. 36/1, p. 1093.
17. John B. Gordon, *Reminiscences of the Civil War* (Atlanta: Martin & Hoyt, 1904); see Gordon's Report of the battle, OR, Series 1, Vol. 36/1, p. 1079.
18. Gordon, pp. 278–79; also see Matter, p. 206, for additional analysis of Gordon's role in the attack plan.
19. William F. Fox, *Regimental Losses in the American Civil War 1861–1865* (Dayton, OH: Morningside Press, 1985), p. 572.
20. William Shakespeare, *Sonnet No. 66.*
21. William Shakespeare, *Henry IV, Part 2,* 3.1.75–6.

Bibliography

Letters and Documents

Duke University, Rare Book, Manuscript, and Special Collections Library, Durham, North Carolina
Abner Perrin, letter to his father, July 16, 1848, from New Orleans, Louisiana.
Maxcy Gregg, letter to Abner Perrin, August 6, 1847, Sullivan's Island, South Carolina.

Rosenbach Museum & Library, Philadelphia, Pennsylvania
Abner M. Perrin, to Abner Perrin, October 24, 1847. Ams 1187/7.
Abner M. Perrin, letter to Mr. Goone, August 16, 1863. Ams 1285/16.

University of Mississippi Department of Archives and Special Collections
Lt. William Cowper Nelson Letters, J.D. Williams Library.

University of North Carolina at Charlotte
Diary of Nicholas Biddle Gibbon.

University of South Carolina, South Caroliniana Library
Abner M. Perrin, letter to Governor Milledge Luke Bonham, July 29, 1863.
"Persona," letter to the sisters of Maxcy Gregg, January 1863.
"Persona," letter to the sisters of Maxcy Gregg, January 9, 1863.
"Persona," letter to the sisters of Maxcy Gregg, March 5, 1863.

University of Southern Mississippi, McCain Library and Archives, Hattiesburg
The Diary of John Smith Lewis.

Newspapers

Seven Days' Battle
Charleston Mercury, July 9, 1862; July 21, 1862; July 26, 1862.
Richmond Examiner, July 18, 1862.
Richmond Whig, July 3, 1863; July 14, 1863; July 19, 1863.

Bibliography

Second Manassas
Charleston Mercury, September 5, 1862; September 13, 1862; September 26, 1862.
Columbia (PA) *Spy*, September 6, 1862, "Battle of Second Manassas."
New York Times, February 1, 1863 (Gen. John Pope's views on the battle).

Antietam
Charleston Mercury, September 22, 1862.
Richmond Examiner, September 22, 1862.
Richmond Whig, September 24, 1862.
South Carolinian, September 27, 1862, "Battle of Antietam."
Staunton (VA) *Spectator*, November 11, 1862.

Fredericksburg
Charleston Mercury, December 14, 1862; December 15, 1862.
Edgefield Advertiser, December 24, 1862, "Battle of Fredericksburg."
Fredericksburg Star, Donald Pfanz, "Behind the Lines," a series of articles on the Battle of Fredericksburg, part 18: "Struggle for Prospect Hill," May 26, 2001.
Richmond Examiner, December 18, 1862.
Staunton Spectator, December 16, 1862; December 23, 1862.

Chancellorsville
Charleston Mercury, May 8, 1863, details of the battle; May 18, 1863, death of Col. James M. Perrin (Gen. Abner Perrin's cousin).
Richmond Examiner, May 6, 1863, battle account; May 11, 1863, review of the positions of the armies; May 12, 1863, battle losses, prisoners, etc.
Staunton Spectator, May 12, 1863, "Glorious victory."

Gettysburg
Charleston Mercury, July 6, 1863, accounts of Lee's army; July 8, 1863, victory on the first day; July 11, 1863, Jackson's movements.
New York Times, July 3, 1863 (three articles); July 3, 1863, General Meade's position at Gettysburg; July 4, 1863 (two articles).
Perrysburg (OH) *Journal*, July 8, 1863; July 15, 1863; July 22, 1863.
Philadelphia Bulletin, July 4, 1863.
Philadelphia Inquirer, July 3, 1863.
Richmond Examiner, July 6, 1863, operations in Pennsylvania.
Richmond Sentinel, July 12, 1863.
Staunton Spectator, July 7, 1863, "Terrible battle in Pennsylvania."
Toledo (OH) *Blade*, July 14, 1863.

Wilderness
Charleston Mercury, May 25, 1864, "Battle of the Wilderness."

Spotsylvania
Charleston Mercury, May 18, 1864, discussion of the Wilderness and skirmishers on post; May 24, 1864, information on the May 12 battle at Spotsylvania; May 24, 1864, more realistic details of May 12 battle (two issues on May 24 of the *Mercury*, both discussing the May 12 battle); June 9, 1864, "Battle on May 12," from an English correspondent.
Democrat Reporter (Linden, Alabama), December 8, 1939, "At 8 o'clock, the organ

pealed...," discussion of the life of Gen. Walter W. Winn of Perrin's brigade, who took command on the brigade after Perrin's death (courtesy of Ms. Betty Hannah).
Edgefield Advertiser, May 23, 1864, discussion of the May 12 battle at Spotsylvania; July 20, 1857, death of Perrin's daughter Julia Duval; December 24, 1862, death of Perrin's wife, Emmala Elizabeth, and her obituary; May 25, 1864, Perrin's obituary.
Greenwood (SC) *Index-Journal*, Perrin Family History: June 12, 1948; June 19, 1948; July 10, 1948; January 1, 1949; January 15, 1949.
Milwaukee Telegraph, September 11, 1887, "The Iron Brigade: A member of it tells some of its experiences."
Richmond Examiner, May 16, 1864, Perrin's death mentioned, along with others reported dead and wounded on May 12.
The Spartan, November 25, 1851, marriage of Abner and Emily Perrin in Edgefield, SC; December 1, 1851.
Staunton Vindicator, May 13, 1863, Gen. Micah Jenkins's death and the May 10 battle; May 20, 1864, Perrin's death mentioned, along with those of other Confederates and some Union generals; also Union losses in the Spotsylvania battle.

Government Records

Edgefield County Archives, Edgefield, South Carolina. Property and other significant public records of Abner M. Perrin III.
National Archives, Washington, D.C.: Military Service Record of Gen. Abner M. Perrin.
War of the Rebellion: Compilation of the Official Records of the Union and Confederate Armies. Washington, D.C.: Government Printing Office, 1880–1901.

Reference Volumes

Annals of the War. Philadelphia: The Times Publishing Company, 1879.
The Batchelder Papers. 3 vols. Dayton, OH: Morningside Press, 1995.
Bowman, John S., ed. *Who Was Who in the Civil War*. Emmaus, PA: JG Press, 2002.
Campaigns of the Civil War. 11 vols. Edison, NJ: Castle, 2002.
Chapman, John A. *History of Edgefield County: From the Earliest Settlement to 1897*. Newberry, SC: Elbert H. Aull, 1897.
The Civil War Book of Lists. Edison, NJ: Castle Books, 2004.
A Compendium of the War of the Rebellion. 2 vols. Wilmington, NC: Broadfoot and Morningside Press, 1994.
Crawford, Mark. *Encyclopedia of the Mexican War*. Denver: ABS-Clio, 1999.
Crute, Joseph H. *Units of the Confederate States Army*. Gaithersburg, MD: Old Soldiers Books, 1987.
Cyclopedia of Eminent and Representative Men of the Carolinas of the Nineteenth Century. Madison, WI: Brant & Fuller, 1892.
Davis, William C., ed. *The Confederate General*. 6 vols. Hanover, PA: National Historical Society, 1991.
Edwards, Bobby F. *The Making of McCormick County*. Columbia, SC: Department of Archives and History, n.d.

Bibliography

Evans, Clement A., ed. *Confederate Military History*. 12 vols. North Augusta, SC: Eastern Digital Resources, 2003.
Fox, William F. *Regimental Losses in the American Civil War 1861–1865*. Dayton, OH: Morningside Press, 1985.
Freeman, Douglas S. *Lee's Lieutenants: A Study in Command*. New York: Scribners, 1998.
Gottfried, Bardley M. *Brigades of Gettysburg*. Cambridge, MA: Da Capo Press, 2002.
Heitman, Francis B. *Historical Register and Dictionary of the United States Army from Its Organization, September 29, 1789 to March 2, 1903*. Urbana: University of Illinois Press, 1965.
Hunt, Roger D. *Colonels in Blue: Union Army Colonels of the Civil War*. Mechanicsburg, PA: Stackpole Books, 2007.
Johnson, Robert Underwood, and Clarence Clough Buel, eds. *Battles and Leaders of the Civil War*. 4 vols. Secaucus, NJ: Castle, 1990.
Jones, Wilmer J. *Generals in Blue and Gray*. Vol. 2. Mechanicsburg, PA: Stackpole, 2004.
Krick, Robert E.L. *Staff Officers in Gray*. Chapel Hill: University of North Carolina Press, 2003.
Krick, Robert K. *Lee's Colonels: A Biographical Register of the Field Officers of the Army of Northern Virginia*. Dayton, OH: Morningside Press, 1992.
Macmillan Library Reference Staff. *Macmillan Compendium: The Confederacy*. New York: Simon & Schuster, 1993.
Martin, Michael, and Leonard Gelber. *Dictionary of American History*. Totowa, NJ: Littlefield, Adams, 1965.
Powell, William H., ed. *Officers of the Army and Navy Who Served in the Civil War*. Philadelphia: L.R. Hamersly, 1893.
Riley, Franklin L., ed. *Mississippi Historical Review*. Oxford: University of Mississippi Press, 1913.
Sears, Stephen. *Civil War Battlefield Guide: Antietam*. New York: Houghton Mifflin, College Division, 1995.
Sifakis, Stewart. *Compendium of the Confederate Armies, South Carolina–Georgia*. New York: Facts on File, 1995.
——. *Who Was Who in the Confederacy*. New York: Facts on File, 1989.
——. *Who Was Who in the Union Army*. New York: Facts on File, 1988.
Southern Historical Society Papers. 52 vols. North Augusta, SC: Eastern Digital Resources, 2003.
Stewart, Richard W., ed. *American Military History: The United States Army and the Forging of a Nation, 1775–1917*. Vol. 1. Washington, D.C.: Center of Military History, U.S. Army, 2005.
Swinton, William. *Decisive Battles of the Civil War*. New York: Promontory Press, 1986.
Tagg, Larry. *The Generals of Gettysburg: The Leaders of America's Greatest Battle*. Mason City, IA: Savas, 1998.
Wakelyn, Jon L. *Biographical Dictionary of the Confederacy*. Westport, CT: Greenwood Press, 1977.
Wallace, David. *South Carolina: A Short History 1850–1948*. Columbia: University of South Carolina Press, 1951.
Warner, Ezra J. *Generals in Blue*. Baton Rouge: Louisiana State University Press, 1964.
——. *Generals in Gray*. Baton Rouge: Louisiana State University Press, 1959.
Watson, Margaret. *Greenwood County Sketches*. Greenwood, SC: Attic Press, 1970.

Bibliography

Who Was Who in America: Historical Volume 1607–1896. Chicago: Marquis Who's Who, 1963.
Wooster, Robert. *Civil War 100*. Secaucus, NY: Citadel Press, 1998.
Wyllie, Arthur. *Confederate Officers*. Printed on demand, 2007.

Periodical Sources

Benson, Berry. "How General Sedgwick Was Killed." *Confederate Veteran* (March 1918).
Brown, B.F. "Some Recollections of Gettysburg." *Confederate Veteran* 31 (1923).
Busha, Charles H. "Lieutenant Colonel Joseph J. Norton, Captain Miles Moore Norton and other Officers of the South Carolina Rifles, CSA." *Carolina Herald and Newsletter* (Spring 2006).
Carmichael, Peter. "D.R. Jones and A.P. Hill Rescue the Right." *Civil War*, no. 74 (June 1999).
Civil War Regiments: vol. 1, no. 3; vol. 4, no. 4; vol. 6, no. 3.
Clark, George. "From the Rapidan to Petersburg." *The Confederate Veteran* (June 1910).
Cox, Jacob D. "McClellan's Own Story." *The Nation* (January 20, 1887).
Crockett, Curtis D. "The Union's Bloody Miscue at Spotsylvania's Muleshoe." *America's Civil War* (January 2008).
De Forest, John W. "Charleston Under Arms." *Atlantic Monthly* (April 1861).
Gambrell, Robert "Fighting at Spotsylvania C.H." *Confederate Veteran* (May 1909).
Gettysburg Magazine: no. 10, 1994; no. 13, 1995; no. 19, 1998; no. 23, 2000.
Hembrix, D.I. "That Bloody Angle Battle." *Confederate Veteran* (September 1909).
James, Robert. "Stonewall's Surprise at Ox Hill." *America's Civil War* (January 1995).
Krick, Robert E.L. "No Controlling Hand: Lee at Malvern Hill." *Civil War*, no. 73 (April 1999).
Martin, Samuel J. "Did Baldy Ewell Lose Gettysburg?" *America's Civil War* (July 1997).
McCall, John T. "7th Tennessee: Battle of Falling Waters." *Confederate Veteran* (September 1898).
Miller, William. "Prelude: Eight Days to Decision." *Civil War: Official Magazine of the Civil War Society*, no. 73 (April 1999).
Mink, Eric C. "The Death, Retrieval, and Remembrance of Brigadier General James S. Wadsworth in the Battle of the Wilderness." *Civil War Regiments: A Journal of the American Civil War* 6, no. 4 (1999).
Neul, Robert C. "Bury Those Men." *America's Civil War* (November 1990).
O'Reilly, Frank A. "Battle of Fredericksburg: Lee's Incomplete Victory." *America's Civil War* (November 2001).
———. "The Real Battle of Fredericksburg: Stonewall Jackson, Prospect Hill, and the Slaughter Pen." *Blue & Gray* 25, no. 5 (2009).
Ouzts, Clay. "Maxcy Gregg and His Brigade of South Carolinians at the Battle of Fredericksburg." *South Carolina Historical Magazine* 95, no. 1 (January 1994).
Purifoy, John. "The Myth of the Confederate Hollow Square at Gettysburg." *Confederate Veteran* 33 (1928).
Ray, Fred L. "The Killing of Uncle John." *Civil War Times* 45, no. 4.
Rhea, Gordon. "The Battle of the Wilderness and Its Place in the Civil War." *Civil War Regiments* 6, no. 4 (1999).
———. "Mule Shoe Redemption." *America's Civil War* (May 2004).
———. "The Overland Campaign of 1864." *North and South* 7, no. 4 (June 2004).

Richards, Miles S. "Pierce Mason Butler: The South Carolina Years, 1830–1841." *South Carolina Historical Magazine* 87, no. 1 (January 1986).
Samito, Christian G. "Patriot by Nature, Christian by Faith: Major General William Dorsey Pender, CSA." *North Carolina Historical Review* 76, no. 2 (April 1999).
Sears, Stephen. "Glendale: Opportunity Squandered." *North and South* 5, no. 1 (December 2001)
Smith, Gene. "The Destruction of Fighting Joe Hooker." *American Heritage* (October 1993).
Snell, Mark A. "The 118th (Corn Exchange) Pennsylvania Regiment at the Battle of Shepherdstown." *Civil War Regiments* 6, no. 2.
Trimble, Isaac. "Gettysburg: General Trimble's Account." *Confederate Veteran* 25 (1917).
Ward, David A. "Of Battlefields and Bitter Feuds." *Civil War Regiments* 3, no. 3 (1993).
Wert, Jeffry D. "Return to the Killing Ground." *America's Civil War* (July 1991).
Young, Louis G. "Pettigrew's Brigade at Gettysburg." *North Carolina Regiments* 5.

Campaign Analyses

Adams, Michael C.C. *Fighting for Defeat: Union Military Failure in the East, 1861–1865*. Lincoln: University of Nebraska Press, 1992.
"Battle of Shepherdstown: September 19–20, 1862." Washington, D.C.: United States Government Printing Office, 2001.
Biddle, Chapman. *The First Day of the Battle of Gettysburg: An Address Delivered Before the Historical Society of Pennsylvania, on the 8th of March, 1880*. Philadelphia: J.B. Lippincott, 1880.
Brooks, Victor. *The Fredericksburg Campaign: October 1862–January 1863*. Conshohocken, PA: Combined Publishing, 2000.
Caldwell, J.F.J. *The History of a Brigade of South Carolinians First Known as Gregg's and Subsequently as McGowan's Brigade*. Philadelphia: King & Baird, 1866.
Cannan, John. *Bloody Angle: Hancock's Assault on the Mule Shoe Salient, May 12, 1864*. Cambridge, MA: Da Capo Press, 2002.
_____. *Burnside's Bridge: Antietam*. Conshohocken, PA: Combined Publishing, 2001.
Catton, Bruce. "Crisis at the Antietam." In *The Civil War: The Best of American Heritage*, Stephen Sears, ed. Boston: Houghton Mifflin, 1991.
Coddington, Edwin B. *The Gettysburg Campaign: A Study in Command*. New York: Simon & Schuster, 1997.
Coffin, Charles C. *Eyewitness to Gettysburg*. Shippensburg, PA: Bard Street Press, 1997.
Doubleday, Abner. *Chancellorsville and Gettysburg*. Edison, NJ: Castle Books, 2002; reprint of the 1882 edition.
Dowdey, Clifford. *The Seven Days: The Emergence of Robert E. Lee*. New York: Fairfax Press, 1954.
Furgurson, Ernest B. *Chancellorsville 1863: The Souls of the Brave*. New York: Vintage Books, 1993.
Gallagher, Gary W., ed. *The Antietam Campaign*. Chapel Hill: University of North Carolina Press, 1999.
_____. *The Richmond Campaign of 1862: The Peninsula & the Seven Days*. Chapel Hill: University of North Carolina Press, 2000.
Gates, Theodore. *The Ulster Guard and the War of the Rebellion*. New York: B.H. Tyrrel, 1879.

Bibliography

Geer, Walter. *Campaigns of the Civil War*. Old Saybrook, CT: Konecky & Konecky, 1926.
Glatthaar, Joseph T. "The Common Soldier's Gettysburg Campaign." In *The Gettysburg Nobody Knows*, Gabor S. Boritt, ed. New York: Oxford University Press, 1997.
Gordon, John B. *Reminiscences of the Civil War*. Atlanta: Martin & Hoyt, 1904.
Harling, Rufus. *At Gettysburg: Recollections and Reminiscences, 1861–1865*. South Carolina Division of the United Daughters of the Confederacy, 1990.
Hartwig, D. Scott. "Who Would Not Be a Soldier: The Volunteers of '62 in the Maryland Campaign." In *The Antietam Campaign*, Gary W. Gallagher, ed. Chapel Hill: University of North Carolina Press, 1999.
Hassler, Warren W. *Crisis at the Crossroads: The First Day at Gettysburg*. Gettysburg: Stan Clark Military Books, 1991.
Krick, Robert K. "Lee's Greatest Victory." *The Civil War: The Best of American Heritage*, Stephen Sears, ed. Boston: Houghton Mifflin, 1991.
Langellier, John. *Second Manassas 1862*. Westport, CT: Praeger, 2002.
Longacre, Edward G. *The Commanders of Chancellorsville: The Gentleman Versus the Rogue*. Nashville: Rutledge Hill Press, 2005.
_____. *General John Buford: A Military Biography*. Cambridge, MA: Da Capo Press, 1995.
Mann, Thomas H. *Fighting with the Eighteenth Massachusetts*. Baton Rouge: Louisiana State University Press, 2000.
Martin, David G. *The Chancellorsville Campaign: March–May 1863*. Conshohocken, PA: Combined Publishing, 1991.
_____. *Gettysburg July 1*. Conshohocken, PA: Combined Publishing, 1999.
_____. *The Peninsula Campaign: March–July 1862*. Conshohocken, PA: Combined Books, 1992.
_____. *The Second Bull Run Campaign: July–August 1862*. Conshohocken, PA: Combined Books, 1997.
Matter, William D. *If It Takes All Summer: The Battle of Spotsylvania*. Chapel Hill: University of North Carolina, 1988.
McGuire, Hunter, and George Christian. *The Confederate Cause and Conduct in the War Between the States*. Richmond: L.H. Jenkins, 1907.
Meyer, Jack A. *South Carolina in the Mexican War: A History of the Palmetto Regiment of Volunteers 1846–1917*. Columbia: South Carolina Department of Archives and History, 1996.
Murray, R.L. *Dedication of the New York State Monument on the Battlefield of Antietam*. Albany: J.B. Lyon, 1923.
_____. *New York's Officers at Gettysburg*. Wolcott, NY: Benedum Books, 2003.
Nevins, Allen. *War for the Union: 1863–1864*. Vol. 3, *The Organized War*. New York: Konecky & Konecky, 1971.
Newton, Steven H. *McPherson's Ridge*. New York: Da Capo Press, 2002.
Osborne, Seward R. *Holding the Left at Gettysburg: The 20th New York State Militia on July 1, 1863*. Hightstown, NJ: Longstreet House, 1990.
Palfrey, Francis W. *Campaigns of the Civil War: The Antietam and Fredericksburg*. Edison, NJ: Castle Books, 2002; reprint of the 1882 edition.
Peabody, James. "The Battle of Chancellorsville." In *From Freeman's Ford to Bentonville: The 61st Ohio Volunteer Infantry*, Robert G. Carron, ed. Shippensburg, PA: Burd Street Press, 1998.
Petty, A. Milburn. *History of the 37th Regiment, New York Volunteers*. New York: Irish American Historical Society, 1937.

Pfanz, Harry W. *Gettysburg: The First Day*. Chapel Hill: University of North Carolina Press, 2001.
Rhea, Gordon C. *The Battle for Spotsylvania Court House and the Road to Yellow Tavern, May 7–12, 1864*. Baton Rouge: Louisiana State University, 1997.
Ropes, John C. *Campaigns of the Civil War: The Army Under Pope*. Edison, NJ: Castle Books, 2002; reprint of the 1881 edition.
Sears, Stephen. *Chancellorsville*. New York: Houghton Mifflin, 1996.
_____. *To the Gates of Richmond: The Peninsula Campaign*. New York: Houghton-Mifflin, 2001.
Southwick, Thomas P. *A Duryee Zouave*. Brookneal, VA: Patrick A. Schroeder, 1995.
Stackpole, Edward J. *Chancellorsville: Lee's Greatest Battle*. Harrisburg, PA: Stackpole, 1958.
_____. *Drama on the Rappahannock: The Fredericksburg Campaign*. New York: Bonanza, 1957.
Steere, Edward. *The Wilderness Campaign: The Meeting of Grant and Lee*. Mechanicsburg, PA: Stackpole Books, 2001.
Stevens, Norman. *Antietam 1862: The Civil War's Bloodiest Day*. Westport, CT: Prager, 2004.
Storrick, W.C. *Gettysburg: Battle and Battlefield*. New York: Barnes & Noble, 1993.
Sutherland, Daniel E. *Fredericksburg & Chancellorsville: The Dare Mark Campaign*. Lincoln: University of Nebraska Press, 1998.
Trudeau, Noah Andre. *Bloody Roads South: The Wilderness to Cold Harbor, May–June 1864*. New York: Little, Brown, 1989.
_____. *Gettysburg: A Testing of Courage*. New York: Harper Collins, 2002.
Tucker, Glenn. *High Tide at Gettysburg: The Campaign in Pennsylvania*. New York: Konecky & Konecky, 1958.
Webb, Alexander. *The Peninsula: McClellan's Campaign of 1862*. Edison, NJ: Castle Books, 2002; reprint of the 1881 edition.
Welker, David A. *Tempest at Ox Hill: The Battle of Chantilly*. Cambridge, MA: Da Capo Press, 2002.
Wert, Jeffry D. *Gettysburg: Day Three*. New York: Simon & Schuster, 2001.
West, Gilmore J. *The Diary of a Soldier*. Perth Amboy, NJ: Pickersgill Press, 1997.
Woodward, Major E.M. *Our Campaigns: The Second Regiment of Pennsylvania Reserve Volunteers*. Shippensburg, PA: Burd Street Press, 1995.

Biographical Sources

Acken, J. Gregory, ed. *Inside the Army of the Potomac: The Civil War Experience of Captain Francis Adams Donaldson*. Mechanicsburg, PA: Stackpole Books, 1998.
Alexander, Gen. Edward Porter. *Military Memoirs of a Confederate*. New York: Scribners, 1907.
Anderson, Nancy S., and Dwight Anderson. *The Generals: Ulysses S. Grant and Robert E. Lee*. New York: Vintage Books, 1987.
Barrett, John G., ed. *Yankee Rebel: The Civil War Journal of Edmund Dewitt Patterson*. Chapel Hill: University of North Carolina Press, 1966.
Beck, Brandon H., ed. *Third Alabama: The Civil War Memoir of Brigadier General Cullen A. Battle*. Tuscaloosa: University of Alabama Press, 2000.
Benson, Berry. *Confederate Scout-Sniper: The Civil War Memoir of Berry Benson*. Athens: University of Georgia Press, 1992.

Bibliography

Booth, George W. *A Maryland Boy in Lee's Army.* Lincoln: University of Nebraska Press, 2000.
Brown, Varina Davis. *A Colonel at Gettysburg and Spotsylvania: The Life of Colonel Joseph Newton Brown.* Columbia, SC: The State Company, 1931.
Cadwallader, Sylvanus. *Three Years with Grant.* Lincoln: University of Nebraska Press, 1996.
Catton, Bruce. *Grant Takes Command.* Edison, NJ: Castle Books, 2000.
Cozzens, Peter, and Robert I. Girardi, eds. *The Military Memoirs of General John Pope.* Chapel Hill: University of North Carolina Press, 1998.
Davis, Burke. *Gray Fox: Robert E. Lee and the Civil War.* New York: Fairfax, 1956.
Dreese, Michael. *An Imperishable Fame: The Civil War Experience of George Fisher McFarland.* Mifflintown, PA: Juniata County Historical Society, 1997.
Govan, Gilbert E., and James W. Livingood, eds. *The Haskell Memoirs: The Personal Narrative of a Confederate Officer.* New York: G.P. Putnam's Sons, 1960.
Grant, Ulysses Simpson. *Personal Memoirs of U.S. Grant.* New York: Dover, 1995.
Hassler, William W. *A.P. Hill: Lee's Forgotten General.* Chapel Hill: University of North Carolina Press, 1962.
Henderson, G.F.R. *Stonewall Jackson and the American Civil War.* New York: Barnes and Noble, 1993.
Jones, Terry. *Campbell Brown's Civil War: With Ewell and the Army of Northern Virginia.* Baton Rouge: Louisiana State University Press, 2001.
Jordan, David M. *Winfield Scott Hancock: A Soldier's Life.* Bloomington: University of Indiana Press, 1988.
Lane, Bessie M., ed. *Dear Bet: The Carter Letters, 1861–1863.* Greenville, SC: Keys, 1979.
Longstreet, James. *From Manassas to Appomattox: Memoirs of the Civil War in America.* New York: Mallard Press, 1991.
Mahood, Wayne. *General Wadsworth: The Life and Times of General James S. Wadsworth.* New York: Da Capo, 2003.
Marshall, Jeffery D., ed. *A War of the People: Vermont Civil War Letters.* Hanover, NH: University Press of New England, 1999.
Maurice, Major General Sir Frederick. *Robert E. Lee: The Soldier.* New York: Bonanza Books, 1925.
Murray, R.L. *In Memoriam Francis C. Barlow: 1834–1896.* Wolcott, NY: Benedum Books, 2003.
_____. *Major-General Abner Doubleday and Brevet Major General John C. Robinson in the Civil War.* Wolcott, NY: Benedum Books, 2003.
Patterson, Gerard A. *From Blue to Gray: The Life of Confederate General Cadmus M. Wilcox.* Mechanicsburg, PA: Stackpole Books, 2001.
Quaife, Milo M., ed. *The Civil War Letters of General Alpheus S. Williams.* Lincoln: University of Nebraska Press, 1996.
Robertson, James I. *General A.P. Hill: The Story of a Confederate Warrior.* New York: Random House, 1987.
Rosenblatt, Emil, and Ruth Rosenblatt, eds. *Hard Marching Every Day: The Civil War Letters of Private Wilbur Fisk, 1861–1865.* Lawrence: University of Kansas Press, 1992.
Sauers, Richard A. *Meade: Victor of Gettysburg.* Washington, D.C.: Brassey's, 2003.
Sears, Stephen W. *George B. McClellan: The Young Napoleon.* New York: Ticknor & Fields, 1988.

Bibliography

———. "In Defense of Fighting Joe Hooker." In *Civil War Generals in Defeat*, Steven E. Woodworth, ed. Lawrence: University of Kansas Press, 1999.

Shugart, Ann, ed. *I Know What I Know: Stories of the Confederate Years*. Vol. 2. Cherokee District, SC: United Daughters of the Confederacy, 2008.

Simkins, Francis B. *Pitchfork Ben Tillman: South Carolinian*. Baton Rouge: Louisiana State University Press, 1967.

Simpson, Brooks D. *Ulysses S. Grant: Triumph over Adversity, 1822–1865*. New York: Houghton Mifflin, 2000.

Survivors' Association. *History of the 121st Regiment Pennsylvania Volunteers*. Harrisburg, PA: 1869–1871.

Townsend, George Alfred. *Rustics in Rebellion: A Yankee Reporter on the Road to Richmond 1861–1865*. Chapel Hill: University of North Carolina Press, 1950.

Walker, C. Irvine. *The Life of Lieutenant General Richard Heron Anderson*. Charleston: Art Publishing, 1917.

Walker, Francis. *General Hancock*. New York: D. Appleton, 1894.

Welch, Spencer G., M.D. *A Confederate Soldier's Letters to His Wife*. Clearwater, SC: Eastern Digital Resources, 2004.

Wilkeson, Frank. *Turned Inside Out: Recollections of a Private Soldier in the Army of the Potomac*. Lincoln: University of Nebraska Press, 1997; reprint of the 1887 edition.

Willard, Van R. *With the Third Wisconsin Badgers*. Mechanicsburg, PA: Stackpole Books, 1999.

Index

Abney, Zachariah 147
Alabama 10th regiment 145–146
Alabama 11th regiment 147–148
Alabama 14th regiment 148–149
Alabama 8th regiment 144
Alabama 9th regiment 144–145
Alston, T. P. 106
Anderson, J. M. (Rev.) 68
Anderson, Joseph 22, 55
Anderson, Richard H. 35, 51, 82, 89, 107; his absence, at Gettysburg 111, 120, 191–194, 209*n*14
Archer, James 78–79, 98, 109

Banks, Nathaniel 39, 41
Barber, M. L. 149
Barnes, Dixon 19; at Antietam 53, 56
Bathany Church 7
Battle of Fair Oaks 83–84
Bell, Jesse T. 146
Benson, Berry: at Fredericksburg 68; at Second Manassas/Bull Run 45; at Wilderness 156
Biddle, Chapman 78; at Gettysburg 100, 103, 105, 107
Birney, David: at Fredericksburg 68; at Second Manassas/Bull Run 45, 48; at Spotsylvania 158; at Wilderness 139, 141
Blackie Hospital 144
Bonham, Millege L. 19; influence on Perrin 10, 19, 70, 116, 120, 172
Branch, L. O'Brien 22, 25, 55, 192; at Antietam 53; at Harpers Ferry 51; at Second Manassas/Bull Run 47, 48; at Seven Days 24
Breckenridge, John C. 150
Brockenbrough, J. M. 52, 55; at Fredericksburg 63

Broome, James A. 148
Brown, Malissa 145
Brown, William S. 146
Buford, John: at Gettysburg 95, 96, 97, 98
Burnside, Ambrose 59, 60, 66, 70–71, 75, 133, 139; at Fredericksburg 62
Butler, Emmaline 11
Butler, Matthew 7
Butler, Pierce 10–11
Byers, Marshman W. 146

Caldwell, JFJ, lieutenant 44, 45, 67, 112–113, 115, 122, 195*n*12
Calhoun, John 11
Cawthen, William W. 149
Cemetery Hill 99, 103, 105, 109, 110, 111, 112, 113, 116, 140, 178, 192, 194
Cemetery Ridge 104, 108, 109, 111, 119, 120, 135, 140, 175
Chickahominy 22, 28
Clark's Mountain 132
Clopton, Mary 5
Colgrove, Silas: at Chancellorsville 84–85
Contreras, battle of 9
"Corn Exchange Regiment" (118th PA): at Shepherdstown 55
Cothran, Wade 6
Crow, James, M. 145
Crumly, Rueben, C. 146
Culp's Hill 111, 112, 120, 178
Curtis, Joseph R. 54

Dana, Charles 136
Daniel, Janius: at Spotsylvania 177, 180
Dare Mark Campaign: Fredericksburg and Chancellorsville 76
Davis, Joseph S. E. 149

221

Index

DeBardelaben, Arthur, M. 144
DeBardelaben, Daniel H. 144
DeShazo, George W. 146
DeShazo, William R. 148
Devin, Thomas: at Gettysburg 96, 97, 98
Dodge, Theodore: Chancellorsville defeat, reasons for 88
Doubleday, Abner 65, 66, 71; at Gettysburg 98–100
Draper, W. W. 147

Early, Jubal 44, 65, 68, 75, 81, 92, 107, 111, 125, 152, 153, 159, 162, 175
Edgefield 12, 13, 16, 17, 73, 166, 170, 172, 189
Edwards, Oliver E. 18, 55, 56.69, 86, 87, 89, 202n29
Emrich, John P. 144
Engelhard, Joseph 121, 190
Ewell, Richard 38, 51, 52, 128, 132, 133, 136–137, 154, 159, 160; at Gettysburg 94, 107–110, 111–112; at Spotsylvania 157, 165; at Wilderness 152

Featherston, Winfield: at Glendale 31
Fellors, Jake 45
Floyd, D. F. 144
Foster, Sarah 5
Francine, Louis: at Chancellorsville 85
Franklin, William: at Fredericksburg 60
Fuller, B. J. 144
Fuller, George 144
Fuller, Jesse 144
Fuller, John T. 144
Fuller, Richard 144
Fush, Henry J. 145

Galphin, George 7
Gamble, William 96, 97, 98, 104, 105
Gates, Theodore: at Gettysburg 178
"General Orders 75" 23
Gordon, John B. 157, 159, 163, 164, 173, 177, 179; at Spotsylvania 160, 162, 164
Grant, U. S. 96, 132, 135, 136, 137; at Spotsylvania 152, 153, 157–158, 159, 161–166; at Wilderness 133–134, 139–141
Gregg, Maxcy 10, 17, 19, 20, 21, 24, 28, 39, 42, 53, 69; at Boteler's Ford 52; at Fredericksburg 58, 62–63, 64–66, 68–69; at Gaines Mill 25–28; at Glendale 29–32; at Harpers Ferry 51; obituaries 70, 72; at Ox-Hill/Chantilly 46–48, 200n24; at Second Manassas/Bull Run

40–45 passim; at Shepherdstown 52, 54, 55–66
Griffin, Goodman 150

Hamilton, Daniel 17, 69, 86, 89; dispute concerning his position 121–122
Hampton, Wade 69, 115; at Spotsylvania 153
Hancock, Winfield S. 9, 177; at Spotsylvania 153, 154, 155, 156, 157, 158, 159, 160, 161, 165, 166, 186; at Wilderness 133, 135, 137, 139, 140, 141, 142
Hardie, Elias B. 146
Harling, Rufus 109
Harper's Ferry 50–51, 52, 53–54, 177
Hartranft, John: at Wilderness 139
Haskell, A. C. 121, 122, 190; at Seven Days 28
Haskell, John C.: at Bristoe Station 127; at Gettysburg 172; at Wilderness 137
Haskell, William T.: at Gettysburg 108, 113
Hawkins, Rush: at Fredericksburg 71, 72
Herbert, Hillary A. 131, 144
Heth, Harry 78, 80, 89, 92, 95, 116; at Gettysburg 96, 97, 98, 99, 101, 103, 109, 114, 115, 123; at Mine Run 125, 126, 127; at Spotsylvania 154, 155; at Wilderness 134, 137, 140
Hill, A. P. 20, 22, 23, 24, 26, 39, 45, 47, 83, 89, 94, 113, 122, 126, 132, at Chancellorsville 79, 82, 83; at Fredericksburg 63–64, 65–66, 70, 79, 80, 81, 82, 83, 86, 89; at Gettysburg 97, 98, 99, 107, 108, 109, 110, 113, 114, 115, 120, 117, 118, 121, 122, 123; at Glendale 30–32, 36, at Mine Run 124, 126–127, 128, 132, 134, 135; at Second Manassas/Bull Run 42–45, 47, 141; at Seven Days 24, 25, 29, 30, 31, 35; at Shepherdstown 52–53, 54, 55, 56; at Spotsylvania 152, 153, 156, 157, 163, 165, 173, 174, 176, 177, 186, 191, 192, 194; at Wilderness 135, 136–137, 140, 141
Hill, Daniel 79, 89, 118, 167; at Seven Days 24, 30, 32
Hobbs, T. H. 145
Hodge, Stephen 149
Holmes, T. H.: at Seven Days 29, 30
Hooker, Joseph: at Chancellorsville 75, 76, 77, 78, 81, 82, 83; at Fredericksburg 60, 62, 71; at Gettysburg 91, 92, 97, 99; at Wilderness 141

222

Index

Howard, O. O 79, 119, 193; at Chancellorsville 82, 83; at Gettysburg 98, 100
Huger, Benjamin: at Gettysburg 103, 118; at Seven Days 32
Huot, Doctor (MD) 45

Iron Brigade 177; at Fredericksburg 71; at Gettysburg 102, 103, 104, 105

Jackson, Thomas (Stonewall) 23, 26, 29, 32, 35, 36, 38, 40, 46, 47, 48, 49, 56, 58, 59, 71, 80; at Chancellorsville 81–89 *passim;* at Fredericksburg 62, 63, 64, 65, 66, 70; at Gaines Mill 25; at Glendale 30; at Mechanicsville 24, 25; at Second Manassas/Bull Run 39, 42–45
Jeff Davis Blues 145
Johnson, Edward 128, 157, 159, 160, 161, 162, 165, 186
Johnson, L. W. 145
Jones, D. R.: at Shepherdstown 52

Kearny, Philip 31, 48; at Ox Hill/Chantilly 49; at Second Manassas 44, 45
King, Joseph, H. 144

Law, Evander M.: at Spotsylvania 177
Lee, Robert E 49, 50, 56, 73, 74, 80, 87, 88, 89, 90, 92, 98, 121, 122, 127, 128, 130, 132, 133, 171, 174, 177, 179, 183, 186, 187, 188, 192; at Chancellorsville 77, 78, 81, 82, 83; at Fredericksburg 62, 63, 67, 71, 72; at Gettysburg 97, 108, 109, 110, 111, 113, 117, 118, 120; at Mine Run 125, 126; at Ox Hill/Chantilly 46; at Second Manassas/Bull Run 40, 42, 46; at Shepherdstown 52, 53; at Spotsylvania 152, 153, 154, 157, 158, 160, 161, 165, 166; at Wilderness 133, 134, 135, 136, 140, 141, 142
Liberty Academy 8
Longmire's Store 7
Longstreet, James 49, 63, 74, 87, 88, 92, 118, 124, 131, 132, 152, 154, 161, 177, 192; at Chancellorsville 78, 87; at Fredericksburg 63, 70–71; at Gettysburg 99, 110, 108, 109, 111, 112, 113, 120; at Seven Days 24, 25; at Wilderness 133, 135, 137, 141, 142

Magnolia Cemetery 144
Magruder, John: at Seven Days 24, 30, 32, 34
Mahone, William: at Chancellorsville 90; at Gettysburg 118; at Spotsylvania 154, 161; at Wilderness 137, 138
Marcy, Ellen 23
Marye's Hill 73
McCall, George: at Gettysburg 99; at Seven Days 29, 31
McClellan, George 22, 25, 29, 30, 32, 33, 38, 55, 56, 58, 60, 64, 76 83, 100, 108, 156, 193; at Second Manassas/Bull Run 39; at Seven Days 23–24, 34, 28; at Shepherdstown 52–53
McDowell, Irvin 39, 40, 41, 100, 141
McFarland, George 104, 105
McGowan, Samuel 8, 14, 17, 20, 21, 23, 36, 73, 80, 83, 92, 130, 187; at Antietam 53; at Chancellorsville 76, 78, 84, 85, 86, 89, 90; at Fredericksburg 69, 73; at Gaines Mill 28, 35; at Glendale 31; at Second Manassas/Bull Run 46; at Spotsylvania 163
McIntosh, David, at Chancellorsville 87
McLaws, Lafayette 92, 118
Meade, George 31, 128, 141, 193; at Bristoe Station Engagement 125, 126, 127; at Fredericksburg 65, 66, 67, 68, 73; at Gettysburg 98, 107, 111; at Spotsylvania 153, 155, 166; at Wilderness 130, 136, 141
Meadows, T. C. 149
Meredith, Solomon 102, 103
Morgan, John H. 23
Mosely, Emily C. 147
Mott, Greshom: at Spotsylvania 157, 158, 161; at Wilderness 161
Mundy, Frank 148

Nall, Duke 144

Orange Court House 21, 38, 39, 59, 76, 78, 92, 128, 133, 134, 135, 137
Orange Plank Road 134, 135, 136, 137, 138, 139
Orange Turnpike 47, 81, 134, 135, 136
Orr, James 18
Ox Hill/Chantilly 46–48

Palmetto Regiment 10, 11
Parker's Store 135, 136, 139
Patterson, Mary 5
Pegram, John: at Gettysburg 97, 99; at Harpers Ferry 51; at Spotsylvania 161
Pender, Dorsey 22, 24, 25, 78, 79, 80, 90, 92, 108, 109, 113, 114, 116, 123, 131, 187; at Chancellorsville 87, 89; at Fred-

Index

ericksburg 63; at Gettysburg 95, 98.105, 107; at Harpers Ferry 51; at Ox Hill/Chantilly 47; at Second Manassas/Bull Run 44; at Shepherdstown 52, 55
Perrin, Abner M. 5, 6,7, 8,9, 10, 11, 12, 13, 17, 18, 22, 38, 50, 56, 73, 74, 75, 86, 88, 89, 94, 105, 107–108, 110–111, 121, 122, 128, 129–130, 143–145, 145–148, 151, 168–169, 170–171, 172, 177, 189, 186; at Antietam 30; at Berryville 58; at Castleman's Ferry 58; at Chancellorsville 84–85, 87; death 163, 166, 168, 177, 180, 185, 189; at Fredericksburg 58–59, 64, 65; at Gettysburg 95, 100–101, 102, 103–104, 106, 107, 110, 114–115, 121, 123, 189; at Harpers Ferry 50, 51; at Mexican War 8, 9,10, 11, 12, 15; at Mine Run 125, 128; at Second Manassas/Bull Run 61–64; at Shepherdstown 52, 54, 55; at South Carolina Military battles 21; at Spotsylvania 162, 163, 164, 165, 166, 179; at Wilderness 133, 137–138, 139–140, 141
Perrin, Arthur 7
Perrin, James 7
Perrin, Joisah 7
Perrin, Joseph 5
Perrin, Margaret 7
Perrin, Napoleon 7
Perrin, Robert 6
Perrin, Robert 7
Perrin, Telemachus 7
Perrin, William 5
Perrin, William 7
Perry, Simon G. 149
Pettigrew, James 80, 90, 97, 166, 169, 187; at Gettysburg, 102, 103, 104, 109, 111, 115, 117
Pickens, Francis 16, 18, 21, 69
Pierce, Franklin 9
Pope, John 38, 46, 49, 64, 96, 141; at Second Manassas/Bull Run 39–44
"Pound Cake" regiment 17
Powell, Ben 156
Price, Francis: at Chancellorsville 85
Prince, John 147
Pryor, Roger: at Glendale 31

Quincy, Samuel: at Chancellorsville 85

Rains, John B. 147
Rainwater, Albert 148
Ramseur, Stephen 123, 164, 167, 173, 177, 179, 194; at Gettysburg 106, at Spotsylvania 159–160, 162
Rapidan River 39, 40, 77, 82, 92, 124, 125, 128, 132, 133, 134
Rappahannock River 22, 40, 59, 63, 76, 77, 78, 82, 91, 92, 124, 127, 128
Reynolds, John 64, 123, 193; at Fredericksburg 65, 66; at Gettysburg 97, 99, 100, 119
Robinson, Beverly: at Second Manassas/Bull Run 45
Rodes, Robert E. 86, 92, 177; at Chancellorsville 81, 82, 83; at Gettysburg 98, 106, 107, 111; at Spotsylvania 154, 157, 162, 164
Rowley, Thomas: at Gettysburg 100, 103
Royston, Young L. 131, 143
Ruger, Thomas: at Chancellorsville 84–85; at Second Manassas/Bull Run 40

Sanders, C. C. 131, 132; at Spotsylvania 164
Second Manassas/Bull Run 39, 42, 45, 46, 48, 49, 55, 56, 64, 96, 118, 177, 186
Sedgwick, James 33, 75, 88, 156, 158; at Mine Run 128; at Spotsylvania 153, 155; at Wilderness 134–135
Seminary Ridge 98, 99, 101, 107, 110, 117, 118, 123
Seven Days battles 17, 20, 22, 23, 28, 34, 35, 36, 42, 56, 80, 118, 130, 131, 144, 149, 177, 194
Shady Grove Church 136
Shelley, James E. 145
Shepherdstown 20, 50, 51, 52, 54, 55, 56, 93
Sheppard, John 8
Sheridan, Phillip: at Spotsylvania 153
Sigel, Franz 39, 41; at Second Manassas/Bull Run 42
Slocum, Henry W.: at Gettysburg 111; at Seven Days 33
Smith, Gaynes, C. 144
South Carolina 1st, 12th, 13th regiments, origins 19
Stapp, M. C. 147
Stevens, Isaac: at Second Manassas/Bull Run 47, 48
Stoneman, George 23
Stuart, J. E. B. 7, 40, 79, 120, 193; at Bristoe Station 127; at Chancellorsville 81, 83, 86; at Gettysburg 97, 108, at Spotsylvania 152
Summer, Edwin: at Fredericksburg 60

224

Index

Sykes, George: at Seven Days 26

Tayloe, George E. 131, 147
Taylor, George W. 148
Tillman, Ben 7
Tompkins, Daniel 103
Trimble, Isaac 92, 111, 112; at Chancellorsville 86; at Gettysburg 109
Troy 6
Truss, James 145

Ulster Guard 103, 178

Veracruz 9

Wadsworth, James: at Gettysburg 100, 102; at Wilderness 137–138, 139
Warren, Gouverneur K.: at Bristoe Station 126, at Gaines Mill 27; at Spotsylvania 153, 156, 157; at Wilderness 136

Warrenton Pike 47
Watlington, C. 148
Welch, Spencer 46; at Bristoe Station 126–127; at Gaines Mill 27; at Falling Waters 115; at Gettysburg 94, 113; at Second Manassas/Bull Run 45
White, Julius: at Harpers Ferry 50
Williams, Alpheus: at Chancellorsville 85
Williams, Roger 146
Williamson, James S. 149
Winn, Walter 149, 150; at Spotsylvania 163; at Petersburg 164
Winterseat, description of 6–7
Woodward, John W. 145
Wool, John: at Harpers Ferry 50

Young, Louis G. 111, 117, 120

Zouaves: at Gaines Mill 26, 27

www.ingramcontent.com/pod-product-compliance
Ingram Content Group UK Ltd.
Pitfield, Milton Keynes, MK11 3LW, UK
UKHW041948140426
5217IPUK00014B/700